THE SUBURBAN SOCIETY

The Suburban Society

S. D. CLARK

University of Toronto Press

To Ellen, Sam, and Edmund

Preface

THIS STUDY was made possible by a grant from Central Mortgage and Housing Corporation. I am deeply indebted to the Corporation. Though financially supporting the study, the Corporation granted to me the greatest possible freedom. No research foundation could have been more understanding of scholarly interests or more patient in face of the scholar's slow pace of work. I would have difficulty singling out the names of various people associated with the Corporation who have been helpful, but I cannot allow to pass the opportunity to publicly thank Mr. Alan Armstrong, now with the Canadian Council on Urban and Regional Research, and Mr. Humphrey Carver, Chairman of the Corporation's Development Group. Mr. Armstrong read an early draft of the manuscript and made many detailed and helpful criticisms. Throughout the study, Mr. Carver was always there, ready to offer advice, criticism, encouragement, but never interfering, never prodding, though the work was planned to be completed long before it was. I am deeply in his debt. Need I add that for the views expressed in this study the Corporation is in no way responsible.

To my field workers I owe thanks—Robert Van Alstyne, Mirvyn Hanna, Michael Sylvester, Robert Gill, and Alice Phené. Two of my colleagues, Professor O. Hall and Professor J. R. Burnet, read and criticized an early draft of the manuscript; I owe them many thanks for their help and encouragement. I also owe thanks to the members of my family who at various times came to my help, in the assembling and analysis of the field notes and in reading the manuscript. Finally, I wish to thank Mr. Jeanneret, Miss Harman, Miss Halpenny, and Miss Houston of the University of Toronto Press for their help in securing the publication of the study.

Agincourt, January 26, 1965   S. D. CLARK

Contents

THE SUBURBAN SOCIETY

1 | The Process of Suburban Development

A BOOK HAVING to do with the suburbs can scarcely lay claim to uniqueness. For the past quarter century in America there has been perhaps no social phenomenon more in the news. A mounting flow of popular magazine articles and paperbacks has appeared, devoted to an examination of the way of life of the suburban resident. Particular suburban areas have been intensively scrutinized; the whole general phenomenon of suburbanism has been brought under review. It would seem there could be little more about the suburbs to be said.

Yet there is little attempt in the extensive literature which has grown up about the suburbs to examine how the suburban society comes into being and develops. Emphasis has tended to be placed upon those characteristics of social organization, patterns of social life, which appear to be distinctive to a suburban society. What has been sought are the outlines and internal structuring of an ordered social system which can be described in much the same way as urban or rural society is described. Underlying a good many of the efforts which have been made to analyse the suburban society is the assumption that it is a new kind of social creation, a product of forces in American social life which only recently have come into play. Thus has developed, however much there may be differences in matters of detail, the image or stereotype of suburbia.

Unwittingly, suburban residents have contributed to the building up of the suburbia image. The mass movement of population into the suburbs suddenly created for publishers a vast new reading public to be exploited, and suburban residents, whatever else they

may be, are egotistical enough to want to read about themselves.
A good deal of the literature on suburbia has been of a sort bordering on the sensational. The more the facts about suburban life have
been distorted the more certain has been the interest in what was
written. Myths tended to become built on to myths to produce a
caricature of the suburban dweller so grotesque that few people
living in suburban areas have been able to resist the temptation of
seeking to discover what they are supposed to be like. If lurid
details about the sexual misdemeanours of the population could
be related a lively reading public was that much more assured.

Not everything written about suburbia has been designed to
appeal to the suburban housewife seeking amusement or instruction
in light reading. Suburbanism as a social phenomenon has had its
serious students. Yet the suburbia myth, which has served so well
the writer seeking a popular appeal, has served no less well the
writer seeking an appeal to that large and growing body of readers
pleased to go by the title of intellectuals. Here the object has been
to shock not the lone miserable suburban housewife but the
American Public as a whole. What is happening in suburbia has
been made to appear symptomatic of what is happening in American
society generally. The suburban dweller, it is claimed, gives expression in stark form to a way of life or attitude of mind becoming
increasingly characteristic of the North American wherever he may
reside. Thus it was in suburbia that David Riesman could most
readily find his "other directed" and William H. Whyte his "organization" man. By his escape from the city, and from the country,
the suburbanite is believed to have let himself become exposed to
the full force of certain changes taking place in the society of North
America.

In such an interpretation of present-day trends and tendencies
in American society, certain very decided value judgments are
apparent. "I speak in this paper," Riesman wrote, in the opening
sentence of a paper entitled "The Suburban Sadness," "from the
perspective of one who loves city and country, but not the suburbs."[1]
A generation ago, the student of American society, then in background truly a man of the country, could find in the big city all

[1]William M. Dobriner, ed., *The Suburban Community* (New York, 1958),
p. 375.

that was evil, depraved, and corrupt in the American way of life. A highly romantic picture of rural society, the product of not a little nostalgia, served to bring into sharp relief the undesirable qualities of urban society. In the quarter century or so that has since passed, the student of American society has learned to love the city in the manner that he has long loved the country, and now it is suburbia, portrayed in terms of a slavish conformity, fetish of togetherness, and craze for organization, which is set over against a romantic image of the city with its narrow and cluttered streets, its quaint shops and picturesque tenements, its strange and ever changing assortment of people of many colours, nationalities, and languages, producing a way of life which seemingly brings out all that is best in man.

It is difficult to believe that some of those writers who have been prepared to pass judgment on the character of American society know any better the suburbs they profess to dislike than "the country" they profess to love. Yet the suburbia myth cannot be dismissed as the product simply of the imagination of urban-bred intellectuals intent on finding in the suburban way of life the symptoms of "the sickness of our times." Interest in the phenomenon of suburbanism has led to much research and faithful reporting of research findings. So deeply imbedded in sociological thinking, however, is the suburbia myth that it has determined the very design of much of the research undertaken. Students of suburbia have gone from reading Riesman to reading Fromm and Whyte, and nothing to them appears more sociologically righteous than the effort to discover in the suburban society a basic personality type, a dominant ethos or outlook on life, a distinctive structure of social relationships. Here, indeed, is a society which seems to exemplify to a high degree the character of the socializing process at work in all societies. The very emphasis upon values of child rearing in the suburban society appears to reflect the underlying concern of the population for conformity and the creation of the condition for social consensus and integration.

By concentrating attention upon certain suburban areas, it has not been difficult to build up a particular image or stereotype of suburbia, or, indeed, of a suburban personality. For instance, from the picture presented in *Crestwood Heights* of what was reputed to be a North American suburb, much could be made of the suburbanite's overwhelming concern for conformity, his enslavement to the values of a society which placed prime emphasis upon the future welfare of the child, his deeply rooted social and political conservatism and distrust of anything which threatened his accepted way of life.[2] The Crestwood Heighter appeared very much to be an other-directed organization man.

Had those students of suburbia who have thus used the Crestwood Heights study, however, known Toronto better, known something about the hundreds of subdivisions spreading east to Whitby, north to Newmarket, and west to Brampton and beyond, known even more that Crestwood Heights at the time it was being studied had been settled for twenty-five years or more and was made up of an upper middle- or upper-class population half Gentile and half Jewish, they would have realized how little typical of a suburban community this community was, if, indeed, in any sociological sense it could be considered suburban at all. What was really being studied in Crestwood Heights was not the social process of suburbanism but the culture of a particular urban social class and, in large degree, a particular ethnic group.

A good many of those residential areas selected for investigation by the student of suburbia have possessed characteristics not unlike those of Crestwood Heights. Though they may not have had as wealthy a population, they have been areas which tended to attract people rising in the social scale and highly conscious of their social status. Very often, they have been heavily populated by middle-class or upper middle-class Jewish people anxious to find in the suburbs a social world where they could be sheltered from the assimilative or culturally disintegrative forces of a Gentile urban environment. Almost all of them have had something of a ready-made quality. Residential communities like Park Forest and the Levittowns (or in the Toronto area Don Mills and Thorncrest Village) did not simply grow up. They were created, often on the initiative or under the direction of one man. They were "packaged" suburbs, residential developments which were designed to offer the family settling in them everything that was required to live a full community life.

---

[2]J. R. Seeley, R. A. Sim, and E. W. Loosley, *Crestwood Heights: A North American Suburb* (Toronto, 1956).

Suburban communities such as these thus had something of the character of social oases, residential areas created outside the city and sharply set off not only from old established urban areas but as well from other suburban residential areas growing up about.

Why it is residential areas of the packaged type which so often have been selected for study is not at all hard to understand. The very isolation of such areas from the built-up sections of the urban community, their physical compactness, and their development around well-defined centres make them easy to study. They have clear-cut boundaries and there is an orderliness in the structure of their social life. They appear to have some sort of ethos or character and they appear to produce a distinctive personality type. Such can scarcely fail to be the case in view of the fact that only certain kinds of people choose to settle in them.

In such areas the sociologist finds a society which can be described and analysed in the same manner the anthropologist describes and analyses the primitive society. The characteristics of the population can be readily determined, sampling techniques employed where necessary, patterns of behaviour searched out and meaningfully re-lated to the values and goals of the group as a whole, processes of socialization identified and measured, and the major institutions of the society fitted together into something that appears to have the characteristics of a social system. In methodological terms, indeed, the packaged suburban community offers an almost perfect socio-logical laboratory for investigation and analysis within a functional theoretical framework.

In the very selection made of suburban communities for study, however, a bias becomes built into the sociological conception of suburbanism. A high degree of order is found characteristic of suburban society, but it is those suburban societies displaying a high degree of order which have tended to be selected for study and investigation. With theoretical tools borrowed largely from the anthropologist and psychologist, what the sociologist has been look-ing for in suburban society is a system of order and nowhere can he find such a system better than in the packaged type.

Where, of course, the sociological interest is in the examination of such social processes as those of socialization, integration, and the creation of social consensus, there can be no quarrel with the selection that has been made. There is an order in suburban society as there is an order in all societies and the nature of this order can be most clearly discerned in those suburban communities which are a product of planning and direction. But suburbanism is not only an order, it is also a process, and an understanding of suburbanism as a process involves looking at those suburban areas not where a sense of order is the most prominent but where it is the least. It is in these latter areas, not in those which are a product of planning and direction, that are to be discovered the dynamics of suburban growth. There is a pattern of suburban development, but it is a pattern in the direction away from as well as towards a state of order. The suburban society is not something created whole and complete, to be examined primarily in terms of the way it is structured. Rather, it is something which grows up, develops, and it can therefore only be understood in terms of the process of its growth. What suburban development essentially means is the process of transformation of the country into the city. It is in the nature of this transformation that are to be found the distinctive characteristics of the suburban society.

Had there been after the Second World War no sudden mass movement of population beyond urban boundaries but rather a steady, continuous spreading of urban residents outwards, suburbanism as a social phenomenon would have attracted little attention. The suburbs gained their social significance because they were areas into which great masses of people suddenly moved. Throughout the development of society on the North American Continent there have been long intervals when economic, political, and other conditions (war, in particular) discouraged any great movement of population. When conditions developed favourable to such movement, it tended as a result to take place in the form of a great "rush." In such manner were the Western Canadian Prairies occupied in the years after the turn of the century and in such manner has the countryside surrounding such cities as Toronto become occupied in the years since the Second World War.

Census figures, which do nothing more than indicate the over-all increase of population, reveal nevertheless in striking fashion the nature of the development which took place in the Toronto area. Between 1941 and 1961, while the population of the City of

Toronto grew only from 667,457 to 672,407 (it declined in the decade 1951–61), that of the twelve surrounding municipalities which were to become a part of Metropolitan Toronto grew from 242,534 to 946,380. More significant still was the fact that of this 703,846 increase of population in the twelve surrounding municipalities, 82 per cent of it, 577,036, occurred in the three outer municipalities of Etobicoke, North York, and Scarborough. By 1951 the nine inner municipalities had become almost fully occupied. Indeed, in the years 1951–61, these municipalities increased in population by only 57,352, from 245,748 to 303,100 (see Table I). It was not here, in these older built-up areas, but in the countryside beyond that occurred the phenomenal growth of population in the years after the Second World War.

In 1941 the combined population of the three townships of Etobicoke, Scarborough, and North York was 66,244. By 1956 it was 413,475. Five years later it had become 643,280 (see Table II). Beyond these townships, in areas reaching out twenty-five miles or more from the City of Toronto, the growth of population was almost as phenomenal, but here census figures can provide no

TABLE I
POPULATION OF THE NINE INNER MUNICIPALITIES

	1941	1951	1961
York	81,052	101,582	129,645
East York	41,821	64,616	72,409
Leaside	6,183	16,233	18,579
Mimico	8,073	11,342	18,212
New Toronto	9,504	11,194	13,384
Weston	5,740	8,677	9,715
Forest Hill	11,757	15,305	20,489
Long Branch	5,172	8,727	11,039
Swansea	6,988	8,072	9,628

TABLE II
POPULATION OF THE THREE OUTER MUNICIPALITIES

	1941	1951	1961
Etobicoke	18,973	53,779	156,035
Scarborough	24,303	56,292	217,286
North York	22,968	85,897	269,959

accurate measure. The increase in the population of such townships as Toronto, Vaughan, Markham, and Pickering, and, further out still, Chinguacousy, Nelson, Trafalgar, King, Whitchurch, East Gwillimbury, and Whitby was striking enough (see Table III), but it was in certain specially favoured parts of these townships that the real increase occurred. By the end of the nineteen-fifties places like Port Credit, Brampton, Georgetown, Woodbridge, Markham, Richmond Hill, Aurora, and Newmarket had lost their character of small-town communities in becoming the centres of large urban concentrations of population (see Table IV).

TABLE III

POPULATION OF TOWNSHIPS BEYOND METROPOLITAN TORONTO

	1941	1951	1961
Toronto	12,481	28,528	62,616
Vaughan	5,829	9,766	16,701
Markham	7,134	10,625	13,426
Pickering	6,602	10,371	17,201
Chinguacousy	3,716	5,225	7,571
Nelson	4,169	8,193	Annexed
Trafalgar	4,585	8,118	31,743
King	5,357	7,469	12,845
Whitchurch	3,294	5,157	7,391
East Gwillimbury	3,647	4,400	10,357
Whitby	2,310	2,972	6,312

TABLE IV

POPULATION OF TOWNS BEYOND METROPOLITAN TORONTO

	1941	1951	1961
Port Credit	2,160	3,643	7,203
Brampton	6,020	8,389	18,467
Georgetown	2,562	3,452	10,298
Woodbridge	1,044	1,699	2,315
Markham	1,204	1,606	4,294
Richmond Hill	1,345	2,164	16,446
Aurora	2,726	3,358	8,791
Newmarket	4,026	5,356	8,932

However much allowance may be made for population increase resulting from local economic growth, it would seem apparent that by 1961 the population of what was in a very real sense the Toronto urban community had grown to about two million, over one-half of which was to be found beyond the borders of the city and the nine inner municipalities. What this growth meant was that for every person living in an old built-up residential area in 1961, one other was living in a residential area at the very most not more than fifteen years old. Indeed, considering that the main increase in the population of the suburbs took place after 1953, there probably was at least one person out of four in the Toronto urban community at the end of the nineteen-fifties who was living within a residential area not more than five years old. What clearly had occurred was a great mass movement of population out of the city into the country. In terms of how particular areas of the countryside were occupied, the movement, indeed, assumed the character of a "rush." Where in many areas there had been only three or four scattered rural families, a year later as many as five hundred or a thousand suburban families could be located.[3] The country was suddenly taken over and made into a part of the urban community. It was this sudden taking over of the country by an urban population which was the dominant feature of suburban development as it took place in the Toronto area in the years after the Second World War.

Though what resulted was a suburban society, it was a suburban society which did not conform to any stereotype of suburbia. It had no structure; indeed, it had no boundaries which could be readily determined. It could not be mapped in the way a Park Forest or Thorncrest Village could. It consisted of little more than a great and undifferentiated mass of dwellings, street blocks, and subdivisions, beginning and ending nowhere that could be seen clearly. Where the new residential developments crowded down on the immediate borders of older established residential areas, what was suburban became almost completely indistinguishable from what was urban. Where, on the other hand, urban residents had spread themselves out in areas far distant from the city there was no easy

[3]There is no end of examples of subdivision developments which illustrate the pattern of growth in particular areas. In East Gwillimbury Heights outside the town of Newmarket, for instance, the first houses were ready for occupancy in the midwinter of 1957–58. By the autumn of 1958 virtually all of the approximately five hundred homes in this subdivision were occupied. Though more than one subdivision development was involved, the increase in population of census tract 162 in Scarborough, an area bounded by Victoria Park, Lawrence Avenue, Birchmount Road, and Highway 401, illustrates the same process of rapid growth. In 1951 the population of this tract was 321. In 1956 it was 14,995!

telling where the suburban left off and the rural began. Clearly, the city was taking over the country but in a manner that produced no readily recognizable form or structure of community life. Conspicuous because of the type of people they attracted, their well-defined boundaries, and their distinctive forms of community life were those suburban residential developments of the packaged type, and little less conspicuous were those cottage-type communities far out from the city developing as havens for the urban poor. But these were residential developments providing housing for only an insignificant proportion of the total suburban population. Stretching for miles beyond the city, and with boundaries which had little meaning other than marking the limits of particular subdivision developments, were residential areas which had no clear or distinctive qualities about them. If the plans of subdividers, or history, gave them a name, they seemingly possessed nothing which could identify them as suburban except that they lay beyond the community that was urban.

If the term suburban is to be used to describe all such residential areas developing beyond urban borders it can be given sociological meaning only by being made to apply to a type of society which while not yet urban is in the process of becoming urban. The suburban is a society coming into being. It is its lack of a form or structure which gives it its distinctive character. When it comes to possess a form or structure it has to that extent lost its suburban character and taken on a character that is urban.

Only as a theoretical construct, of course, can such a "pure" suburban society be conceived. In any suburban residential area there is in fact from the very beginning something of the established urban society built into its social structure. People cannot move from the city to the country without bringing with them at least some of the equipment necessary for building an urban society. As well, there are few suburban communities which in their beginnings did not take over and transform for their purposes some part of the society which was there before the occupation by an urban population began. Urban and rural are not so far apart, in the structure of their social life or in their social values, that the making over of the country into the city leads to the complete dissolution of the society of the one in the establishment of the society of the other.

If no suburban society can come into being, and take a shape sufficient for it to be recognized as a suburban society, without its already having become something of an urban society, there is no suburban society, on the other hand, which is not in a small degree at least a rural society as well.

Any examination of the process of suburban development must necessarily take account of those forces which secure the easy and almost imperceptible transformation of the society of the country into the society of the city. The packaged residential development is only one example of how the country is made into the city without serious disturbance to the values and ways of life of the people involved. The growth of the rural village into a community urban in character is another example. Certainly, where the movement of population to the suburbs involves people of different social classes, religions, and ethnic backgrounds these differences are reflected in the character of the residential areas which develop. A working-class suburb, as Bennett Berger has convincingly demonstrated, is not the same as an upper middle-class suburb.[4] Some of the new society is simply a re-creation of the old society long known.

Yet this does not mean that suburban society is only a projection, as William M. Dobriner tends to argue,[5] of the forms and ways of life of the urban society. If a working-class suburb is not the same as an upper middle-class suburb, neither is it the same as an old established working-class residential area. What is important is not what gets carried over from the urban to the suburban society but what fails to get carried over. Something happens to the way people live, to the social structure in which they participate, when they move out of the city to the suburbs.

Given the character of suburban development, it would be hard to imagine how such could fail to be the case. The very act of moving involves some upset of established ways of life, social attachments, and values. Even the packaged suburban community does not come into being without disturbance in the manner of life of the residents. Where suburban development involves the movement all at once of great masses of people from the city to the country the disturbance can be very great.

[4]Bennett M. Berger, *Working-Class Suburb* (Berkeley and Los Angeles, 1960).
[5]William M. Dobriner, *Class in Suburbia* (Englewood Cliffs, N.J., 1963).

Thus the study of suburbanism is a study of social change. What results in the end is an urban society. But the suburban society is made into an urban society only after an interval of time. It differs from the urban society in that it is an urban society not yet complete. Much of what makes up a society is carried with them by people moving from the city to the country but much is left behind. What emerges is a simpler society, a society less elaborately structured, less socially differentiated, less ordered. Indeed, at that point in time when settlement in the suburban community has just taken place, the society is one almost totally lacking in structure and form.

In methodological terms, what such a conception of suburbanism means is that there can be no easy determining the boundaries and limits of the society being analysed. Where the form and structure of this society can be perceived, it has to that extent lost its suburban character. It is the society without form and structure—and thus without identifiable boundaries—which is truly suburban. Yet, of course, no social analysis is possible if the limits of what is being analysed cannot be determined. It is this fact which justifies the emphasis in sociology upon order and structure and leads to the effort to construct, however it may be defined, some sort of boundary-maintaining social system. The suburban society must be talked about as if it really were a society with identifiable boundaries.

To talk about the suburban society in this manner does not mean, however, that analysis has to proceed in terms of one model only of the society. If the way the suburban society comes into being and develops is to be analysed, what is required is a model of the society as it was and a model of the society as it has become or is becoming. The suburban society must be distinguished from the urban society even though it may be nothing more than a less perfect form of this society. As well, one suburban society must be distinguished from another in terms of the degree to which it conforms to the model of the urban—or "pure" suburban—society. Within such a framework of analysis interest shifts from an examination of those forces in the suburban society securing its character as an ordered social system to an examination of those forces bringing about its change from one kind of social system to another.

In the study here undertaken of the Toronto suburban community it was not possible to find a social creation, of course, which fully conformed to any analytical model of the suburban society. What was inevitably required were a number of compromises with actuality. Not only was there no "typical" suburban society to be found, there were to be found no clearly demarcated types of suburban societies. The population of the city, in truth, had spilled itself out in the country in every conceivable manner. In the over-all view, it was this formlessness which was the most distinctive characteristic of the suburban community.

Yet, while form may have appeared to be lacking, it was lacking in different degrees in different suburban areas. There could be no mistaking the suburb five years old from the suburb which had just come into being. Nor could there be any mistaking the suburb which had grown up as a result of careful planning and direction— the "packaged" suburb—from the suburb which had grown up without any planning or direction at all. However treacherous the effort to classify suburban areas into broad types, only by such classifying can the pattern of suburban development be perceived and analysed. There is a pattern of development of suburban society as there is a pattern of development of any society. It is the recognition of such a pattern which distinguishes comparative sociological from historical analysis.

In all, fifteen different suburban residential areas were selected for field study. Though no two of these areas were exactly alike, they could be divided into six fairly distinct types:

I. THE SINGLE-FAMILY RESIDENTIAL DEVELOPMENT OF THE "PURE" SUBURBAN TYPE

(1) Lyons subdivision in Newmarket, about thirty miles from Toronto. An area of homes which sold for about $15,000. Though lying within the town borders of Newmarket, Lyons subdivision developed separated geographically from the old town. Three years old at the time it was studied.

(2) Crosby Heights in Richmond Hill, about twenty miles from Toronto. A subdivision of $15,000 homes, geographically completely separated from the town though within the town's borders. Three years old at the time it was studied.

(3) Richmond Acres in Richmond Hill, immediately south of

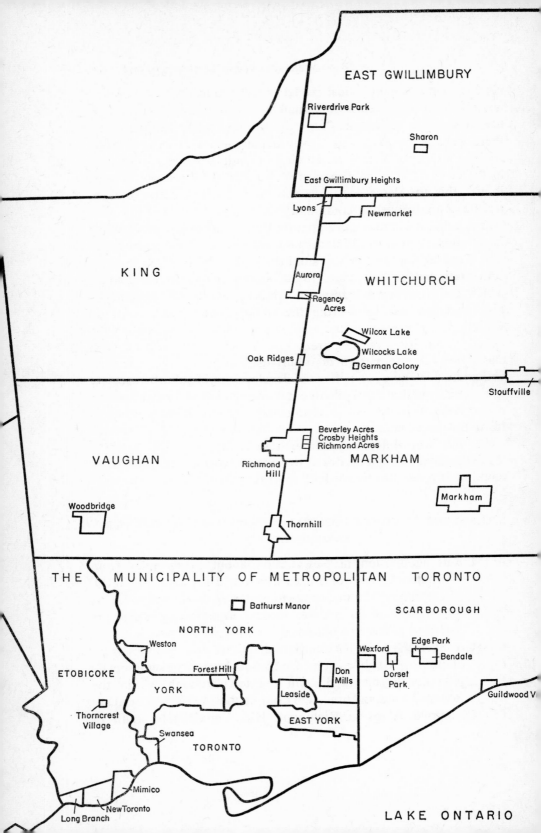

Crosby Heights and indistinguishable from this subdivision except that homes here had been built to sell for about $13,000. Developed one year before Crosby Heights.

II. THE SEMI-DETACHED RESIDENTIAL DEVELOPMENT OF THE "PURE" SUBURBAN TYPE

(1) East Gwillimbury Heights, lying immediately outside the borders of Newmarket, within East Gwillimbury Township. Homes built to sell for less than $11,000. Less than a year old at the time it was studied.

(2) Beverley Acres in Richmond Hill, immediately north of Crosby Heights. Homes built to sell for about $11,000. Developing about a year later than Crosby Heights.

III. THE SINGLE-FAMILY RESIDENTIAL DEVELOPMENT IN A BUILT-UP AREA

(1) Bendale in the Township of Scarborough, about fourteen miles from Toronto. An area of about $15,000 homes, situated in the very centre of the township. About two years old at the time it was studied.

(2) Edge Park, adjoining Bendale, and similar in character except that it was just under development at the time it was studied.

IV. THE "PACKAGED" OR SEMI-PACKAGED RESIDENTIAL DEVELOPMENT

(1) Thorncrest Village in the Township of Etobicoke, about twelve miles from Toronto. Homes of varying prices, ranging from $18,000 to $35,000 or more, two hundred in all. Fully built up at the time it was studied; had developed over a period of seven or eight years.

(2) A residential area, partly semi-detached and partly single family, in Don Mills, a planned community of several thousand people, about ten miles from Toronto. Homes in the area studied ranged in price from $15,000 to $19,000. About four years old at the time it was studied.

(3) A Catholic co-operative residential development, outside the hamlet of Sharon, in East Gwillimbury Township, about thirty-five miles from Toronto. Homes of a value of about $13,000. Still developing at the time it was studied.

(4) A German colony of twenty to thirty homes, south of Wilcocks Lake in Whitchurch Township, about twenty-five miles from Toronto. Homes largely of a value of about $13,000, though a few ranging considerably higher. From one to three years old at the time it was studied.

V. THE COTTAGE-TYPE RESIDENTIAL DEVELOPMENT

(1) Riverdrive Park in East Gwillimbury Township, about eight miles north of Newmarket, almost forty miles north of Toronto. A subdivision of almost 300 homes built up in the early nineteen-fifties. Homes built to sell for a total price of $1,900, $200 down-payment. About eight years old at time it was studied.

(2) Wilcox Lake[6] in Whitchurch Township, about twenty-five miles from Toronto. Several hundred homes, most of which had been built as summer cottages and about half of which were rented. Homes sold ranged in price from $2,500 to $4,000. Area had developed as permanent residential about ten years before studied.

VI. THE RESIDENTIAL DEVELOPMENT OF THE "PURE" SUBURBAN TYPE, NOW FIVE TO TEN YEARS OLD

(1) Wexford in the Township of Scarborough, about ten miles from Toronto. An area of $15,000 homes. Eight years old at the time it was studied.

(2) Dorset Park in the Township of Scarborough, about twelve miles from Toronto. An area similar to Wexford except about five years old at the time it was studied.

There can be no claim that any of these areas was thoroughly studied. Very early in the field work any effort to secure a "true"

[6]The spelling of the name of the lake is "Wilcocks" but the spelling of the name of the settlement which surrounds most of the lake is "Wilcox."

sample of the suburban population was abandoned. Rather, the effort was directed to learning as much as possible about all the various types of residential development which had taken place in the Toronto area in the years since the war. A good part of the early field work consisted of nothing more than "exploring" this vast expanse of suburban growth. People in all walks of life were talked to, but more particularly those persons who in one way or another were involved in the developments taking place; assessment rolls were examined, newspaper files searched, and various other sorts of material studied. In all, about twelve hundred interviews were carried out by the field workers. Of these, about nine hundred were in the fifteen areas selected for intensive study. Here, apart from the interviewing of the "important" people in the area— church ministers, officers of the ratepayers' associations, service clubs, and such—an effort was made to secure a representative sample of the local residents. The remaining three hundred or so interviews were carried out in a great variety of other areas, partly as a check upon whether there was anything unusual about any of the areas under intensive study, partly as a means of securing a better view of the over-all development taking place.

In the presentation here of the findings of the field research, no effort is made to offer these findings as conclusive evidence. Indeed, only a part of the interview material finds its way into this study. What is presented here can be considered as nothing more than an exploratory essay. In reporting upon the findings of the study in this manner, however, no apology is necessary. By the very nature of the suburban society, any examination of it other than one of an exploratory character would have been impossible. To lay claim to scientific precision in the study of such a phenomenon would be to falsify the field of competence of Sociology. What there is about suburban society that lends itself to study by precise scientific methods is not worth study, if what is sought is an understanding of how this society comes into being and develops.

In the end, study of the suburban society can be considered only an aspect of the study of the larger society. Thus, in any examination of suburban development in the Toronto area, there can be no avoiding issues and problems relating to the development of the

Canadian society in general. With urban growth have come far-reaching changes in the character of life in the rural community and small town. What is being transformed is not only the country into the city. Urban influences are reaching back from the city to make something different out of what has been known as rural and small-town society. Nor has the development stopped at this point. Urban complexes like Elliot Lake, Kitimat, and Arvida represent something in the nature of new social creations. So as well, in a smaller way, do some of the developments taking place in the heart of our larger cities. Community planning has come to play a new role in the task of society building. Even more, the state has taken on a function in the determination of how people should live in a manner that to a nineteenth-century laissez-faire social theorist would have been beyond comprehension. The sociological dictum that stateways cannot make folkways was proved by the experience of war and revolution to be largely false, and today no limits are known to the power of the state to bring into being, and to destroy, the society of man. There is, it is true, too much toughness about this society for it to be easily made over by the state, if the state had such a will. Much that is about us still is a social creation that has just happened. But however restrained may be the state in the exercise of its power, and however tough may be the material with which it has to work, the student of society can no longer view the social as something distinct from and independent of the political. Too much of what is happening to our society is a product of the dictates of political power.

Nowhere perhaps has the new role played by the state been more apparent than in the recent development of the suburban society. This society as it developed in the early years after the war was a creation of people moving largely without direction or control from the city to the country in search of a home for themselves. It is this undirected and uncontrolled development which receives primary emphasis in this study. But as attention shifts from developments of the early nineteen-fifties to developments of the late there become evident certain very marked differences. The small subdivision developer gives way to the large, and municipal authorities, and, indeed, the provincial and federal governments as well, come to play a much more important part in determining the character of the development taking place. To some extent, the change represented nothing more than the passing of one phase of suburban development for another. To some extent as well, however, it represented a fundamental shift in the character of the development. By the end of the nineteen-fifties suburban residential areas were not permitted to develop in the manner that they had developed at the beginning of the nineteen-fifties.

How this change came about in the character of suburban development receives nothing more than passing notice in this study. Here attention is focused on the effects of that sudden bursting of urban boundaries and overrunning of the countryside by masses of people which in the Toronto area took place in the years roughly from 1952 to 1958. In such a limitation of the study is reflected the bias of the sociologist interested in the problem of social change, but, given the nature of the phenomenon being examined, the bias finds justification. Too much of the effort directed towards an understanding of our society has proceeded from an inadequate appreciation of the nature of the forces of change at work within it. Sociology has suffered from accepting too readily the economic materialist's interpretation of social phenomena. But it has suffered even more from developing a framework of analysis heavily influenced by psychology. In the writings of Simmel is to be found perhaps the best statement of the ends and aims of sociology, and the work of such sociologists as Robert E. Park and Everett C. Hughes attest to the influence he has had in the development of a truly sociological approach to the study of social phenomena. But in much present-day sociology the important distinction Simmel made between form and content has been largely lost sight of, and the consequence is a serious confusion between processes which are truly social and processes which are largely psychological. This is not to suggest that a psychologically oriented analysis of suburbanism cannot be revealing of important facets of the structure of suburban society. Indeed, in the study of this phenomenon, there is perhaps as much to be found out by the psychologist (and psychiatrist) as by the sociologist. And, if the work of Robert C. Wood may be taken as an example,[7] the political scientist as well has important contributions to make. But what is

[7]Robert C. Wood, *Suburbia: Its People and Their Politics* (Boston, 1959).

important is that the social process of suburbanism should not be confused with the psychological—or political—process. It is this fact which offers justification in this study for the emphasis upon the consequences of mass movement of population from the city to the suburbs. In the nature of these consequences can be seen most clearly the social forces at work leading to the creation of the suburban society.

2 | The Creation of the Suburban Community

BY THE END of the nineteen-fifties the Toronto suburban community, not including the nine inner municipalities of the metropolitan area, had a population of close to a million people. In territory, it consisted of a great arc based on Lake Ontario and sweeping over the top of the city. To the east, what was part of the Toronto suburban community became at a certain point indistinguishable from what was a part of the community of Oshawa, while, to the west, Toronto suburban development met and joined forces with suburban development growing out of Hamilton, to be confounded still further by the efforts of Oakville in between to maintain an independent existence. To the north, however, the residential development which had taken place was clearly and unambiguously related to the expansion of Toronto. In this direction, the Toronto suburban community extended almost as far as Lake Simcoe, a distance of fifty miles.

It would be no easy task to describe, even in very broad, general terms, the way in which this vast sprawling suburban community had come into being. What appeared most striking was the suddenness of the development. Farm fields almost overnight had given way to massive housing tracts and, where once perhaps farm buildings stood, great shopping centres came into being. It seemed that there had been everywhere in evidence a great impatience to have done with anything rural. The bulldozer quickly had done the work of destruction and by the time the house-builder moved in nothing of the country remained. The large-scale subdivision development made easy and rapid the taking over by an urban population and establishment of a community that was suburban.

Yet such a development did not come until long after the first initial settlement of urban people in the country had taken place. In this respect, there was no difference between the way the suburbs developed and the way any other new area of settlement developed. In the new area of settlement there has to come first a "proving up" of its suitability for occupation, a feeling out of its resources and the bringing of those resources to a certain stage of exploitation, before it can be taken over by great masses of people. What is required, in this early phase of settlement, is enterprise of both an individual and collective sort. The "hard" frontier has to be converted into a "soft" frontier before it is ready for full occupation.

Thus, in the settlement of the Canadian West, there was a long interval of very slow development, extending from about 1870 until after the turn of the century, before there took place that great inrush of settlers which resulted in the rapid occupation of large parts of the country. On the one hand early farm settlement came with the pushing into unknown areas of a few hardy pioneers who, far distant from markets, undertook farming by combining it with native industrial pursuits. On the other hand were those collective efforts of settlement, colonization schemes of various sorts, which, deriving support from outside, were able to take over more completely certain selected areas for farm occupation. Without this early penetration of the country, the settlement that came after would scarcely have been possible. Yet it was only with this later settlement that the occupation of the farm areas of the West really began. In similar manner occurred the settlement of the suburbs.

The suburbs had its pioneers as did other frontiers and it had its share of collective efforts of settlement of various sorts. Because suburban development involved (as, indeed, the development of the West had involved) pushing the line of occupation further and further back into the country, there was no point of time setting off one kind of settlement from the other. At a time when great masses of people had already begun to completely take over the first occupied areas, further out collective types of suburban settlement were being established and further out still the individual pioneering family was only just beginning to penetrate areas which hitherto had been wholly unaffected by urban development. Though the development could not easily be traced chronologically, the pattern was one shaped by time. It was the individual pioneer family which led the way into the suburbs, and after the individual pioneer family came the collectively sponsored type of settlement. Out of this early phase of development grew the forces leading to the later phase of the mass movement of population into the suburbs.

There are no census figures that make it possible to trace easily the movement of individual urban families into the vast countryside surrounding Toronto in the years after 1946. The nature of the highway network, farm land values, and the extent to which rural public services had developed determined the general pattern of the movement, but the choice of location by particular families was largely dependent upon their economic circumstances and individual tastes. The very wealthy were influenced in their choice by one consideration, the very poor by another and very different. The rich moved to the country in search of a better place to live, the poor in search of a cheaper. For the family of moderate means, the choice was determined by considerations which neither the rich nor the poor could wholly ignore: distance from the city and its accessibility by road, a desirable local community environment, the price commanded by lots suitable for building on or of houses available for occupation. In the end, the particular choice depended upon how a great variety of considerations were weighed and balanced. For some persons, the primary consideration was the distance to be driven to work; for others, it was physical surroundings or the presence of a good rural school or other public services. For the very poor, the price of land was of paramount importance. Families moving into the country, at this early stage of development, were very much individualists in the sense that no two families were influenced by the same considerations. It was this motivation in terms of individual preferences which determined the highly haphazard character of the development which took place.

In the years after the war there were few rural or small-town communities within a forty-mile radius of Toronto which did not experience the effects of this intrusion of scattered families from the city. A declining population characteristic of most country districts and villages over the period 1870–1941 had produced a surplus of housing and of school facilities which could be taken up by urban families in the years during and after the war, and public services could be strained to accommodate a few additional families. Thus there occurred a filtering out over the whole vast countryside of urban people. No zoning restrictions stood in the way of locating where they chose or building or occupying the type of residence they saw fit. Where the settlement was of well-to-do families it could engender considerable local pride, or, if it was of families requiring the attention of local welfare agencies, it could engender much grumbling and a feeling of hostility to a city which appeared to be using the country as a dumping-ground for its social unfortunates. But whatever the particular consequences, the settlement of urban families in rural areas resulted in a change in the rural society. The rural society lost something of its rural character.

So long as dependence had to be placed upon rural public services, however, a sharp limit was set on the movement of urban population into the country, and the rural community was not readily transformed into a suburban community. The voting power of the rural population was crucial in maintaining the existing tax structure and blocking efforts to make over public services. The fate of the rural society became closely tied to the fate of the red brick country school house. A point was reached where, to break the voting power of the rural population, only a very few additional urban families needed to have settled in the community, but, with public services at this point taxed beyond their capacity and not yet made over, there was no inducement to further settlement of urban families. Thus, where the resources of the rural community were considerable, and the population had the means and the will to maintain intact its tax structure, there was no easy taking over of rural areas by an urban population moving into these areas one family at a time.

Where, however, the rural community had no considerable resources, the barriers checking the inflow of urban families could be easily broken and the rural society transformed into an urban. Rural villages favourably located in relation to the city, and farm communities bordering on a main highway leading into the city, were particularly vulnerable to suburbanizing influences. What was demanded by urban residents located in the rural village was not so sharply different from what many of the village residents themselves wanted that it was possible for the latter to maintain any kind of solid front. It was so easy to add another room or two to the local village school, and no major making-over of other public services—streets, street lights, fire protection, policing, garbage collection, and such—was required to accommodate a slowly but steadily increasing residential population. Thus a village community like Agincourt to the east of Toronto or Thistletown to the west could become something of a suburban community without any large-scale residential development taking place (though such development outside the immediate borders of the village eventually came).

Similarly, the farm community bordering a main highway leading into the city offered such extremely favourable locations for urban residential settlement that any concern about the inadequacy of local public services was not great enough to check the inflow of population. Urban residents spread themselves along the highway in sufficient numbers that some sort of local community life became possible and the good road fronting their property not only made access to the city easy but brought near, in terms of driving time, what local services and facilities were essential. Thus developed along roads leading into the country from the city that ribbon kind of suburban settlement so familiar in the environs of any large city and so much the despair of the town planner.

Where suburban development took place, however, either in the rural village or in the farm community bordering a main highway, there occurred no replacement of the original population. The village still offered a means of livelihood to those people who had been there before the urban residents arrived, and in the farm community the land back from the highway still had value only for farm purposes and continued to offer support to a substantial farm population. There remained in village and country alike a mixing of rural and urban, a suburban community which clearly was not wholly suburban.

Where, however, the countryside remained unoccupied before the coming of an urban population, or was occupied in such a way

that no stable form of community life developed, a complete transformation of rural into urban could occur if the population was
one which made no heavy demands in terms of the kind of services
it was prepared to accept. Here and there, in the countryside surrounding Toronto, there grew up after the war small isolated
residential communities built up entirely through the undirected
movement of individual families out of the city.

A few of these communities were established by people of lower
middle-class social standing. Such was the community which
developed in the mid nineteen-fifties south of Wilcocks Lake, along
and back of Bayview. Its rolling and wooded hills made the land
in this area unsuitable for agricultural purposes but invited its use
for a place of residence. The proximity of a large and undesirable
residential development around Wilcocks Lake and poor access roads
to the city (Bayview at this point was nothing but an uncleared
right of way), however, discouraged the building of homes here
by well-to-do people from the city. The result was the settlement
in the area of people of modest means, largely recent German
immigrants, who possessed the skills and the enterprise which made
possible the building of their own homes, solid six-room structures
which if built for sale would have had a value of about $12,000.

It was to be a bitter discovery on the part of these people just
how exceedingly inadequate were the public services in the area and
how impossible it was to secure improvement except at exorbitant
cost. A small group of residents could not by themselves build up
and support the kind of community services required and, so long
as these sorts of services were not available, there was not likely
to be any increase in the number of residents. What had been
created was a little residential pocket, almost idyllic in superficial
appearances, but doomed to be deprived for a long time to come
of much that was essential to the existence of an urban residential
community.

The obstacles to the establishment of middle-class residential
settlements in the country by the movement out from the city of
individual families on their own were almost insuperable and not
many such settlements came into being. Where the movement,
however, was of a population which had little concern about the
quality of public services there was virtually no limit to the develop-

ment which could take place in areas where land had little value for any purpose other than residential use.

Thus it was that the taking over of the countryside in this early phase of movement of population from the city was most successfully accomplished by people in impoverished circumstances prepared to accept whatever the country had to offer them in preference to what was available to them in the city. There were all kinds of areas surrounding Toronto which could be occupied by people such as these in the years after the war. One such area was the summer-resort colony.

With the growth of Toronto in the years after the war, such summer-resort colonies within fifty miles became so easy to invade by week-end visitors from the city that they ceased to serve as desirable places of retreat for the urban middle class. They became lower-class summer-resort areas and ultimately, wholly or in large part, areas of lower-class permanent residence. Services which had developed to meet the needs of summer residents, local grocery stores in particular, were available to meet the needs of permanent residents. Tar paper and used lumber served to convert crudely constructed two- to four-room frame structures (the urban middle class of the nineteen-twenties' era had no high standard of cottage building) into habitable dwellings and, where vacant land was available and could be bought at a low price, further building took place. Such was the character of the development of the Wilcox Lake area. Here what was before the war a fully developed summer-cottage area was in the years after the war transformed almost completely into an area of permanent residence. What there had been in the area in the way of a rural society had been largely destroyed by the summer cottage and few obstacles thus stood in the way of the taking over of the community by families moving out from the city.

The very character of such residential areas, however, meant that a sharp limit was imposed upon the extent of their development. What was here demanded was cheap land, and land remained cheap only so long as there was no vast influx of population. Isolation was a condition of the development of the lower-class residential area. What emerged were small residential pockets lying back from the main routes of travel, their very existence often unknown to people about. It was not in this way that the country was to be made over into the city. Its making over depended upon a very much more concerted effort to promote urban residential development.

In terms of what actually took place, of course, no clear line set off this later type of residential development from the earlier. Such was particularly the case with respect to those "soft" areas of development where the small speculative builder could very early move in and offer to prospective residents virtually the whole range of services available in an urban community. Thus in the small villages about Toronto it was not long after the war before private builders or developers had taken up what small parcels of land lay within their boundaries, and sufficient building took place to result in a sudden substantial increase in population. Throughout the Toronto area there developed a number of such relatively small-scale suburban residential areas in the years immediately after the war. Almost invariably, however, such developments took place in areas where already, as in the case of the village community, a number of individual urban families had settled, and only in those exceedingly "soft" areas did these developments result in the complete taking over by an urban population. As in the case of the movement of individual families from the city, the small-scale residential development could most readily lead to the complete taking over of the community for urban residential purposes where the population moving in made no heavy demands in the way of public services. Such was the case of Riverdrive Park.

Developed before the war as a small summer-cottage colony on the banks of the Holland River, eight miles north of Newmarket, Riverdrive Park had already in the early years after the war been partially converted to a place of permanent residence. Unlike Wilcox Lake, however, this area had never attracted any great number of summer residents and, with the river becoming polluted, the community might well have virtually disappeared had not an enterprising local farmer who owned the land stretching back from the river undertaken to develop the area for permanent residential use. A subdivision plan accepted by an unwary East Gwillimbury Township council led to the building of some three hundred homes in the years 1950–52, crude frame structures set on cedar posts which were sold for as little as $1,900, with a $200 down-payment and monthly payments of $25.00 on a mortgage which was carried without interest.

Most of the homes were purchased by families moving out from the city. Available here were no public services other than those normally provided by a rural community. The subdivision was laid out on a street plan but the streets were little more than trails leading past the fenced lots. No street lights, sewerage, or running water were provided; every house had its outside privy and water was carried from a well. As part of a rural school district, an elementary school was within two miles of the settlement. The township provided what police protection there was and two small grocery stores were established by private enterprise. A gravel road led to the highway, five miles distant. It was forty miles to the city. Ultimately, East Gwillimbury Township could not escape a substantial charge upon its operating budget resulting from this development. But immediately, provided in effect with no public services except those already in existence, the community could be established at no great cost to the township and at a profit to the developer. Land that had no other use was made to serve the purpose of providing a place of residence for people who were being crowded out of the city by post-war immigration and a rising birth rate.

There could, however, be few residential developments of the Riverdrive Park type as there could be few residential developments of the Wilcox Lake sort. The market for the kind of housing which Riverdrive Park had to offer was exceedingly limited. Not a great number of Toronto families were prepared to move forty miles out of the city, and five miles from the nearest highway, to accept accommodation in four-room, unlined, frame cottages situated in a residential area which had no urban public services of any sort. In Riverdrive Park one small part of the country had been made over by the city, but such a development had been possible only in an area many miles from the city, away from main routes of travel, where land had little value for farming purposes and where there was a township council seemingly unaware of what the establishment of such a type of community meant in terms of municipal finances. If any part of the countryside lying closer in to the city was to be taken over by an urban population there were required types of subdivision development providing housing for a market much larger than that for the Riverdrive Park type of development.

Yet the barriers were formidable to any massive overrunning of the countryside by an urban population. Except in those areas close in to the city, the rural structure remained intact. Urban residents had crowded along country roads, but there remained no serious break in the concession road pattern. Residential development back from the road involved heavy capital outlays in the building of streets and the provision of other essential services. In the undertaking of such development, private enterprise hesitated unless it had a very special and assured market.

Thus there was nothing curious about the fact that it was subdivision developments providing housing for the rich that tended to follow into the country subdivision developments providing housing for the poor. The poor were prepared to forgo public services if offered the opportunity to secure the housing they required; the rich, on the other hand, were prepared to bear the full costs of providing such services themselves. If the rich, of course, were very rich, they could afford to move out of the city into the country on their own and enjoy all the advantages the country had to offer while giving up none of the amenities of urban living. If not quite so rich, however, they could still afford to move into the country by taking advantage of that type of residential development where all the services and amenities of the urban community were provided in advance and where planning and physical isolation offered a protection against possible undesirable developments outside. Such on a large scale was the Don Mills housing development; on a much smaller scale, Thorncrest Village.

What the community or "packaged" housing developments had to offer, which the ordinary subdivision development did not, was the structure of a society whole and complete. In theory at least, everything that was required for full living within a community was provided: paved streets, sewers, garbage collection, recreational facilities and such, and as well, and even more important, congenial and socially acceptable neighbours. For Don Mills what this meant was the building up of the structure of a small city; for Thorncrest Village the structure of a country village.

Thus the packaged residential development was in no way dependent upon an earlier residential development in the area. Rather, it depended upon the absence of any other such development. What was required was the entire taking over of the area to be developed, and the less previous development there had been the less had to be made over. A condition of the packaged residential development was its separation from the city. Where enormous financial resources were available and farm land could be gradually and quietly acquired over a long period of time such a development was able to take place no great distance from the city and at a time when the countryside beyond had already been developed residentially. Such was the case of Don Mills. With more limited financial resources, the developer of Thorncrest Village could build, whole and complete, a residential community so near to the city only by restricting it to the dimensions of a village, and even as such there was much that Thorncrest Village lacked which a rural village would have provided. But it had something of an air of completeness, and it was its isolation from other residential developments which provided it with such an air. People moving to Thorncrest Village, to a degree, were not dependent upon what in the way of services and amenities the local community outside the village had to offer. Socially at least, they could lead their lives complete within the village.

It was the lack of previous urban residential development which made possible the establishment of packaged communities like Don Mills and Thorncrest Village. At the same time, it was their isolation in the country which made such communities attractive to the kind of people who settled in them. They were something of a backlands utopia. They represented experiments in community building, efforts to construct, where no previous development stood in the way, the perfect urban society.

Where such residential areas developed no great distance from the city, it was only the rich or near rich who could afford to settle in them. The person locating in Don Mills or Thorncrest Village was able to rationalize that in the long run property values would hold more firmly in such an area than in other kinds of residential areas, but he had to be a person who could afford the additional immediate cost of a home in this type of area. The market for the kind of housing offered by the packaged residential development tended to be highly selective. It was made up of people who were prepared to pay the premium price of a house in such a develop-ment in return for the advantages offered.

Thus it was that while struggling individual families were hap-hazardly occupying the countryside, it was the very poor far out and the near rich closer in who were making over completely the country into the city. Riverdrive Park and Thorncrest Village were opened up for development in the same year, 1950. Though vastly different in character, there was nothing incongruous about the development at about the same time of these two different types of residential areas. For the residents of Riverdrive Park the com-munity was as complete as was Thorncrest Village for its residents. The people settling in Riverdrive Park asked for nothing in the way of an urban society except what was provided by such elementary forms of association as those of kinship which they easily carried with them. In its own peculiar fashion, it like Thorncrest Village and Don Mills had some of the characteristics of a backlands utopia.

Between these two types of residential development—the one providing housing for the well-to-do, the other for the poor—were other types of a partly packaged character. One was that resulting from the movement of a large industry to the country and the establishment by the industry of a housing area for its workers. Another was the housing area developed through the co-operative efforts of the residents themselves. Such a housing area was that established on the outskirts of the crossroads hamlet of Sharon in East Gwillimbury in the late nineteen-fifties.

Sponsored by the Catholic Church, the Sharon development had its beginnings in a study group in Toronto where a number of interested people were brought together to learn how to go about to build houses for themselves co-operatively. After several months of study and planning, when everything involved in the building of a house from the purchase of the land to the sodding of the front lawn was gone into, a site was chosen and the homes built. Some-thing like forty families took part in the project.

What the co-operative residential development secured was a pooling of the financial resources, the knowledge, and the skills of a number of people. Without such co-operative effort, few of the families involved could have undertaken the building or purchasing for themselves a house in the country. More important still than the financial considerations, however, were the considerations of a social character. Though when first brought together, the families taking part in the project were strangers to one another (some of them were not even Catholic), by the time the project was completed they had been made into a cohesive social group. In effect, it was the community which was built first; the houses in which the people were to live were built afterwards. There was not required of the residents here, any more than in Thorncrest Village, the painful experience of trying to build up from the very beginnings the structure of a society.

What the residential development of the co-operative type—or of other packaged or partly packaged types—secured was a considerable widening of the market for suburban housing. There were many people prepared to move into a residential area like Sharon or Riverdrive Park, or like Thorncrest Village or Don Mills, who would not have been prepared to locate along some country road or even in the environs of an old established village. They were assured that neighbours would be reasonably congenial, sharing the same interests and possessed of the same aspirations, and, especially in the case of the fully packaged development, they were assured as well that what had started out to be one kind of residential community would not suddenly become another kind. Enough of the structure of the community was built up at the very beginning that it could not be easily changed.

Yet the market, though made wider, remained sharply restricted. Not just anybody was prepared to move into a packaged residential development, however well provided it may have been with urban services and amenities. Important social advantages were offered by such a development, but in return a heavy price was exacted. There were obligations owing to the group, and to the sponsoring body or individual. People had to be prepared to fit in, to join in the collective effort which such schemes of settlement required. Neighbourliness could not be secured without an effort to be neighbourly. For people interested only in acquiring a house for themselves such obligations could appear highly onerous.

It was thus that the vast widening of the housing market came only with that large-scale type of residential development which did not involve building into the development the structure of a community. In terms of what actually occurred, of course, there was no clear and sharp break between this type of residential development and the type which had gone before. The one led into the other. A residential development like Bathurst Manor in North York, providing housing for middle-class Jewish people, possessed something of the "packaged" quality characteristic of Don Mills, while, in Etobicoke Township, Thorncrest Village soon became scarcely distinguishable from some of the "smart" residential developments growing up nearby. Yet, in terms of the over-all picture, there was a vast difference between the community residential development and the residential development pure and simple. The former type of development depended upon reaching out far enough into the country so that it was possible to build up, in some fashion or other, the structure of a complete community. The residential development pure and simple, in contrast, depended upon being near enough already built-up residential areas that the structure of a community could be expected to grow up on its own, without being provided for within the development itself.

Thus the occupation of the countryside had to reach a certain point before there resulted this type of residential development. Once this "break-through" point was reached, however, there was virtually no limit to the development which could take place. Precisely what point had to be reached before such a "break-through" occurred depended, of course, upon the size and character of the residential development. The conditions necessary for a residential development which involved building homes to sell in a price range of $25,000–35,000 were not the same as those necessary for a residential development which involved building homes to sell in a price range of $11,000–15,000. The price of land near the built-up areas of the city, driven high by speculation, forced developers to open up areas further out for large-scale residential building, but how far out was determined by the prices the houses were built to sell for. High land costs could be absorbed more readily by higher-priced houses.

But whatever the price the house was built to sell for, until the upper price ranges were reached, what was offered for sale was primarily a house. The whole paraphernalia of a community was not included. People buying a house in Thorncrest Village were buying the village with the house. People, on the other hand, buying a house in a large-scale subdivision development were buying a house and nothing else. What community was to be found here was one outside the subdivision, not built into it.

The large-scale residential development was able to reach a very different kind of market than that reached by the community residential development. The major effort was directed towards making the house competitive in price for a mass market. This was true of the high-priced as well as the low-priced house although the conditions of building for a mass market were most completely reached in those residential developments where houses were built to sell for a price ranging from about $11,000 to $20,000. As the price advanced beyond $20,000 something of the "mass" quality went out of the market; beyond $35,000 it almost completely disappeared. People prepared to pay $35,000 for a house wanted something more than simply a house; they wanted a "good place to live" and they wanted a place where property values would be protected. If the $35,000 house could not be built in an area where previous development had secured the conditions of residential exclusiveness, it almost necessarily had to be built in an area given up to a packaged residential development. At the other extreme, people unable to pay as much as $11,000 for a house were effectively excluded from the mass market. The cost of the land and its assembly, and the conditions of the mortgage market, made impossible building on a large scale houses selling for less than $11,000. Somewhere about $11,000 at the bottom and $20,000 at the top the break occurred between the house that was built for what was unmistakably a mass market, and the house that was not.

It was people able to afford a $11,000 to $20,000 house who were the creators of the Toronto suburban community. Settling in the country were the rich and the poor but together they were able to occupy only small bits and pieces of it; there were not many rich and most of the poor lacked the means or the will to undertake the hazardous move out of the city. The real occupation of the countryside came only with the mass building of homes for those people, neither rich nor poor, who, prospering with the boom economic conditions of the nineteen-fifties and crowded in the city by overseas immigration and a rising birth-rate, were made increasingly house hungry. What had been a trickle in the earlier phases of the movement of population into the country became now a great flood. In this manner were the townships of Etobicoke, North York, and Scarborough occupied in the years 1953–58 and in this manner are being occupied today the townships lying beyond.

The character of development of Scarborough Township from the first settlement there of urban people affords an indication of the way in which the occupation of the country by an urban population led to the transforming of a rural community into an urban. In 1951 the population of the township was 56,292. By 1961 it was 217,286. It was the growth in these years which determined the urban character of the community. With the coming of the large-scale subdivision development after 1951 whole vast areas were transformed from country into city in a few months.

Yet this development after 1951 was not unrelated to developments which had gone before. The sudden and almost complete overrunning of the township by an urban population in the years 1953–58 stands in sharp contrast to the long, halting efforts to bring about its residential occupation in the years leading up to 1953. The history of Scarborough during this early period of development is the history of a suburban community coming into being.

The original rural settlement of the township had taken place in the early nineteenth century. Because of its proximity to the town of York (later the city of Toronto) and the scenic attractions of the Scarborough Bluffs, much of the land along the lake was taken up by persons who had earned the favour of the government or by such government-favoured institutions as King's College; in a modest way, this area became one of landed estates with a predominantly English population. Further east, in that part of the township cut through by Highland Creek, the land was mostly sandy and swampy, and here early attempts to farm proved largely unsuccessful. By the middle of the century, the prevalence of fever in this area had given it the reputation of being one of the most unhealthy places in the province. Trade, shipping, and the development of local extractive industries, however, led to an early economic prosperity with the result that Highland Creek and West Hill grew up as thriving towns. Early church registers provide an indication of the diversified occupations of the people. After 1860, however, decline set in. Depletion of local resources, new technological developments, the building of the Grand Trunk Railway, and improvements to the Toronto harbour led to the disappearance of industry and shipping and the shift of trade to more strategically located centres. The towns of Highland Creek and West Hill became little more than place names on the map. Population over the next half century moved out rather than into the area, a development reflected in the decline of the total population of the township from 4,615 in 1871 to 3,845 in 1901.

In contrast, the northwestern part of the township was good farm country and here, in the first half of the nineteenth century, a substantial farming population established itself, mostly Scottish Presbyterian, with ties developing early with the village of Markham and later with the village of Agincourt. These were the people who, not favoured by the provincial administration located in the capital of Toronto, found themselves in 1837 sympathetic to the cause of William Lyon Mackenzie, and who, in the years which followed, voted Grit on election day, attended church faithfully on the sabbath, carefully tended their fields, husbanded their savings, and built fine brick or stone homes, some of which are still standing today. Though this area, like similar agricultural areas throughout the province, lost some population during the years 1860–1900, the loss was probably not great.

As late as 1911, Scarborough was still largely undisturbed by the growing city a few miles to the west. Then, in the years immediately after, there occurred the first penetration of the township by an urban population. With the spreading out of the city and the establishment of street car service on the main roads leading into the township, the old landed estates in the southwestern corner were broken up and the area developed residentially. Along the lakefront, where the view was sufficiently tempting to attract people able to afford spacious lots, fine homes made their appearance, but immediately to the north small one- or two-storey houses were built close together on narrow lots, to accommodate a working-class population being crowded out of the city by high rents. Within a few years after the First World War, this area was almost wholly built up with houses of cheap and shoddy construction. The population which established itself here was mainly of British origin; a large proportion was made up of British immigrants. What had grown up in the southwestern corner of the township during the early nineteen-twenties was a typically urban, working-class district.

With the economic boom of the nineteen-twenties, however, the kind of residential development which took place in the southwestern corner of the township quickly gave way to another kind involving the subdividing for residential purposes of the area beyond, almost to the eastern extremity of the township. The land was acquired cheaply and, even allowing for substantial profits, was sold off at a low price in one- or two-acre lots. A radial railway extending out to West Hill provided transportation to the city. Many hundreds of urban residents, looking for a place to build a small house, bought lots and established themselves, but the area remained largely given up to bush and forest. By 1930, there was a scattering of population extending from the western to the eastern border of the township. Thousands of vacant lots, waiting to be taken up for residential purposes, eloquently bespoke the optimism of the nineteen-twenties. Few subdivisions could boast more than a handful of residents. The types of homes built were generally poor and urban services were non-existent. There were no industries to provide a local market for labour.

The problems of Scarborough during the depression of the nineteen-thirties were largely problems resulting from the kind of residential development which had taken place during the nineteen-twenties. Unemployment became general, property taxes remained unpaid, essential services could not be provided, and poor relief became an intolerable burden. The bankruptcy of the township under such circumstances was inevitable.

The war years made recovery possible and the municipal government might well have taken advantage of the long halt in residential growth to prepare for the problems which the post-war boom would bring. Instead, the township encouraged the very kind of development which at the onset of the depression had brought about its ruin. Most of the vacant lots in subdivisions stretching across the township had been taken over for taxes during the nineteen-thirties. Now, with the mad clamour for housing, the township saw a means of realizing a substantial revenue by selling lots to prospective home-owners. Between 1946 and 1951, almost exactly the same sort of development took place as had taken place before 1930. People desperate for any sort of housing bought these lots for $300 or so and built small frame homes or basement dwellings. They settled down with the hope that the vacant spaces about them would eventually be filled and services which were lacking would ultimately be provided. At the same time, farmers along the main crossroads of the township seized the opportunity to realize some ready cash by selling building lots along their fronts. Approval for such subdividing was readily secured and homes were erected of various types, ranging from four-room frame cottages to substantial brick dwellings.

To the northeast, during these same years, there grew up an even more erratic type of residential community. Here, after the First World War, many Toronto residents with tastes much less exacting than those generally prevalent today had built summer cottages at favoured spots along Highland Creek. These cottages, small, poorly constructed, and built close together, were winterized in a manner that added nothing to their appearance and little to their comfort. During and after the Second World War, they became the permanent homes of people moving out from the city. In this way grew up the little residential community known as the Willows. Isolated from the outside and treacherously situated in terms of flood hazards (as Hurricane Hazel so dramatically demonstrated), the Willows quickly degenerated into a slum. Only with urban growth, and the action of a township council, grown wise with the years, in converting the whole Highland Creek area into parkland, could it be rescued from such a state.

Not all of the residential development that took place in Scarborough in the years after the war was of the type described above. Extending along the cliffs east of the Fallingbrook district, there grew up a fine residential area of large homes, spacious grounds, and paved streets. At the same time, within the old established village of Agincourt and on its immediate outskirts, considerable residential development took place during the years 1946–51—the population of the village grew from 607 in 1941 to 971 in 1951. Developments such as these did something to improve the over-all condition of the Scarborough community, but, had depression come after 1950, the township might well have faced a financial crisis like that of the nineteen-thirties. Lack of control of residential development permitted the population to scatter over the whole breadth of the municipality. Great open spaces made the provision of services extremely costly. Only 5.23 per cent of the total assessment in 1949 was industrial and only 5.94 per cent was commercial; 19.82 per cent was still agricultural; the remainder, 69.01 per cent, was residential. Housing conditions generally were among the poorest in the Toronto metropolitan area. Of the 14,604 occupied dwellings in the township in 1951, only 77 per cent of them were provided with furnaces, 72 per cent with flush toilets, 57 per cent with electric or gas refrigerators, 63 per cent with telephones.[1] Dependent upon jobs several miles from its place of residence, the population of the township, as the township itself, was as economically vulnerable in 1950 as it had been twenty years earlier. A sudden halt in growth would have left Scarborough with a great number of basement dwellings, a still greater number of ramshackle shacks or poorly constructed and ill-kept frame or cement-block houses, a large part of the population unemployed or employed only in casual work, inadequate municipal services, and no means of substantially increasing municipal revenues.

Instead of depression, however, with the Korean War there came the great boom of the early nineteen-fifties. The residential development which took place completely altered within a few short years the character of the Scarborough community. Before 1950, apart from the southwestern corner of the township where the transportation link with the city was close, it had been economically impossible to convert large blocks of good farm land to urban residential use; a price of between $300 to $1,000 for building lots had encouraged spotty development. Now, however, with real estate values soaring, and good residential lots advancing in price to $2,000, $3,000, and, before long, $4,000, development capital became available which made possible the buying up of whole

[1]Census of Canada, 1951. *Population and Housing Characteristics by Census Tracts: Toronto*, Bulletin CT-6.

farms and their conversion to residential use. The day of the small frame or cement-block cottage had come to an end in Scarborough. With the rise in real estate values, and the increasing insistence by the township government that the land built upon be serviced, the quality of homes constructed and the general character of the residential areas steadily improved. Something of the old, spotty residential development continued for a time, but it was quickly submerged in the new kind of subdivision development where whole farms were suddenly swallowed up and, almost overnight, hundreds of six-room, neat, brick bungalows or two-storey houses made their appearance. In strategic crossroad locations, the establishment of large shopping centres soon gave the township an urban air.

This new burst upon Scarborough of an urban population, however, brought its own distinctive problems. For a brief period, industrial growth almost kept up with residential growth and there could be hope that the imbalance between industrial and residential assessment would correct itself. But the pressure for new housing was so intense that residential building continued to outstrip industrial development, and the imbalance remained. Lack of effective control over the plans of subdividers intensified the problems of the township. Before 1951, prospective home-owners had leaped over one another to occupy lots here and there across the township. Now real estate developers did the same thing by opening up subdivisions in various parts of the township without reference to the large open spaces left in between. The speculator was as active as the builder, and for every parcel of land built upon, another was withdrawn from the market.

Other kinds of problems quickly made their appearance. Where new subdivisions were opened up in areas that hitherto had been devoted almost wholly to agriculture, the problem of fitting the new into the old was not particularly great. Most of the apparatus of the old rural community could be scrapped, or converted to the use of the new residential communities. The old rural school sites had not been well chosen in relation to the needs of the new residential suburbs, but such sites were few and far between, and many new schools were needed. Barns were torn down and farm houses were remodelled to fit into the new landscape. The farm population which had occupied the land was pushed out of the way.

The new suburban community was able to grow up free of the encumbrances of the old rural community. In a large part of the township, however, the residential development of the early nineteen-fifties involved the redevelopment of areas which had been developed earlier. The old residential streets, the old five-room frame or cement-block houses, the old lots wide enough to be divided into two narrow lots, the old schools and school sites, and the old ill-kept family stores and domestic industrial establishments still stood. The new capital investment was not yet sufficiently great to justify the scrapping of such a substantial investment of the past. Along many roads in the township, one side could be flanked by modern residential subdivisions and the other by lawnless, ramshackle frame dwellings situated on one- or two-acre lots, littered with torn-down automobiles or trucks, cement mixers, lumber, and trash of various sorts. Establishment of the services, and amenities, of an urban residential community became almost impossible where so much of what had developed in the past continued to intrude itself.

However, further urban growth in the years after 1956 brought an end to the mixture of old and new in most areas. Land between built-up areas became too valuable to lie undeveloped, and by the end of the decade not much of it remained. At the same time, the increase in the size of the capital investment in new development and the greater willingness of a township government (supported now by a metropolitan municipal structure) to invest in the future made possible the razing of much that had been built before 1951. The Willows was not alone in suffering destruction before the bulldozer. Subdivision developments like Guildwood Village led to a complete making over of one kind of suburban community into another. Roads were converted into four-lane lighted streets and vastly improved bus service into the city ushered in a new phase of development marked by extensive apartment-house building. Here and there, tough remnants of the past remained—only the dictates of the planner could force an old established village like Agincourt to make itself over—and far off, in the northeastern corner of the township, the farmer and farm community struggled to survive. But urban growth had done its work and what had once been country had become now almost wholly city. Scarborough had nearly passed through the stage of transforming a rural community into an urban.

Suburban growth, however, which in Scarborough (and in North York and Etobicoke), by the close of the nineteen-fifties, was almost at an end, was only beginning to make its effects felt in those townships further out. In Markham, Vaughan, Pickering, and Toronto Township, and, beyond these, Chinguacousy, Nelson, Trafalgar, King, Whitchurch, East Gwillimbury, and Whitby, there were still to be found suburban areas representing all the various stages of residential development. There was much in evidence the settlement along country roads of individual urban families. Indeed, in certain areas, it was not easy to tell the difference between the urban family taking up residence in the country and the farm family, now squeezed by mounting taxes and a higher standard of living, turning to urban forms of employment. Neither was there lacking the residential development which came with the movement of the urban poor to the country and the building up in small isolated pockets of what in effect were transplanted urban slums. Wilcox Lake was only one example of such a development. So too, here and there, and particularly where the rural scenery was inviting, residential communities of the packaged or partly packaged type had come into being, small enclaves of urban idealists or European immigrants offering a new variety and richness to the social life of rural Ontario. Such was the settlement of German immigrants south of Wilcocks Lake or of Catholic working-class people on the outskirts of Sharon. As well, in its own fashion, such was the settlement in Riverdrive Park.

It was the great subdivision, however, which was fast turning, by the end of the nineteen-fifties, the country lying beyond the old built-up townships into a part of the urban community. Suburban residential development followed the main highways out of the city, though areas near old established towns were most favoured by subdividers. Thus were established on the east side of Richmond Hill such subdivisions as Beverley Acres, Crosby Heights, or Richmond Acres, and, within the town of Newmarket or its immediate environs, such subdivisions as Lyons or East Gwillimbury Heights. Between these and other residential developments great open spaces remained. Not all the country had yet been made city. But already the land speculator had moved in, and there was not much country left within forty miles of Toronto which had not felt the effects of urban growth. Though towns like Richmond Hill, Markham, Stouffville, Uxbridge, Aurora, Newmarket, Woodbridge, Brampton, and Georgetown struggled still to maintain an independent existence, they, like the country, were fast becoming city. It was here in this vast area of countryside extending out to and beyond these towns that was to be found, indeed, by the time the decade of the nineteen-fifties had come to an end, the Toronto suburban community.

The Choice of a Suburban Home

IN THE FIFTEEN YEARS after the war Toronto's urban growth had resulted in the occupation by a million or so suburban inhabitants of an area of countryside large enough to provide housing for several times that population. Though to the west and the east the growth of the cities of Hamilton and Oshawa had led to the establishment of an almost unbroken line of residential settlement out from Toronto, to the north suburban residential development had taken place in very much a leap-frog fashion. New subdivisions had grown up before those already established had been fully developed, and often several miles of country separated one group of subdivisions from another. Only the presence here and there of old established towns gave the residential development some sense of order and direction.

Viewed from the perspective of the urban planner, there was much that could be deplored about the character of suburban residential development. It seemed almost as if every suburban resident had been determined to get as far away as possible from the city. The more isolated the residential development the more it appeared to have appealed to the family taking up residence in it. While the economies of large-scale production favoured building several hundred houses together, there seemed virtually no limit to the distance beyond the city such building could take place. In the pushing ever further into the country of large-scale subdivision developments, escape from the city for vast numbers of people was made possible.

Yet it was not a desire of people to escape from the city which led to the scattering of subdivision developments over the country-side many miles from the city. Rather, it was the drive to keep house prices down which forced subdivision developers further and further into the country. Where people wanted to live had very little to do with where houses were built. Under different conditions, it is true, particularly with respect to the sale and taxation of land and the provision of mortgages, a very different development might have resulted. It would not have been impossible, indeed, had provincial and municipal authorities had the will, to have completely pre-vented the spread of urban population beyond fully developed resi-dential areas. There was nothing inevitable about the development which did occur. But it is no part of this study to pass judgment upon how Toronto's residential growth should have been planned and controlled. What is important here is an understanding of the development which actually did take place. To explain this develop-ment in terms of a desire of people to escape conditions of life in the city (or, as Wood would have it,[1] to re-create the conditions of small-town life) overlooks the simple fact that only in areas distant from the city could houses be built at a price to be sold in a mass market. It was not a desire to escape the city but a desire to secure a house in which to live that led to the movement of people into suburban areas.

There was much about the city, it is true, as it had developed over the years, that offered people good reasons for moving beyond its borders. Crowded streets, smoke-laden air, mounting taxes, crime, and political corruption were only a few of the manifesta-tions of what appeared to be a general disintegration of the urban way of life. The city had become not a wholly pleasant place in which to live. Certainly, urban planner and social reformer alike could make much of its faults and find little in it to commend. Talk of the "flight from the city" seemed to have real meaning when the move to the suburbs was viewed against the background of what the city had to offer.

Yet such talk, though it may have served a useful purpose in stirring city fathers to action, came far from touching upon the true reason for the movement of people to the suburbs in the years

[1]Robert C. Wood, *Suburbia: Its People and Their Politics* (Boston, 1959).

after the Second World War. Within the inner reaches of the city there were, certainly, areas where residence had become exceedingly unpleasant. But the people who lived in these areas were not the ones who came to populate the suburbs. People who are poor do not move out of the city except under very special circumstances, while those who, once poor, now have become rich move usually only into those areas of the urban or suburban community where their newly found status can be preserved. Thus the "old Canadians" of downtown Toronto after the war, still poor, remained where they were or settled in an area like Riverdrive Park, far out from the city; "new Canadians," now rich, took up residence in one of the packaged residential developments not too distant from the city. It was, however, neither the poor, nor the poor become rich, who filled up the vast expanse of the suburbs in the years after the war. The new suburban population came, predominantly, not from the downtown urban area but from the old established residential areas extending out to the very limits of the city and, indeed, beyond.

To a fifty-year-old, grown sensitive with the years, residence in many of these areas could appear unpleasant enough. Wherever in the urban community single-family dwellings had given way to multi-family, aesthetic values had suffered. Trees had been slaughtered to make room for widened streets, and stately homes of the past had crumbled before the bulldozer, their place taken by high-rise apartment dwellings. The noise of traffic alone may have been sufficient to make living in these parts of the city intolerable to a person accustomed to the peace and quiet of a secluded residential area.

But to those young people who made the move to the suburbs, their surroundings in the city had appeared of no great importance. What was important to them was to be near their place of work and to the downtown shopping and entertainment area. They could be indifferent to the district in which they lived. There was thus nothing about the city which led these people to seek to escape residence in it. The city offered them everything they wanted except a house. It was the search for a house which forced them out of the city into the suburbs.

In the twenty years 1941–61, the population of the Toronto

metropolitan area more than doubled, growing from 909,928 to 1,824,481. For every person provided with residential accommodation in 1941, another had to be provided with such accommodation by 1961. A part of this new population could secure accommodation within the city by taking over the homes of people moving out. Few recent European immigrants settled beyond old built-up urban areas. The result was a "moving up" of older elements of the population in terms of type of neighbourhood and residential area. Municipalities like Forest Hill Village, Leaside, and York Township became occupied after the war very largely by people who had previously owned homes in the city. Within the built-up urban community, the least desirable areas of residence were those closest to the centre. The further population moved out from the centre the more likely was it to be a population which had already owned homes and which was taking advantage of urban growth to secure an improvement of residential environment.

There was such a movement until the outer limits of the urban community were reached. Beyond those limits, the pattern reversed itself. Like the downtown areas of the city, the great expanse of the suburbs did not attract people who already owned homes. People who already owned homes moved only if the move held the promise of an improvement in their residential state. Such people were able to be selective—they didn't have to move—and consequently they could look around before making a choice and take into consideration not only the value offered in the house but the desirability of the area as a place of residence. Where they were most likely to locate, therefore, was somewhere within the built-up urban community or, if beyond, in a suburban residential area of the packaged type which appeared to have something special to offer in environment.

Thus the more "purely" suburban the residential area was the more likely was it to be made up of people owning a house for the first time. Of the 379 families settling in Regency Acres, a subdivision of single detached houses outside the town of Aurora, only 62, or 16.3 per cent previously owned homes; in Beverley Acres, a subdivision of semi-detached houses outside the town of Richmond Hill, the number was 94 out of 293, or 32.1 per cent.[2] Of a research

[2]C.M.H.C. records.

sample of 78 residents in three other subdivisions, Lyons outside Newmarket and Crosby Heights and Richmond Acres outside Richmond Hill, only 14, or 18 per cent, previously owned homes.

In contrast, over half of the 196 families settling in Thorncrest Village, 113 or 57.6 per cent, were previous home-owners.[3] In Don Mills the proportion was almost as large. In 1954, of 707 families surveyed by the Don Mills Development Company, 46.2 per cent had previously owned homes; in 1955, of 932 families surveyed, the proportion was 45.2 per cent; in 1956, of 1,835 families surveyed, 53 per cent; and, in 1958, of 1,932 families surveyed, 46.2 per cent.[4] Had the survey been limited to owners of single-family dwellings, the proportion almost certainly would have been larger. Of a research sample of Don Mills residents in an area of single-family dwellings, 50 per cent of the original home-owners had previously owned homes, whereas, in an area of semi-detached houses, the proportion was only 31.3 per cent. Don Mills had something of the character of the mass residential development and this was revealed by the proportion of the residents, in areas given over to semi-detached housing, who had not previously owned homes. Because of its size, it could not be "packaged" to the extent that Thorncrest Village was. But in areas where single-family dwellings predominated it had an unmistakable packaged character. Here about one-half of the residents had given up homes they had owned in older residential areas to settle in Don Mills.

The proportion of residents previously owning homes, of course, was not always a certain indication of the extent to which a residential area was "packaged." Of the 251 original residents of Edge Park subdivision in Scarborough Township, as many as 95, or 37.8 per cent, had previously owned their own homes.[5] In 1959, when Edge Park developed, the area nearby had been largely built up, and families moving in had immediately available to them schools, churches, shopping centres, and other community facilities. A family living in an older residential area could give up the home it owned and move into a new house in Edge Park without suffering any great loss in the way of community services or amenities. The

[3]Village records.
[4]"Statistics Re House Owners and Tenants in Don Mills," survey carried out for Don Mills Development Co. Mimeographed.
[5]C.M.H.C. records.

change could represent for it a "moving up" in type of residential accommodation and environment. For the family not owning a home and now forced to buy, however, the advantage of locating in Edge Park was much less apparent. A house of equal quality could be bought for less money further out from the city. Thus, where the interest was in securing a house rather than exchanging a house in an old residential area for a house in a new, the subdivision developing in an area not yet built up (where houses were cheaper) was strongly favoured.

On the other hand, residential areas that were developed to provide housing for people of very limited financial means were populated almost wholly by families owning homes for the first time. None of the residents interviewed in the Catholic co-operative development outside Sharon had been previous home-owners. Among the German immigrant families settling south of Wilcocks Lake, likewise, there were no previous home-owners. In Riverdrive Park, of a research sample of twenty-two home-owners, only two had previously owned homes. The residents of an area like Riverdrive Park were made up very largely of a displaced population drawn from the centre of the city. Those who did not come from the centre of the city came largely from country districts or small towns—or from overseas. They belonged to a social class which characteristically rented rather than owned a home. There was thus on their part a "moving up" both in type of residential accommodation and in type of residential environment; they were escaping not only from residence in an undesirable area of the city but from rental accommodation.

Among the families settling in the mass-developed residential area there were certainly some who made the same choice as those settling in an area like Riverdrive Park (or as those settling in an area like Thorncrest Village, Don Mills, or Edge Park). But, for most, the choice was not between rental accommodation and home-ownership, or between residence in an undesirable area of the city and residence in the suburbs. The suburban population, though largely made up of non-home-owners, belonged to the home-owning class. For such a population home-ownership at a certain stage in life was something that was taken for granted. It did not represent a move upward in the social scale. A house, like a baby carriage (and, indeed, for most, a car) was considered simply one of the necessities of family living and, like the baby carriage (and the car) was shopped for and bought in terms of what could be afforded. Given the nature of the housing market and the general character of the development taking place, there was nothing surprising in the fact that it was to the suburbs these people turned once the house search began. Any other considerations that influenced their decision seldom had to do with the character of the district in the city where they had been living. It is true, there were not many families interviewed who did not express a preference for the suburban way of life. But the indication of such a preference offered no certain clue to the reason for the move to the suburbs. Having settled in a suburban residential area, it was not difficult for these young people to convince themselves that this was where they preferred to live. But there was no mistaking, in the answers they gave to various questions, why in fact the move had been made. What the vast majority of them wanted was a house. If other considerations entered into the decision to move, they were almost always secondary to this one.

Of a sample of seventy-eight families who had bought homes in Crosby Heights, Richmond Acres, Lyons, or Beverley Acres, forty-six had previously been living in apartments or flats in Toronto or its immediate environs and only three of these forty-six indicated that they had moved at least in part because of dissatisfaction with the area in the city in which they resided. The first had been living in a flat in the Rogers Road area of York Township where both the husband and wife had grown up. They had moved and bought a house in Lyons subdivision, they said, because they needed more space and wanted to own their own home. But the area in which they had lived, "now becoming occupied by immigrants, mostly Italians," where "fights and arguments were everyday occurrences," was described as unsatisfactory. The second family had been living in an apartment and had bought a house in Beverley Acres, as they put it, "just because of the children," but the area in the city where they lived, which they described as "international," would appear to have been one of the reasons for the move; "it was too noisy downtown and stinky—bad for the children." The third family had been living with the wife's parents in the Lansdowne–St. Clair area.

They had bought a house in Beverley Acres because the parents had moved to Orillia and the Toronto house was sold. Nothing was said about the area in the city as a reason for moving out, but it was described as having once been good, middle class, which, "with many immigrants moving in, had become practically a slum."

Five other families had given up apartments in the city to buy a house in the suburbs for reasons which may have been related to the character of the neighbourhood lived in. The first of these families, a couple both forty years of age with no children, had been living in an apartment on Mount Pleasant Road, in an area described as a "rather anonymous city neighbourhood." They had decided to move and buy a house in Richmond Acres because they "could not see paying rent." The second family, with three children, living in a flat, had moved and bought a house in Lyons subdivision because the rent was too high and they "might as well be putting money into something"; however, the neighbourhood in which they had lived was described as "west end residential—mostly foreigners" and may have had something to do with the move. The other three families, moving from the city to buy homes in Beverley Acres, gave no indication of having lived in an unsatisfactory residential area. Two asserted that the reason for the move had been to avoid continuing to pay rent. "Renting an apartment was expensive and we wanted a place of our own," the one expressed it; the other, "because we wanted a place of our own, that's all." The third family, living in a flat in a neighbourhood described as a "sort of suburb," had moved because, as they put it, "we were fed up with living in other people's houses"; relations with the landlord were described as having been very disagreeable.

Not one of the remaining thirty-eight families gave any indication of having moved out of the city because they had found the area in which they lived unsatisfactory. At worst, the area was described in some such fashion as "an older neighbourhood of older people," or "it wasn't a neighbourhood at all." Most of the replies were in the character of a "nice neighbourhood," "downtown—pretty good neighbourhood," "fairly nice area, pleasant," "just a middle-class area," "very good area," "quiet—older people—nice." A few families spoke of having had many friends where they had lived, but many admitted having known only a small number of people.

"There is not much neighbourhood life in an apartment," one resident expressed it; "only said 'hello' to the person next door," another had to confess. Such casual neighbourhood ties as these did little to root people in the urban community. The city was an easy place from which to move. On the other hand, this type of neighbourhood did not lead to an urge to escape. All thirty-eight families were very clear in the reason they gave for moving from the city and buying a home in the suburbs. They needed more residential space. It had been this urge to secure larger living quarters rather than dissatisfaction with the area lived in which had been uppermost in their minds.

The following statements were typical:

Flat too small with three children. Bought house because more room and you think you can be by yourself.

Apartment satisfactory but too small with baby.

Apartment served its purpose. Bought house because of kids; we're having a family.

Well, how is it in a flat with a two-year-old child!

Bought house on account of family.

Two-room flat much too small.

Basement apartment all right. Bought house because we had two children.

Flat was terrible—much too small. Bought house because we didn't have enough room.

Basement apartment on the whole very good but we bought a house because we needed room, for the sake of the children.

Apartment not very satisfactory. It was pretty tough to get a place in 1954; had to take what you could get. Bought house because with kids it's easier than living in an apartment.

Flat in mother-in-law's house. Not too good after first baby came, two rooms and bath. Bought house for growing family.

We bought house because of the impending birth of our child. With the two of us alone we didn't need a house.

Bought a house because it was no life for kids in two rooms.

For those thirty-two families in the sample who had not previously been living in apartments or flats in Toronto, the reasons for the move to the suburbs were more mixed. The purchase of homes in Richmond Acres by two of these families and of homes in Lyons subdivision by eight can be readily accounted for. The two in Richmond Acres had their place of work (and had been living) in Richmond Hill. Of the eight locating in Lyons, three had been renting apartments and two had been renting houses in Newmarket, and three others had been transferred there by their employers from other Ontario centres, one from Toronto. Four other families had simply shifted their place of residence without moving far out of the area in which they had been living; one had been renting a house in Elgin Mills on the outskirts of Richmond Hill before buying in Crosby Heights; one had owned a house in Wilcox Lake which they had sold to buy in Beverley Acres, one had been living in a farm house in King Township, and one, a widow, had moved from a rented house in Aurora to a house she purchased in Lyons subdivision.

Of the other eighteen families, all from Toronto or its environs, two had owned and six had rented houses which they had found too small or in some other way unsatisfactory, one had rented a house which was torn down, one had made the house purchase before marriage, and two others, renting houses, had bought out of a desire to save rent. One, owning a house in Scarborough, had moved "for a personal reason, having to do with the church," and another, also owning a house in Scarborough, had sold it because the taxes were too high. One other couple, both fifty-four years of age without children who had twice previously owned homes but had given them up "because they cut into the wife's golf time," had moved from the city, and bought a house in Crosby Heights, for no very clear reason. Three other residents, previously owning homes, could offer no reason for the move to the suburbs.

Only three of these eighteen families in any way indicated that the district in which they had lived might have had something to do with their moving. One of these, buying a home in Richmond Acres, gave as the reason for moving that the house they owned in Toronto was too small, but they also said that the district in which they had been living was "too close to Yonge Street." The second, buying a house in Beverley Acres for the professed reason of saving rent, almost certainly were influenced in the decision by their place of residence; "we were living," the wife asserted, "right in the centre

of the city, around Grange and Spadina—I didn't like the district."
The third, having shortly before buying in Beverley Acres moved
into a rented house in the Woodbine district, had earlier been living
in an apartment at Grange and Augusta; "odd, mixed races, densely
populated neighbourhood," the wife described the area, "but nobody
ever bothered us."

In the case of the other fifteen families, nothing was said about the
district lived in to suggest that dissatisfaction with it entered into
the decision to move. When described at all, the description was
of the sort: "more the old type of neighbourhood, you know, more
friendly"; "area of older people, mostly with grown-up families";
"area of small single-family houses—knew almost everybody there";
"quiet neighbourhood—dead end street"; "more or less like this
one [Beverley Acres]—mixed shall we say"; "Don Mills—a spread-
out community." Like the families moving out of apartments in the
city, these people giving up houses they had owned or rented only
very rarely hinted that they had been reluctant to move from the
area in which they had been living. But similarly there had been,
in the type of neighbourhood lived in, little that had led to an
urge to move.

The four subdivisions from which these samples were drawn
represented a type of suburban residential development that had
little other than housing to offer. Even so, for some people, residence
in them could appear more desirable than residence in the city.
But to the vast majority of the families settling in them the city
they had left behind had been good. It was in the city they had
their place of work and it was there that were available most of the
things they were interested in, shopping and entertainment facilities,
friends, relatives, and, for those so inclined, libraries, night schools,
art galleries, and such. To leave the city meant giving up much.
But in return there was offered the one thing the city withheld, a
house in which to raise a family.

It was different for people moving into residential areas like
Thorncrest Village and Don Mills. Among the residents of these
areas who had been living in flats or apartments in the city, there
had been the same urgency to secure housing space. But a far
greater proportion of the people moving out of the city into Thorncrest Village or Don Mills had already owned their own homes,

and a far greater proportion, whether owning their own homes or not, had been influenced in making the decision to move from the city by the desire to secure an improvement in their residential environment. This is not to say that people locating in Thorncrest Village or Don Mills had been living in less desirable parts of the city than had those locating in such mass residential developments as Crosby Heights, Richmond Acres, Lyons, or Beverley Acres. But they were people who, owing to their occupation, education, and social standing tended to be much more sensitive to their residential surroundings. It was this sensitivity which had accounted in large part for their decision to move from the city. The difference showed up in the reasons given by residents of these areas for the decision to buy a house in the suburbs. Even those families living in apartments in the city, many of whom were clearly in need of more space, were inclined to give a reason other than this one for the move. In the case of those families who already owned their own homes in the city, few failed to make reference to the character of the area in which they had been living even if another reason for the move had been given.

Information provided by a sample of residents of Don Mills offers an indication of the extent to which the decision to move had been influenced by the character of the area previously lived in. Of fifty-seven residents owning homes in Don Mills, thirty-seven had moved from the City of Toronto or its immediate environs, twenty-one from apartments or flats, thirteen from houses owned, and three from houses rented. Only five of the twenty-one who moved from apartments or flats gave as the reason for the move that they needed more space. Six others offered this as one of the reasons but indicated that the desire to own their own home had influenced their decision as well. The remaining ten gave as the sole reason for moving the desire to own their own homes. For these people, the character of the district lived in may have had nothing to do with the decision to move, but it is not perhaps without significance that five who gave as a reason the desire to own their own homes described in unfavourable terms the district in which they had been living and three others made reference to it. The following were some of the statements made:

Bought a house to give the child a home and be my own master. Had an apartment at Bloor and Spadina. It wasn't what we were used to; lived there to save money to get the house as fast as possible.

Bought house to have our own roof over our head as well as for privacy. Had just one room in downtown Toronto, between King Street and the Lake. It was old immigrants from England, and well, the district was getting worse and worse. We didn't like it; lived there just to save money to buy the house.

Bought house because it was more space for less money. Lived on Kingston Road in an apartment which though adequate would have to be described as mediocre. Would say that it was lower to middle class; not as good as here.

It was, however, the families who already owned their own homes or who had been renting a house who clearly were most influenced in moving by the character of the district in which they had been living. For six at least of these sixteen families there was no mistaking the reason they had moved from the city:

The house we had owned was excellent but my wife wanted to move to a new district. The old district was getting run down.

Traffic was getting too heavy for children where we lived. Not the sort of place where we wanted a permanent home.

It was our first house and all we could afford. We wanted a better house and district. Judging by this area, the one we were in was lousy. We had no friends there.

The house we were renting was pleasant. We wanted a better atmosphere in which to raise our son. The house was on a busy, through street. We didn't know many people in the area.

The house we owned was fine but they changed the zoning and built a garage just around from us, and that did it.

Owned a house in east-end Toronto. It was quite congested there, pretty close to slums, I guess—lower middle-class neighbourhood and it was slowly deteriorating. We had no friends in the area.

Five other families, though not attributing the move to the district they had lived in, suggested in their reference to the character of this district that it was probably an important consideration: "area was working class people who had made a little money," "neighbourhood was fifty-fifty Jewish and Gentile—were not at ease with so many Jews," "an area of smaller lots and houses," "a low-cost housing area," "neighbours were older, belonged to odd religious groups and frowned on a lot of things," were the way these residents described their previous neighbourhoods. Only five of the sixteen explained the move as having had nothing to do with the area lived in. Three had moved because they needed larger houses, one because the wife had a heart attack and they wanted a bungalow instead of a two-storey house, and one because they "had got in too deep" with the house previously owned.

Though the sample questioned in Thorncrest Village is too small to make possible any estimate of the proportion of people who moved from Toronto or its environs to seek an improvement of residential area, the proportion probably was even greater than in Don Mills. Of nine residents who previously had lived in the City of Toronto, two clearly attributed the move to dissatisfaction with the area lived in. "Well, it wasn't a very good area," one resident confessed, "the foreigners were starting to get in; this was the thing that really made us want to move." The second bluntly asserted: "We were driven out by immigrants." Four other residents, in descriptions offered of the area previously lived in, strongly suggested that it had something to do with the move. "I would say it was a working man's district," one resident described the area; "working class and lower middle class," was the description offered by a second; "average" and "an area of older people" were the way the other two put it. Only three of the nine families gave a reason for the move that had nothing to do with the character of the area in which they had been living. Two, with their children now grown up, had wanted a smaller house, and the third, meeting with trouble financing the house they owned, had been forced to give it up.

Of a total of forty-six residents who had moved to Don Mills or Thorncrest Village from the City of Toronto or its environs, only twelve accounted for their move in terms of unsatisfactory or unsuitable residential accommodation. When the reason given for the move, by those living in apartments, was the desire to own their own homes, or, by those already owning their own homes, the desire to secure a better house, the character of the district in most cases almost certainly had something to do with the move. Such reasons suggest strongly that the motivation to move grew out of feelings not unrelated to considerations of status. Twenty-five, or more than one-half of the total sample, made some reference to the district in which they had lived in explaining the decision to buy a house in Don Mills or Thorncrest Village. "Flight from the city" may not accurately have described the reason for the move to these areas, but it came closer to doing so certainly than in the case of the move out of the city of people locating in the mass-developed residential areas.

At the other end of the scale, in terms of type of residential development, areas like Riverdrive Park and Wilcox Lake also tended to attract people who sought to escape residence in the city. Almost all those families moving into such areas from the city had been living either in the downtown district or in one of the poorer residential districts on the outskirts. Many of the older of these people had witnessed over the years the deterioration of the part of the city in which they had lived. What neighbourhood life there was had been largely destroyed. For the younger families who had moved to Riverdrive Park or Wilcox Lake, residence in the city would have meant going on living in a cheap rental district, where no satisfactory form of neighbourhood life existed, through those years their children would be growing up.

There was nothing surprising, therefore, in the fact that few residents of Riverdrive Park or Wilcox Lake who came from the city had anything favourable to say about the district in which they had lived. A number were non-committal, brushing off questions about their previous residential experience with such replies as "it was all right" or "they were nice people there." Those who answered more fully, however, left little doubt about its character. Thus one old man in Riverdrive Park could express the view, in explaining why at the age of seventy-four he moved from the city: "This is God's country you know; where we lived five thousand cars used to go through between five in the morning and nine in the evening." A number of other residents of Riverdrive Park and Wilcox Lake expressed little less forthrightly their opinion of the area in which they had lived. "It was a working man's district—cabbage town," one Riverdrive Park resident asserted, "It was rough and run down but you get that all over the world. Yet I raised three children and they never had any trouble." Another answered: "The area in

which we lived was no good. It was Parliament and Carlton Street—
that explains it. I didn't want my daughter to go to school in that
district." One other had this to say: "The neighbourhood was O.K.
as far as I was concerned other than bringing children up. It's
why I came out here."

For one element of its population, a residential development of
the Riverdrive Park or Wilcox Lake type exemplified in extreme
form the effect of those forces leading to the mass exodus of people
out of the city into the suburbs in search of a place to live. This
was a population in desperate need of housing which was forced
to move from one part of the city to another, or from the city to the
country, without being greatly concerned about its residential surroundings. For another element of its population, however, this
type of residential development exemplified the effect of those
selective forces which led to the movement of people out of the
city into the suburbs as a matter of choice. The choice, of course,
was between residence outside the city and residence in the least
desirable areas of the city, but even so it was not everyone who
was prepared to give up the sorts of things life in the city had to
offer for the advantages associated with owning a home in the
country. The older the person was in age, the more deliberate was
likely to be the choice. "I gave up my house in the city to come out
here and die in quiet," was a true expression of the aspirations of
the old man of seventy-four in Riverdrive Park who for thirty-five
years had known no other place of residence than a downtown
district in Toronto. For such a person the move represented in a
very real fashion an escape from life in the city.

But it was not only persons ready for retirement who found the
prospect of residence away from the city pleasant. For one young
couple in Riverdrive Park, aged twenty-eight and twenty-one at
the time of the house purchase, the move to the country was
described as "a good break from the hot and noisy city—it's a lot
quieter here." For another couple in the same area, thirty-seven
and thirty-six when they made the move from the city, a concern
about the raising of their children was given as the reason for the
choice, though here the pressure to find a place to live was evident
as well: "We bought it for the sake of the children, just to get away
from the busy streets; it was the only house we could afford to buy
at the time." A young woman, twenty-six when she moved with

her husband of the same age and their one-year-old son to Riverdrive Park, replied to the question of why they had moved: "I didn't
like it in Toronto, I hated it. I can't stand looking out the window
and seeing a brick wall in front of me." Also expressive of a dislike
for the city were the remarks of the following residents of Riverdrive
Park:

We didn't like it in Toronto because the house where we lived they
brought all drunk men and it was not a good place for the children.

I don't like the city. There's too much hubbub and noise and not the
fresh air. You worry about the children in the city.

I don't like the city—it's too crowded.

They all seem to be in such a hurry in the city.

There's no room to breathe in the city.

It's too mad and busy in the city.

It's too congested in the city.

I don't like it in the city. I spent a good many years there and I always
had it in mind that when pensioned off I would come to the country.

I hate the city. Everybody is in a rush and you can't make friends there.

I don't like the city. The class of people in Toronto now, they don't
consider anybody but themselves.

In the city, could I sit here and talk to you with my kids playing out
there and not worry?

The city could have done much in the years after the war
to make itself a more attractive place for people to live. With
large-scale overseas immigration, the rebuilding of the downtown
residential areas advanced too slowly to provide satisfactory accommodation for the population which could not afford housing in
the city's better residential areas. Yet the very deterioration of the
older residential areas of the city meant that there was in the years
after the war a growing supply of cheap rental housing. The poor
took over what had once been the housing of the rich. There were,
of course, people at the very bottom of the income scale who could
not afford even the cheapest of residential accommodation available
in the city. But neither could such people afford even the cheapest
of residential accommodation available in the country (except perhaps in those squatter settlements which in the Toronto area the

winter climate made almost impossible to develop). For the vast majority of the urban poor, however unsatisfactory the type of housing available to them in the city, this housing appeared more satisfactory than anything that was offered by the country; only a small fraction of them ventured out of the city to take up residence in the country. For the most part, those who made such a move were people who had a strong dislike for residence in the city; for residence, that is to say, in those parts of the city in which they could afford to live.

In this respect, thus, there was no great difference between the selective forces at work determining the movement of people out of the city into areas like Riverdrive Park and Wilcox Lake and into areas like Thorncrest Village and Don Mills. For the people moving either into Riverdrive Park or Wilcox Lake, or into Thorncrest Village or Don Mills, in terms of what they could afford, satisfactory housing was available in the city. What they could not secure in the city, at a price they could afford, was housing in an area they considered suitable as a place to live. For the urban poor, intent on an improvement of their residential environment, what this meant was moving far out from the city to an area like Riverdrive Park or Wilcox Lake. For the urban rich who were not yet rich enough to locate in an exclusive residential area in the city, the attainment of a desirable residential environment meant moving out of the city into a residential development of the Thorncrest Village or Don Mills type.

There was, of course, no clear and sharp line between those forces determining the movement out of the city of people settling, on the one side, in mass-developed residential areas like Crosby Heights, Richmond Acres, Lyons, and Beverley Acres and, on the other side, in packaged areas like Thorncrest Village or Don Mills or areas offering housing for the urban poor like Riverdrive Park or Wilcox Lake. Whatever part of the suburbs was turned to, there could be found a mixture of reasons for the move from the city. But, in terms of the general development which took place, the line was clear enough. In residential areas like Thorncrest Village and Don Mills, and like Riverdrive Park and Wilcox Lake, were to be found a large number of families who had moved from the city because they found residence there unpleasant. In contrast, in residential areas like Crosby Heights, Richmond Acres, Lyons, and Berverley Acres, the vast majority of families had moved from the city because they could not find there the house they could afford.

If there was nothing about the city which impelled these people to move out of it, there was nothing about the suburbs, on the other hand, which impelled people to move into them. This is not to say that no regard whatsoever was paid to what may have appeared to be the advantages of a particular suburban location. Real estate advertisements and, where the residential development was on a massive scale, literature of a board of trade sort made very vigorous efforts to play up the attractions of the suburban area in which homes were being sold, and such efforts were not without effect, whether what was offered was "an exclusive residential environment," "quiet country living," or nothing more than "sewers and paved streets." Where the price of the house was high, a good deal of effort went into selling the district in which the house was located, but even in areas of lower-priced housing the character of the residential surroundings were never completely neglected in the sales talk. The city street could be made to look drab indeed when compared with the beautifully landscaped residential development of the newspaper advertisement.

Yet even the newspaper advertisement made clear, when the residential development was a large-scale one, what was likely to make the greatest appeal. Every advertisement featured a picture of the house being offered and carried in large block print its price and the down-payment required. In the mass housing market as it developed after the war, house-buyers were sorted out in terms of their housing needs and their capacity to pay. People bought the type of house they required and could afford, and it was the availability of such a house that determined whether they settled in the city or the suburbs, or if in the suburbs, in what area.

What particular considerations influenced the choice of a house differed, of course, with different people. There were some who were very much alive to quality of construction, and others, more artistic in temperament perhaps, who had a ready appreciation of good design and appearance. For still others, the distance to be travelled to work or the availability of good schools may have weighed heavily. The new suburban resident did not completely lack ideas of what he wanted.

Yet, for the most part, he stumbled—or rushed—into buying a house in the suburbs without giving consideration to anything much except his need for better residential accommodation. The more "purely" suburban the residential area was, the more completely did this need for better residential accommodation determine the move. Where the residential development involved the building into the house of a number of "extras," there was attracted a class of people who could afford and had reason to consider the quality of the residential surroundings. The greatest difference in this regard was between the mass-developed residential area and the fully "packaged," but between different mass-developed residential areas as well there were differences. It was in those residential areas developing away from old established towns and attracting almost wholly their population from the city that the need for better residential accommodation dominated over all other considerations in the choice made of a place of residence.

Where the person buying a house in a suburban area was employed nearby or had for a number of years been living not far away, this proximity was in itself sufficient reason for the choice made. Many of the families settling in new subdivisions near old established towns had for years resided in the area. Their purchase of a home in what to them was a suburb of the town represented a move up in type of house and in type of district. As well, for some persons, settlement in the suburbs represented a move back to the town where they had spent their childhood. It was here that were centred cherished associations of the past: "My husband went to school in Newmarket," one resident could offer as a reason for locating in the nearby Lyons subdivision. For the vast majority of the families who moved from the city to the suburbs in search of a house, however, it did not greatly matter in what residential area they settled. Indeed, all areas looked very much alike. However much subdivision developers may have sought to introduce distinctive features in their plans, the drive to make the house competitive in price imposed sharp limits upon such efforts, and, to the prospective home-owner, there was nothing much which distinguished one residential area from another except the price of the house. The difference in this respect in many cases may have been only slight, a matter of a few hundred dollars, but where people were buying in terms of all that they could afford, even a slight difference could be decisive in the choice, as the replies of residents questioned in the field study made clear.

Of 102 residents interviewed in East Gwillimbury Heights, a new subdivision development of semi-detached homes outside the town limits of Newmarket, fifty-eight indicated that price was the only reason they had bought a house in the area. Sixteen others, making a total of seventy-four, gave this as the main reason though coupling with it other considerations such as its location near where they worked or that "it was a good place to raise kids." Twelve failed to give any reason. Only sixteen had a reason other than price for choosing a house in the area. Six of these residents worked in the district; one worked in the subdivision itself. Two older couples located here because their daughters had settled in the area and one couple because the wife's sister lived in Newmarket. One other chose the area because they liked the house. Only six offered a reason that had anything to do with the residential environment: "wanted small town near," "wanted to get out of Toronto because of the kids," "disliked Toronto—like small towns," "liked area," "always wanted to go north from the city," "better for children—less traffic," were the considerations mentioned. What was significant in the replies of the residents interviewed was the lack of any clear expression of a preference for a house in the suburbs. Only sixteen indicated, apart from the consideration of price, that they preferred to live outside the city, while as many as five indicated that they would have preferred a house in the city or on its immediate outskirts but none was available that they could afford. "We chose this house," one resident informed the field worker, "because of the low price and low down-payment. We also thought it was a good value. We looked at the houses in Scarborough but we thought they were too expensive; we also looked at several other places and found them all too high in price. We didn't want to move away from Weston. Friends now living here told us of this subdivision." Another resident replied to the same question:

We chose this house because of the price. It was the best we saw for the money. We drove around on Sunday afternoons looking for a place and found this one. We wanted something out of the city—a good place to bring up children. I don't think it is right for children to have to grow up in the city. We may have come a little far out—I would prefer a place in closer, you know; what everybody wants: a place that has the advantage of both, all the conveniences of the city and plenty of room and good country air besides. That seems impossible around Toronto, except for a good price; and so it is impossible for us now. We drove out one afternoon and saw this house and we decided to take it.

Of the fifty-eight families of East Gwillimbury Heights who indicated that the price of the house was the reason they had located in this area, there were unquestionably a number who had a preference for residence in the suburbs, though, could they have afforded it, they would have chosen a different location. None of these fifty-eight families, however, clearly expressed a preference for a suburban way of life. By far the majority of the residents of East Gwillimbury Heights had been living in Toronto, in flats or apartments. They had gone looking for a house to buy, typically by reading the advertisements in newspapers, by enquiring from friends, and by Sunday afternoon drives. They had an idea what they could afford. They were led to the suburbs and to this particular area by the price of the houses offered for sale. Among the similar answers to the question of the reason for this location were the following:

We were frantic. Had to buy this house. Could not find any other place to live with children. Heard about it from co-workers of husband.

The house was cheaper than one with comparable features located in Toronto. We feel we got good value for the amount of money spent.

It was a good buy for the price. Couldn't buy the same house anywhere else for the same amount. We also looked at houses in Richmond Hill and Georgetown but they were more expensive for the same type of house.

Moved here because the houses were cheap.

Came to this subdivision because we wanted to buy a house and the downpayment was low. We wouldn't have moved here if we had lots of money.

Located here because homes were cheaper than anywhere else.

Why did we move to this subdivision? Well let's face it! The houses are cheap and a low downpayment.

In Beverley Acres, a subdivision like East Gwillimbury Heights of semi-detached houses, of a sample of twenty-nine residents who had previously lived in Toronto, twenty-three indicated that they had located in the area because of the price of the house and the size of the down-payment. Thirteen of these gave no other reason for their choice. The ten who did suggested such considerations as "the district was handy to the city and the bus service was good," "figured it would be better for the kids," "it's nearer here to the lakes for swimming," "liked the north of Toronto area very much," "it's not in the city and yet it's not too far away from it," "close to work for husband." Of the six who gave a reason other than price for locating in the area, two claimed to have been pressured into the choice by real estate agents. One, born in Richmond Hill nearby, had always wanted to live in the town and chose the house they did because they "liked the look of it inside." Another claimed to have made the choice "just because we liked the house." Only two of the twenty-nine residents claimed to have been influenced in their choice by the character of the residential area. "It is more our type of district when we get more children," one of these residents replied when asked why they had located in the area. "Thought the district was well planned," was the answer given by the second.

Though three of the residents interviewed indicated a preference for living in the suburbs, as many as five suggested that they had moved so far out of the city only because they could not afford a house nearer to it. Twenty of the twenty-nine admitted having no knowledge or experience of suburban living before buying a house in Beverley Acres. "Always were city folk," one resident confessed. "I never know very much [about suburban living]," another replied, in broken English, "and like I say I don't know yet. We didn't know anything about the district, what kind of people live here and we just didn't care. We came up, took a look at the house, and bought it. We live our own way." A third resident replied: "I didn't know nothing about houses. My husband, he didn't know much either. We knew nothing about living in suburbs. One thing I knew it couldn't be more difficult than in the city." Of the nine residents who professed some knowledge or experience of suburban life, five had come from small towns or villages where they had owned their own homes or had been renting a house, one couple had grown up on a farm,

and one had recently immigrated from Holland. The families settling in Beverley Acres were predominantly from the city, who,
because of their circumstances, could know little about what residence in a suburban community was like. What was significant,
however, was not their lack of knowledge about suburban living but
lack of concern. A good many made an effort to learn something
about houses before undertaking the purchase of one; indeed, a
number had been in a building trade or had had some experience
in building. But very few indicated having made any effort to learn
about the area in which they were buying a house. "I was green—
we got this place in a week," "We had a friend living here and they
told us all the things we needed to know," "I read only advertisements when I was looking for a house," "We didn't know too much
about the district—we just came up and when we saw the houses
it was nothing but mud," "We bought this house from ads in paper
—a real estate man brought us out—we looked at it and we signed
the papers within one day if not the same day," were the ways
some of the residents described their embarking upon a career of
home-ownership. Clearly, it was not the search for a certain type
of residential environment that brought people to such an area as
Beverley Acres. What was sought was a house which could be
afforded and it was such a house that was offered here. What else
was offered was a matter of little consequence.

East Gwillimbury Heights and Beverley Acres were areas of
low-priced housing. It could be expected, therefore, that in the
choice of a house in either of these areas price would be a dominant
consideration. Given the general preference for the single-family
dwelling, only those people who could afford nothing better bought
a house that was semi-detached. None of the residents interviewed,
in East Gwillimbury Heights or Beverley Acres, indicated a preference for a semi-detached house. It was clearly price that determined the choice of this type of house, and as a consequence it
was price that determined the choice of the area in which semi-
detached housing was available. "We wanted a detached house,"
a resident of Beverley Acres confessed, "but they were too expensive. We chose this district because semi-detached were cheaper."
"We would rather have had a detached house," asserted an East

Gwillimbury Heights resident, "but this one was easier to carry because of the smaller down-payment."

But in areas of single-family dwellings as well it was mostly price that determined the choice made. There may have been, for single-dwelling houses in the price range of $13,000–$16,000, a greater degree of choice, and thus more consideration could be given to location. But if there was such a difference, for most people it was of no great consequence. Whether the house was located in Crosby Heights, Richmond Acres, Lyons, or other such subdivision did not really matter. What did matter here, as in East Gwillimbury Heights or Beverley Acres, was its price.

Of thirty-five families interviewed in Crosby Heights, Richmond Acres, or Lyons who had previously lived in Toronto, twenty-one indicated that the price of the house was the chief reason for their choice of location; indeed, eleven gave this as their only reason. Two of the thirty-five offered no reason for their choice. Of other reasons given, only a few had to do with the character of the district as such. In the case of three families in Lyons, it was the desire to live near Newmarket that had determined the choice; in the case of one family in Richmond Acres, the desire to live near Richmond Hill. For two other families of Richmond Acres, the only reason for the choice of residential area seems to have been that it was here that a particular builder was building houses, while one other chose Richmond Acres because the services were in. One resident of Crosby Heights could offer no better reason for the choice of residential area than that "we liked coming north rather than east" and another because "it would be good for commuting." Still a third confessed: "I didn't have no choice in the matter. I was in the hospital and my husband picked it. Being a carpenter he knew a lot about houses. We didn't know very much about the district but thank goodness it turned out Anglican." For one family in Lyons, the choice of location was made by the husband's father, who lived in the area and bought the house for them. Only one of the thirty-five residents interviewed, a family in Richmond Acres, offered a reason for their choice that had anything directly to do with the character of the residential area: "we liked the house and district," they asserted. But even in the case of this family it was obvious that price was an important consideration; at the time, they admitted, houses in the east and west end of Toronto were considerably higher in price than the one they bought.

There was on the part of only a small number of these people any clear indication that they preferred a house in the suburbs. Indeed, only three of the thirty-five gave expression to such a preference while as many as nine asserted they would have bought a house closer to the city if they had found one they could afford. More than half of the residents interviewed confessed to having no knowledge of suburban life before they made the move from the city. "We didn't even know," one resident admitted, when she and her husband bought their house, "the size of the lot." There could be little doubt from the answers given by most of the residents that, however much they may have sought other reasons, the fact that they could afford the house was the thing that determined their choice. The following replies of residents interviewed offer an indication of how important was this consideration:

It didn't matter where the house was too much. We bought a house here because it was several thousand dollars cheaper than houses in Willowdale. My father-in-law was in real estate and had told my husband it was a good buy.

I chose this house because of the picture window; my husband for the value.

We bought here because it was too expensive to buy in Toronto. We didn't know too much about the district.

We chose this house because it was cheap. The only one we could afford. We chose the district for the same reason. It all falls in together. Land values were cheaper up here. There was just no choice.

We chose this house because others weren't ready. It met our price range. Chose the district because of price. We knew nothing about houses or suburban living. We were told a lot which we chose to ignore and got into a lot of trouble we could have avoided.

The house had some good points but we bought it because it was a good buy, I guess. We didn't have time to look around. We went to a real estate agent to get information.

We couldn't afford a down-payment on a house closer to Toronto. We would have gone to Scarborough if we could. Read a good deal about houses—C.M.H.C. booklet. We didn't know very much about the district other than we enquired about hydro and had spoken to people (my sister was one). When we first saw the district it was a wheat field.

We bought this house because it was what we could afford. We liked the house—the floor plan and brick outside. We knew absolutely nothing about the area. Got information from fellows my husband worked with. This place we got out of the paper.

For many of those families who previously owned their own homes, either in the city or in small centres outside, the decision to move to the suburbs was almost certainly influenced in part by the desire to "move up" in type of residential area. These were people with an experience of living in a community and they could not help but be sensitive to the effects of the residential environment on property values. But such families represented only a small proportion of the total locating in suburban areas. Forty-six, or 72 per cent, of the sixty-four residents interviewed in Crosby Heights, Richmond Acres, Lyons, and Beverley Acres who had moved from the City of Toronto or its immediate environs had previously been living in apartments or flats. For these forty-six residents, suffering inadequate residential accommodation, there could be no strong expression of a desire to move up in type of residential area. This is not to say that they had no urge to improve their social position; to very few did a house in the suburbs fail to make some appeal as a status symbol. The very desire of people "to own their own home" was not unrelated to aspirations for a higher social status. But for few sections of the urban population did such aspirations mean less than they did for the section forced into the mass housing market in the years after the war. In the choice of a home in the suburbs the urge to secure an improvement of social position found not the fullest, but the least, expression. The suburban population, in its choice of a place to live, had had to act out of motives that had little to do with considerations of social status.

In contrast, considerations of social status led the population locating in residential areas like Thorncrest Village and Don Mills to make the choice it did. It is true that at a time when there was a mad scramble for houses, even such residential areas could not wholly escape the mass push of population into the suburbs in search of suitable housing without regard to location. Two of the families interviewed in Thorncrest Village confessed they had bought their homes without any realization that they were situated in the village. But, given the fact that comparable houses were obtainable elsewhere at a lower price, there could not have been many families locating in areas like Thorncrest Village or Don Mills who were not aware of the advantages which such locations offered. Typical of residents of Thorncrest Village were such statements as the following:

We chose this district for the suburban living and for the sake of the children.

We chose this district because of the ideas and ideals that represent it.

We were quite taken by the space around and the community centre.

We liked the open type of area; the planning is such that you don't feel hemmed in. We knew all about the special regulations of the village.

Had friends who had lived in the village and we were quite fascinated by it.

In the application for membership in the Thorncrest Homes Association, prospective members were asked among other questions, "what features of Thorncrest Village attract you most?" Only 27 of the 199 persons who became residents of the village failed to answer the question. Though some of the answers given had little to do with the character of the village as such, almost all of them gave emphasis to the desirable type of residential environment offered; phrases like "exclusiveness of the village," "organized community life," "way of life," "country atmosphere," "planned community," "restricted membership," "quiet country living in protected area," "community identity," "good neighbours," appeared over and over again in the answers given. Whatever may have been the particular features of the village that appealed, there was no one who bought a house in this area who had no knowledge of what the area was like. Even the two persons who claimed to be unaware that the house they had chosen was in the village could not have been uninfluenced in their choice by the house's location. If it was not made known to them in other ways, the Thorncrest Home Association took pains to see that prospective members were informed about life in the village before locating there. Families buying a house in Thorncrest Village brought with them a clear conception of what the community should be like. It was this conception of what was the good community that largely determined the choice made.

It was not quite as discriminating a house-buyer who located in Don Mills. Here the mass quality of the development was evident in the purchase of homes by people who were more interested in the type of house offered than in the type of residential area. Yet an overwhelming majority of the residents interviewed gave as the reason for buying a house in Don Mills the character of the area. Indeed, only seven of the sample of fifty-seven home-owners failed to give this as at least one of the reasons. As many as thirty-three indicated that this was the chief reason for their buying a house here. The following were some of the answers given:

Area was recommended to us by friends.

Don Mills is considered one of the top-flight areas for middle-class professional people.

We were first attracted to the area—school, shops, planning.

Loved the district.

Chose house here because most of our friends in this area.

We thought this the nicest subdivision within reach.

It is a planned community—like Silver Heights in Winnipeg—don't like a jungle.

We liked Don Mills—like the idea of more young professional people here.

Had heard about Don Mills from friends. One family we knew had lived in Willowdale but weren't satisfied and they looked all over Toronto and then settled in Don Mills. They were a meticulous family so we took their experience as our own.

My husband's company had advised him to buy a house in Don Mills; that it was a good area to live in.

We spent about one year while waiting to sell our house and during the year we looked all over and liked Don Mills best. It's a good place to raise children.

Don Mills is a well planned community, with schools, parks, shopping centre close by.

Bought a house here because it was a suburb and Don Mills is a respectable district.

It's a nice professional district—a middle-class district.

There were few people who knew nothing about Don Mills before they bought a house there. Many, living in the city, had watched the development of the area from the beginning. A considerable number reported learning about it from friends living there. Magazine articles, newspaper stories, and pamphlets published by the Don Mills Development Company offered other means of gaining information. They were for the most part sophisticated house-buyers who located in Don Mills. They may have known little about how the house they purchased was constructed (in contrast to the people who settled in an area like Beverley Acres they were not likely to have had any building experience) but they could be expected to be very alive to the advantages of good community planning. Although as many as twenty-eight residents claimed that they had no knowledge of houses before buying in Don Mills, only thirteen claimed to have had no knowledge of the area and twelve to have had no knowledge of living in the suburbs. Knowledge about houses was something considered not very important; of greater concern was the character of the residential environment. One resident commented: "We didn't know too much about houses. We were concerned mostly with styling and area rather than the construction of the house. We did a lot of looking around in the years my husband was in law school. We didn't like the houses in Scarborough; there wasn't any planning. We had both lived under crowded downtown conditions—this area looked like paradise."

Among the people settling in Thorncrest Village and Don Mills were a considerable number who had moved from other urban centres to Toronto and had sought in the Toronto environs the type of residential area they had known. Such people could be exacting in their demands. The sale of one house provided the means for financing the purchase of another and social pressure (and very often pressure from the employing company) compelled the search for a "good address." These people did much to set the tone in a residential area like Thorncrest Village or Don Mills. They were "organization men." For them, "suburbia" had a special meaning. Settlement in an area outside the city represented a means of escape from a type of residential environment considered undesirable. There could be here no ready acceptance of a suitable house regardless of location. What was called for was a desirable residential environment and such a desirable residential environment could be found only where it was "built into" the very structure of the development.

Not everybody who located in the packaged residential development made exacting demands in terms of residential environment. Indeed, one resident of Don Mills claimed that he had not liked the community but had located there because he liked the house. One other, a housewife, reported that, having "read a lot of things about life in suburbia" in magazines like *Harpers*, she had been apprehensive about locating in Don Mills and had come "prepared to resist the undesirable things." But these very negative reactions of people were indicative of how important was consideration of the area in the choice of location made. It was impossible to settle in an area like Don Mills or Thorncrest Village without having some opinion about it. In contrast, people settling in a mass-developed residential area were likely to have no opinion about it. They seldom liked or disliked what was offered there in the way of a residential environment. In truth, of course, there was nothing much about such an environment that could be liked or disliked.

Although very different from Thorncrest Village or Don Mills, a residential development like Riverdrive Park also had a character which made it almost impossible for people to choose it as a place of settlement without having formed some opinion of its desirability as a residential area. There were, of course, people settling in Riverdrive Park for no other reason than that they could find no other place to live. This was particularly true of the younger families with several children. But even they did not wholly lack an opinion about the area, largely unfavourable though it may have been. "We just figured we had to start somewhere with a house," one such resident could assert, "and up here was cheap. We couldn't afford a down-payment in the city. I didn't know nothing, to tell you the truth, about living in the country; my husband pushed me. We didn't know too much about the district, just what I heard from other people. It's kind of a rowdy district." Another resident similarly responded: "It's pretty hard to get rooms when you have three children; any place you can get is too small. Then we didn't have much money to buy elsewhere. We chose this district because this is a place where you could buy cheap and we did not have much money and I thought that this place was better for the children because they can play outside free. There's not much traffic. I have always lived in a big city so I didn't know much about living in the country."

People desperate for a place to live and without financial means had to take whatever residential accommodation they could get without much regard for location. Certainly, not everyone residing in Riverdrive Park had moved there as a matter of choice. Indeed, there was here a considerable floating population; for a number of people the only interest in locating in Riverdrive Park was to secure temporary shelter. Yet Riverdrive Park was far from being simply another housing area. It had a very distinctive character. However crudely constructed may have been the homes, and however lacking was the community in social amenities, there was an atmosphere about the place. No two houses on any street looked alike, and every street (in all, about four) extended the length of the settlement to come to an end in heavy woods. Flanking the whole settlement was the Holland River. People in search of a community which was alive with children and yet offered to old people "quiet country living" could find it here. Riverdrive Park was a sort of haven for the urban poor; for those urban poor who disliked life in the city and who yearned for the things the country had to offer.

For the most part it was a population heavily represented in the older age groups and predominantly of a rural background. More than one-third of the residents interviewed in the area had been born and brought up on farms or in country districts. Many of the residents had had an experience of moving back and forth from the city to small towns or rural areas. Few of them had formed any strong attachments to urban ways of life. They were people who had been living on the very fringe of the urban society. For them, what the country seemed to offer had a strong appeal. In Riverdrive Park could be found, it was felt, that freedom and independence which life in the big city denied. "I came out here to stay out here," one resident could assert; "it's a good district— sixteen years ago I spent my holidays here and I like the country." "Our children have a chance here," a second asserted; "they're like Indians up here—the freedom they've got." Another reported:

"I'm used to country life. The further away from the city I am, the better I like it." Of the twenty-two residents interviewed in the area, twelve indicated that they knew at least something about it before moving there. A number, indeed, had friends or relatives living in the area.

For a person not familiar with the geography of the country stretching back from Toronto, Riverdrive Park would not have been an easy place to find during the years after the war when it developed. No sign on a main highway gave any hint of its existence; what roads led to it were not of the sort which were likely to be taken by a family seeking a pleasant Sunday afternoon drive. People could not stumble into Riverdrive Park in search of a house to buy. It had to be "discovered." It was people who knew something about the area who found their way there in search of a house.

On the other hand, once discovered, there was no mistaking such a residential area. It was like no other. Given its extreme isolation, such, of course, could scarcely fail to be the case. Here had been at work no large-scale subdivision developer or builder, turning hundreds of acres of farm land into a massive housing project. Riverdrive Park, unlike Thorncrest Village or Don Mills, had grown up without plan, direction, or control—even the East Gwillimbury Township Council was scarcely aware of its existence until after it had become established—but, for all that, it was far from lacking in a character of individuality. Every family that settled in such an area contributed to such a character, even, indeed, to the extent of giving to each house occupied a quality all of its own.

It was this character of distinctiveness, of being "hard to find," that distinguished a residential area like Riverdrive Park from the mass-developed residential area. It was, as well, such a character that distinguished from the mass-developed residential area such packaged residential areas as Thorncrest Village or Don Mills or such partly packaged residential areas as the Catholic co-operative development outside Sharon or the German colony south of Wilcocks Lake. Compared with Riverdrive Park or even Sharon, of course, Thorncrest Village and Don Mills were not really hard to find. Their names soon came to appear on most city maps and to both places good roads led out from the city. Yet in a very real sense they were "discovered" by the people who found their way to them. The people who located in Thorncrest Village or Don Mills, like the people who located in Riverdrive Park, Sharon, or the German colony south of Wilcocks Lake, were looking for a very special kind of residential development. If they found what they were looking for in one of these places, they were not likely to find it anywhere else. A residential development like Thorncrest Village or Don Mills had the character of being a special creation.

In contrast, residential areas of the mass-developed type had little about them that was distinctive. Few people went looking for a particular mass-produced residential development. They could drive out of Crosby Heights into Richmond Acres and Allen Court without knowing the difference, and, indeed, unless they had made note of the towns along the way, they would have found little to distinguish between any of the subdivisions stretching west from the city to Brampton, north to Newmarket, and east to Markham, Stouffville, and beyond. The signs that pointed the way along the highway for the vast majority of those people in search of a home in the suburbs did little more for them than indicate the price and the down-payment of the houses offered for sale. Very often, only after they had moved into the house they had purchased did people discover in what particular subdivision they had located. It was in such an indiscriminate manner that the vast expanse of the suburbs became occupied.

In the over-all view, what suburban development seemed to mean was simply the shifting from the city to the country of that section of the population which could not find in the city the kind of housing it required. The suburbs attracted more than just those people who desired to live in them. People were forced into the suburbs in search of living space.

Yet not everybody in need of space turned to the suburbs. For every individual family there was a choice offered. Persons determined to remain in the city could choose to do so for the reason that many chose to move out. It was, by and large, those people the least reluctant to abandon residence in the city who made the move to the suburbs. To this extent, in the populating of the suburbs, there were selective forces at work. The suburban population had about it a negative quality at least. If the people who moved to the suburbs were largely indifferent about where they lived, the same was not true of the people who remained behind. They had a clear idea of the kind of social world in which they wanted to live. In one way or another, they had a strong commitment to the urban way of life.

4 | The Suburban Population

THE KIND OF SOCIETY which developed in the suburbs was determined, to some degree, by the character of its population. Though for the most part people had to learn from experience how to think and act as members of a suburban society, they could not abandon old established habits of thought and behaviour; their aspirations, hopes, conceptions of the good and right, were written into the structure of the society they built themselves.

How far there was a carrying into the suburban society of values and ways of life acquired in the urban society depended very largely upon the extent to which the new suburban population had been rooted in the urban social world. People with strong social, ethnic, religious, political, or other ties are not likely to abandon lightly the values and ways of life upon which these ties depend. Thus, when people with such ties made the move to the suburbs, much that they had known in the urban society became projected into the suburban. Indeed, with their way of life threatened within the urban environment, the suburban society which was created by such people could be made more urban than was the urban society itself.

In the settlement of the suburbs, however, it was those elements of the population the least deeply rooted in the social life of the urban community, the least identified with the class, ethnic, religious, political, and other such groupings of the urban society, which were most involved. This was almost inevitably so, given the character of the forces which led to suburban development. People with a strong attachment to an urban way of life did not leave the urban community unless offered the opportunity of preserving the way of life which they valued. It was people with no great stake in the urban society, no heavy commitment to urban values, who were prepared to move to the suburbs without regard to what the suburbs were like. Thus if there was a selection of population in the settlement of the suburbs, the selection tended to be of a negative character. The poor and the rich, by and large, did not move to the suburbs, nor did the old, the halt, and blind, the community-minded, the socially class conscious, the religiously devout, the politically involved, the kinship bound. There could be many qualities of a population which determined its remaining within the urban community. For the population moving to the suburbs only one quality gave distinctiveness: the need for the kind of housing the suburbs provided. What general characteristics the suburban population possessed were related, directly or indirectly, to the fact that it was the search for a house which determined the move to the suburbs.

In no respect was the relationship between the characteristics of the suburban population and its position in the housing market more evident than in its age structure. Old people by and large were not in need of the kind of housing available in the suburbs. If they were rich, they already had a house; if they were poor, they had no means of securing one. There were some important exceptions. Economic prosperity, in the years after the war, had lifted many older people out of the middle into the near upper class and such people, although owning homes, now desired better ones. For some of these people, the search for a better home meant returning from the suburbs to the city. For others, however, it meant moving from an urban (or suburban) area of medium-priced housing to a suburban area of high-priced housing. Residential areas offering housing in the higher price ranges tended to attract a population of previous home-owners and thus a population in the older age bracket. As well, economic prosperity after the war lifted many older people out of the lower into the middle class, and such people, hitherto dependent upon renting, could now aspire to home-ownership. Residential areas offering housing near the bottom of the price range, and with second as well as first mortgages available, tended to attract considerable numbers of people of middle age entering the house market for the first time in their lives.

In over-all terms, however, the number of people moving to the suburbs and buying homes (whether or not for the first time) who were in the upper age brackets of the population was not great. It was people under forty-five years of age who swarmed into the suburbs in such vast numbers in the years after the war.

The general youthfulness of the suburban population can be readily shown. It is scarcely necessary to do more than compare the age structure of the population of such a "new" residential area as Scarborough in 1956, at the peak of its residential development, with the age structure of the population of the City of Toronto the same year (see Table V). In Scarborough, 45.6 per cent of the adult population fell in the age group 20–34, 26.3 per cent in the age group 35–44, and 28.1 per cent in the age group 45 and over. In Toronto, 35.4 per cent of the adult population fell in the age group 20–34, 19.5 per cent in the age group 35–44, and 45.1 per cent in the age group 45 and over. Almost three-fourths of Scarborough's adult population in 1956 was under 45 years of age; only slightly more than one-half were under this age in the city.

But the city in 1956 was not without its "new" population, particularly in areas heavily settled by immigrants, and Scarborough had within it, in areas bordering the city, an "old" population. More meaningful, then, is a comparison of the age structure of the population of those parts of Scarborough occupied as a result of the great "push" of population after 1951 with the age structure of the population of those parts of Toronto unaffected directly by post-war immigration. There is no easy way of separating the new from the old population in either the city or the township. But census tracts 164 and 165 in Scarborough, consisting of an area bounded by Victoria Park, Eglinton, Brimley, and Lawrence, where the combined total population grew from 1,309 in 1951 to 18,400 in 1956, offers an example of an area made up largely of a new population, and census tract 81, in Toronto, north of Briar Hill and west of Yonge Street, where the population grew only from 6,418 to 7,046 in the 1951–56 period, is perhaps as good an example as any of an area with a well-established and highly stable urban population. In the Scarborough area, with an adult population of 10,190, 57.6 per cent fell in the age group 20–34, 30 per cent in the age group 35–44, and only 12.4 per cent in the age group 45 and over. In the Toronto area, in contrast, with an adult population of 5,410, 23.6 per cent fell in the age group 20–34, 16.8 per cent in the age group 35–44, and 59.6 per cent in the age group 45 and over.

TABLE V

AGE COMPOSITION OF THE ADULT POPULATION OF TORONTO, ETOBICOKE, NORTH YORK, AND SCARBOROUGH IN 1956 AND 1961*

	Toronto		Etobicoke		North York		Scarborough	
	1956	1961	1956	1961	1956	1961	1956	1961
20–34	35.4%	33.7%	37.7%	33.5%	41.0%	36.9%	45.6%	40.3%
35–44	19.5	19.9	27.5	28.3	27.4	27.3	26.3	29.2
45 up	45.1	46.4	34.8	38.2	31.6	35.8	28.1	30.5

*Census of Canada.

Five years later, as would be expected, the difference in the age structure of the population of Scarborough and the city had become less marked (see Table V). There was little change in the city, but in Scarborough the proportion in the younger age group had dropped to 40.3 per cent, while that in the middle and upper groups had risen to 29.2 and 30.5 per cent respectively. The contrast, however, between areas in Scarborough occupied by a new population and areas in the city occupied by an old population remained as great as ever. Census tract 280 in Scarborough, stretching east of Markham Road to Highland Creek and north of Lawrence to Highway 401, and growing in population from 695 in 1956 to 13,827 in 1961, was clearly an area occupied by a new population. Of its adult population, 54.6 per cent fell in the age group 21–34, 30.6 per cent in the age group 35–44, and 14.8 per cent in the age group 45 and over. In contrast, census tract 78 in the City of Toronto, north of Lawrence and west of Yonge, declining in population from 10,218 to 9,921, had an adult population of which only 22.5 per cent was in the younger age group, 15.7 per cent in the middle, and 61.8 per cent in the upper.

Striking as these figures are, even they do not fully reveal the extent to which the suburban was a youthful population. A true measure can only be secured by examining its age structure immediately upon the first settlement of the new residential area. It was at that point that the suburban community was most fully suburban. After a lapse of time, even two or three years, there occurred a replacement of some of the original population. New people moved in to take the place of people moving out, and these new people, settling now in an area to some extent established, were less likely to be new home-owners and less likely, therefore, to be as young.

An examination of the age structure of the first owners of the new residential subdivision developing in an area not yet built up, at the time of the house purchase, reveals a breakdown in the age groups 20–34, 35–44, and 45 up roughly in the order of 70–25–5. In East Gwillimbury Heights, outside the town of Newmarket, of 329 original home-owners, the breakdown was 70.8, 25.2 and 4; in Regency Acres, outside the town of Aurora, of 174 original home-owners, 68.2, 28.1, and 3.7; in Beverley Acres, outside the town of Richmond Hill, of 279 original home-owners, 68.8, 27.6, and 3.6; and in Edge Park, in Scarborough Township, of 248 original home-owners, 62.5, 30.2, and 7.3.[1] Research samples drawn from these or similar types of areas revealed an age breakdown of the population little different. In Crosby Heights and Richmond Acres, of a sample of forty-eight residents, all original home-owners, 79 per cent fell in the age group 20–34 at the time of the purchase of the house, 13 per cent in the age group 35–44, and 8 per cent in the age group 45 and up. Of a sample of seventeen original home-owners in Lyons subdivision, 59 per cent were between 20 and 34, 41 per cent between 35 and 44, and no one was over 44; in Beverley Acres, of a sample of eighteen original home-owners, 50 per cent were between 20 and 34, 33 per cent between 35 and 44, and 17 per cent over 44.

The less "purely" suburban the area, the less the population conformed to type with respect to age. Subdivisions far out from the city tended to attract a younger population than did subdivisions near in. Even more, residential subdivisions providing housing for the well-to-do had a larger proportion of older people than

[1]Records of real estate agency and of C.M.H.C.

did those for people of modest means. In Etobicoke Township, where the median value of owner-occupied dwellings in 1961 was $19,355 compared with $16,015 in Scarborough, the proportion of older people in the population was clearly higher—33.5 per cent in the 20–34 group, 28.3 per cent in the 35–44, and 38.2 per cent in the 45 and over. Where the residential area offered very high-priced housing, the age structure of the population came near that of the population of an old established urban residential area. Thus, in census tract 266 in Etobicoke, enclosed by Richview Side Road, Kipling, Rathburn, and Islington, where in 1961 the median value of owner-occupied dwellings was $34,573, only 20.8 per cent of the adult population belonged to the 20–34 age group, while 33.6 per cent belonged to the 35–44 age group and 45.6 per cent to the 45 and over, even though the population was almost wholly "new," increasing from 989 in 1956 to 4,575 in 1961.[2] The residential area comprised within census tract 266 had essentially a "packaged" character. Indeed, the southern portion of this tract was made up of Thorncrest Village. In Thorncrest Village itself, where the median value of homes would be lower than for the tract as a whole, of 197 residents, at the time of the house purchase, 28 per cent fell in the age group 20–34, 43 per cent in the age group 35–44, and 29 per cent in the age group 45 and over.

Don Mills had a population younger than Thorncrest Village. In the 1956 census tract 191, extending north from Eglinton to Highway 401, east of Leslie and west of the Don Valley, where there had been an increase in population from 143 in 1951 to 8,666 in 1956, 59.8 per cent of the adult population was in the younger age group, 27.9 per cent in the middle, and 12.3 per cent in the older.[3] The median value of owner-occupied dwellings in this area in 1961 (now census tracts 191 and 290) was $19,850 for the part north of Lawrence and $20,593 for the part south.[4] A research sample of forty-six original home-owners revealed a population somewhat older: 42 per cent in the age group 20–34

[2]Census of Canada, 1961, *Population and Housing Characteristics by Census Tracts: Toronto*, Bulletin CT-15.
[3]Census of Canada, 1956, *Population and Housing Characteristics by Census Tracts: Toronto*, Bulletin 4-7.
[4]Census of Canada, 1961, Bulletin CT-15.

at the time of the house purchase, 39 per cent in the age group 35–44, and 19 per cent in the age group 45 and over.

Had the creators of Thorncrest Village and Don Mills fully achieved their purpose, to make out of these residential areas communities whole and complete, the age structure of their population would not have differed significantly from that of the population of a "normal" urban community. But the very act of creation of such residential areas led to the selection of a population which in age structure could not be normal. Few old people move no matter what the attractions may be, and thus by virtue of the fact that these were new communities, though created "whole and complete," they tended to attract a population younger than that characteristic of the old established urban community. On the other hand, their character of "wholeness and completeness" meant that they could attract a population older than that attracted by the purely suburban residential development. As reflected in the age structure of their population, such packaged residential developments stood midway between the suburban housing development pure and simple and the established urban community.

In residential areas of the Riverdrive Park and Wilcox Lake type the age structure of the population came even closer to conforming to that of the population of the normal urban community. In Riverdrive Park, of 177 names of heads of households appearing on the assessment rolls in 1959, only 36 per cent were in the age groups 20–34 while 31 per cent were in the age group 35–44 and 33 per cent in the age group 45 and over. The research samples revealed a population favouring even more the older age groups. In Riverdrive Park 27 per cent fell in the age group 20–34, 32 per cent in the age group 35–44, and 41 per cent in the age group 45 and over, at the time of the house purchase; in Wilcox Lake, it was 27, 37, and 36 per cent. Where in a residential area of the mass-developed type the different age groups were represented roughly in the order of 70–25–5, in areas like Riverdrive Park and Wilcox Lake it was closer to 30–35–35. Among the residents of such areas were many very young and some old (three of the research sample in Riverdrive Park and two in Wilcox Lake were over sixty-four years of age) but all groups were well represented. Though in the two areas studied only about 20 per cent of the residents had previously owned homes, the vast majority had been renting houses in older established communities and had moved not to secure more housing space but to better their residential environment. Indeed, of the twenty-two families interviewed in Riverdrive Park, as many as fourteen had previously either rented or owned a house and, of the remainder, at least one had accommodation which was satisfactory in terms of space. Settlement in Riverdrive Park for most of these families meant a "moving up" to a more desirable place of residence in later years of life.

Thus, residential areas offering housing for the "poor" tended to acquire a population with an age distribution similar to that of residential areas offering housing for the "rich." The rich moved on from home-ownership in less desirable residential areas to home-ownership in more desirable and, where the move involved locating in the suburbs, as in Thorncrest Village, the effect was to make for a heavy representation of older age groups in the population. In the case of the poor, the move was largely from rental accommodation to home-ownership, but the effect was to make for a similarly heavy representation of older age groups. Don Mills came near being like Thorncrest Village but lacked something of its "packaged" quality which was reflected in the somewhat younger age distribution of its population. On the other side, though possessing most of the characteristics of a "pure" suburban community, an area of semi-detached housing like Beverley Acres reflected in the age distribution of its population some of the characteristics of an area like Riverdrive Park. Here, with second mortgages providing for an exceedingly low down-payment, there was a "moving up" of people from rental accommodation to home-ownership. Of thirty-seven residents in Beverley Acres who were over forty years of age at the time they purchased their homes (out of a total of 279), seventeen were new home-owners.

Throughout the suburbs, even in those areas most purely suburban in character, there was something of this "moving-up" of people from a less desirable to a more desirable place of residence with the result that nowhere were the older age groups completely unrepresented. Four per cent of the residents of East Gwillimbury Heights, 4.7 per cent of those of Regency Acres, and 3.6 per cent of those of Beverley Acres were over forty-four years of age. This proportion was very small. Yet, given the nature of development of residential areas such as these, what is remarkable is that there were any older people at all. To some extent, there was a "packaged" quality about all suburban areas. Even an area that seemingly had nothing to offer in social amenities could appear to a few people of the older age group a desirable place to live.

Yet, in the mass-developed residential area, it was not the 3 or 4 per cent of the population over forty-five years of age but the 70 per cent or so under thirty-five who determined the character of the society which grew up. Here predominantly was a population lacking in the experience which comes from age. In Regency Acres, out of 174 original home-owners, only one was over sixty; in East Gwillimbury Heights, Beverley Acres, and Edge Park, out of, respectively, 329, 279, and 248 original home-owners, none.[5] To the extent that it is among the older age groups that the values of a society are most firmly rooted, there could be in the mass suburban development no determined clinging to ways of life that had been known. For a considerable element of the population, the taking up of residence in the suburbs marked the beginning of serious adult life. Thus there could not help but be a difference in the character of development of the mass suburban residential area and the residential area of the packaged type. The latter type of residential area could begin by taking advantage of the experience of its population which comes from age. The mass-developed residential area depended largely upon the capacity of the young to experiment and learn.

It was not because of its age alone, however, that the population settling in the vast expanse of the suburbs brought to the task of building a new society no rich store of experience. The suburban population in a very real sense possessed no previous experience of living in a community. Typically, the suburban family was a young couple which had started out in a flat in the city, had moved to larger rented quarters on the birth of the first child, and had made the move to the suburbs before or soon after the birth of the second. Of the total residents of East Gwillimbury Heights, Regency Acres, and Beverley Acres, at the time of the house purchase, more than one-half had at least one child but not more than two.[6] There was

[5]C.M.H.C. and sales office records.   [6]Ibid.

for most residents an interval of approximately five years from the time of marriage to the time of the house purchase. During this interval there were few families which had not moved at least once. Many had moved three or four times. Of thirty-one residents in Beverley Acres interviewed, nineteen, or 61 per cent, had moved from a flat or apartment in Toronto; in Crosby Heights and Richmond Acres, of forty-four residents interviewed, 63 per cent had. Typical of the previous residential experience of the suburban dweller were the following:

Had about five flats all together, all in west end of Toronto. Moved more after the children came.

Had lived in a flat for one year on Winchester Street and an apartment for five years near College and Bay. The house in which we had this apartment was torn down.

Had a basement apartment for one year in the Jewish district of Bathurst and Lawrence. Then our baby was born and we moved to a duplex at Bayview and Mount Pleasant for three years. Had trouble with the dog there and rented a flat on Merton Street and then two and a half rooms in a semi-detached house on Shaw Street.

Rented a flat in Toronto at first and then moved to a four-room apartment. We moved from there because of the birth of our second child.

Rented an apartment on Yonge Street, then a flat at Bathurst and Wilson.

Rented a flat in Toronto, moving three times.

With this background of residential experience, there was no easy referring back to life in another community in undertaking the task of building a new suburban society. Probably a majority of suburban residents, it is true, had grown up in an urban environment and this experience of early life was not without value. Of a sample of twenty-four residents in Crosby Heights and Richmond Acres, fifteen of the husbands and twelve of the wives had been born and raised in Toronto; in Lyons subdivision of twenty-three couples, eight of the husbands and eleven of the wives had. But even where the parental residence had been in a well-established urban area this early experience of urban living could arouse little more than nostalgic memories. The embarking upon a career of earning a livelihood, marriage, and raising a family had led to a tearing up of old community roots. No new roots had been put down before the move to the suburbs.

In one respect, the person seeking a home in the suburbs was not "rootless." He was a member of a tightly knit family group. But if his past residential experience had given emphasis to the importance of family values—had served to draw the family close together as a group—it had done little to develop a sense of attachment to the social world beyond. For such a person, loyalty to the community had little meaning. Life had been led largely on the primary group level, in the associations of work and the immediate neighbourhood. The suburban had not been a population of "joiners." When asked what organizations they had belonged to before moving to the suburbs, in Crosby Heights and Richmond Acres, twenty-seven residents interviewed had declared none, in Lyons subdivision, eighteen of twenty-three, and, in Beverley Acres, eighteen of twenty-eight. Some of the residents who answered that they had belonged to no organizations may have had associational affiliations which they had forgotten. On the other hand, few if any of those who declared that they had belonged to organizations had been actively involved. The new suburban dweller certainly was not a person who had a past experience of lively participation in the organized life of his community. Such, of course, should not have been expected, considering his age and family responsibilities. Of the ten residents in Beverley Acres who claimed they had belonged to organizations, three were over forty-five years of age and four in the age range 36–44; of the three who were less than thirty-six years of age, two were immigrants and the other had belonged to nothing but a church Young People's group.

In contrast, the people who moved to Thorncrest Village and Don Mills tended to be persons with a long experience of participation in community life. Almost 80 per cent of the residents of Thorncrest Village either had owned their homes or had been renting a house or duplex before they had settled in the village. Most of them had come from residential areas not a great deal older than Thorncrest Village itself. In Don Mills, of a sample of fifty-eight residents, only twenty or 34 per cent had moved from an apartment in Toronto. To a much greater extent than the residents of areas of the mass-developed type, those of Thorncrest Village and Don Mills had a character of "transiency"; a good many conformed closely to Whyte's "organization man," moving from city to city as demanded by their careers. Twenty-eight of the 198 residents of Thorncrest Village or 14 per cent had their previous immediate residence in a city other than Toronto. Of the 1,932 families surveyed in Don Mills in 1958, 8.7 per cent had come from outside the Toronto area. As many as one-third of the field work sample of fifty-eight residents in Don Mills had a history of moving from one city to another before locating in this area. Characteristic of the transient, in Thorncrest Village and Don Mills, was the previous residential experience of the following:

Rented a duplex in Calgary. Moved to Edmonton and rented a house. Moved to Toronto and bought a house in East End. Bought a house in Thorncrest Village, 1957.

Rented an apartment in Vancouver and then a house. Bought house in Calgary. Moved back to Vancouver and bought a house. Moved to Toronto and rented a house in older section of city as a temporary measure before purchasing. Bought house in Don Mills, 1955.

Rented flat in Winnipeg and then bought a house. "We had quite a nice little house in Silver Heights in Winnipeg—an area like this." Moved to Toronto and bought house in Don Mills, 1955.

Had done a lot of moving. Had rented apartments in London, Ontario; Ithaca, New York, and then Sarnia. Moved to Toronto and bought a house. Moved to Calgary and bought a house in a Calgary suburb. Transferred to Toronto and bought a house in Don Mills, 1956.

Lived in California, Massachusetts, New York, and Vermont. Rented apartments at first and then houses. Bought house in Don Mills, 1959.

Moving from place to place may have given these residents some of the characteristics which Whyte identified as distinctive of the suburbanite but it certainly did not make them rootless. Rather, out of this experience they developed a very lively appreciation of the values of community life. Not all of them had come, as had the family which had owned "a nice little house in Silver Heights in Winnipeg," from an area like the one into which they were moving, but a great number of them did. They simply shifted their place of residence as they shifted their place of work with the result they did not enter with the move into a new and different social world. As many as twenty of the fifty-eight residents interviewed in Don Mills had belonged to community organizations before the move to the suburbs. More significant still was the type of associational activity. Whereas the person in the mass-developed residential area, if he had formerly belonged to an organization at all, was likely to have been associated with a recreational or church group, the Don Mills resident was likely to have belonged to a service club, a business or professional association, or an organization devoted to some national or international cause. In Thorncrest Village, even a larger proportion of the residents could be expected to have previously belonged to organizations. Only twenty-one of the total of 199 residents of the village declared, when completing their applications for membership in the Thorncrest Village Association, that they had belonged to no organization. Almost all of those indicating their associational attachments, a total of 144, listed two, three, or more organizations to which they belonged, and a great number indicated holding office. Several of these were organizations of considerable prestige and power, boards of trade, exclusive service or golf clubs, professional associations, and the like. The people who settled in Don Mills and Thorncrest Village had been men of the world.

They were a very different kind of people who settled in residential areas like Riverdrive Park and Wilcox Lake. Yet the population of such areas was not one which had had no experience of participating in community life. What distinguished residential areas of this type was their almost complete lack of urban services and amenities. They possessed many of the characteristics of the small town, as well as of the rural community. They could be tight little societies, rich in human association if almost completely lacking in the formal structure of a community. This was certainly true of Riverdrive Park.

Though few of the people moving to Riverdrive Park had previously owned homes, most of them nevertheless had had a rich experience of community living, whether in the downtown area of the city or in a small town or farm area. People like this, it is true, moved around a great deal, but, like the moving around that people settling in Thorncrest Village and Don Mills had done, it was from one area to another very much alike. There developed out of such moving a great resourcefulness and capacity to adjust. With settlement in the suburbs, these people were not faced with a new and very different kind of experience. There was no real tearing up of old roots. Life went on very much as before. Typical was the past residential experience of the following families in Riverdrive Park.

Rented a flat in Toronto at Dufferin and Rogers, then second floor of Mother's house on Gilmour Street, basement apartment of mother-in-law's house in Parliament district.

Rented houses in Niagara Falls, Fort Erie, Crystal Beach, Bradford.

Rented room in London, Ontario, small cottage in Port Stanley, rooms in Hamilton, war-time house in London, farm house in London area.

Rented house in northern Ontario, a half of a house in Stouffville, an apartment in downtown area of Toronto.

Lived in about nine different places in Toronto (St. Clair–Oakwood district) and Wilcox Lake.

Rented apartments and flats in various areas of Toronto, farm house in Mono Mills.

Rented apartment Dovercourt Street, Toronto, basement apartment, New Toronto, cottage Oakridges.

Rented war-time house Parry Sound, two-room apartment Weston, three different farm houses within Toronto environs, house in Willowdale (condemned), cottage Oakridges.

In terms of the wider social world of which it was a part, the population of residential areas like Riverdrive Park and Wilcox Lake represented in extreme form a character of rootlessness. Because of its impoverished circumstances, this population had virtually no experience of participation in the affairs of the wider community. Driven from one area to another in search of a place to live, and existing always to some extent on the sufferance of others, it could take no real part in the life of the larger world. They were important people who located in residential areas like Thorncrest Village and Don Mills and very unimportant people who settled in residential areas like Riverdrive Park and Wilcox Lake.

Yet in terms of their own social world, the residents of Riverdrive Park and Wilcox Lake were as deeply rooted as were the residents of Thorncrest Village and Don Mills. These were a kinship-oriented people. Among the older residents, the ties were not to parents but to brothers and sisters and to grown children, but, whether young or old, except where the family had immigrated to Canada, there was seldom apparent any serious breaking with kinship bonds. Five of twenty-two residents in Riverdrive Park had close relatives living in the area and twelve others had relatives living no further away than Toronto; all seventeen indicated that there was a good deal of visiting back and forth. Of the other five residents, one had no living relatives and the other four were immigrants from England or Scotland who professed having previously enjoyed close family ties. In Wilcox Lake, kinship associations appeared almost as important; at least two of the residents interviewed had relatives living in the neighbourhood and most of the others had them no further away than Toronto. Not all Wilcox Lake residents were on close friendly terms with their relatives—"Listen," one resident of the area declared, "I have got a niece and brother and they wouldn't give me a glass of water"—but expressions of ill-will were the exception and only gave emphasis to the general strength of kinship ties. Where the culture permitted no easy emancipation from the obligations of kinship, disagreeable relations were almost unavoidable when the break did occur. Indications of help received from parents and brothers or sisters were sufficiently frequent to make apparent how dependent a large number of these residents had been upon the kinship group before the move to the suburbs.

In this respect, the population of Riverdrive Park and Wilcox Lake contrasted sharply with the population of Thorncrest Village and Don Mills. The social world of the Riverdrive Park and Wilcox Lake resident had extended no great distance beyond the boundaries of the kinship group. The social world of the Thorncrest Village and Don Mills resident had reached out to the limits of the national and international community. But although the two social worlds were vastly different in their dimensions, each had given to its members a sense of group identity and belonging.

This possession of a sense of group identity and belonging distinguished the people settling in Thorncrest Village and Don Mills, and in Riverdrive Park and Wilcox Lake, from the people settling in the vast expanse of the suburbs. The suburban population generally, of course, was not completely lacking in associational attachments or in the attachments of kinship. Indeed, the population locating in an area of semi-detached housing like Beverley Acres came near to being as strongly kinship-oriented as the population locating in an area like Riverdrive Park. But for most elements of the suburban population, associational and kinship ties, like community ties of a general character, had been negative qualities. There had been no repudiation of the claims of such ties (as there virtually had been of associational ties by the population locating in an area like Riverdrive Park), but neither had there been any great dependence upon them.

In making the move to the suburbs, thus, claims developing out of ties to the community, or to associations of the community, could play no important part in determining what the population was seeking. Most of this population, it is true, was urban in background; indeed, if reliance can be placed upon the data of the field study, there was a larger proportion of Toronto people settled in the mass-developed residential areas than in areas like either Thorncrest Village and Don Mills or Riverdrive Park and Wilcox Lake. But this urban breeding as such gave the population no particular sense of community. A sense of community develops out of the experience of participating in the life of the community—of becoming involved in community affairs and acquiring a stake in the community's welfare. In this respect, the new suburban population had been clearly marginal to the social life of the urban community from which it had come.

To say this is not to suggest that the people left behind—the people in the urban community who did not move to the suburban —were all community-minded. The city was made up of vast numbers of people who had no sense of community. But what was significant in terms of suburban development was that most of those people who were community-minded remained behind. People heavily involved in the life of the urban community were not likely to leave it to settle in the suburbs; except, of course, where there was offered, as in the packaged suburban development, a form of community life more desirable than the one they enjoyed in the city. Thus it was that the new suburban society had to be built by a population which had to learn by living in the suburban community the meaning of community life.

In class, ethnic, and religious terms, there was the same lack of identification on the part of the suburban population. The vast

majority of the people who moved into suburban areas outside
Toronto in the years after the war were Canadian born, predominantly of British origin and Protestant religious affiliation, and, if
questioned as to the social class to which they belonged, would
certainly have answered that they were middle class. It would have
been surprising if such had not been the case. The poor, the rich,
and the recent immigrant could find suitable housing in the city,
and they had good reason to avoid the suburbs. For the rich, there
could be no assurance that the move to the suburbs would not
involve their living alongside people of very different social circumstances, tastes, and upbringing. For the poor, suburban settlement
threatened to destroy those close ties of kinship, neighbourhood,
and friendship upon which they were so dependent in time of need.
Similarly, for the recent immigrant, the suburbs could appear a
frightening world into which to venture. Even if able to afford the
down-payment on a new house, the twenty-year mortgage seemed
to him a distasteful form of debt bondage. In social terms, residence
in the suburbs meant isolation from one's ethnic fellows and a
plunge into a strange and friendless world.

There was thus in a negative fashion an ethnic and class selection
of the suburban population. People highly dependent upon established social ties and associations, and this was very much the case
with respect to the rich and the poor and recent immigrant, were
not prepared to risk the move to the suburbs except where a
sheltered environment was offered. It was people of no strong ethnic
or social class attachments who were the most likely to make the
move. These were people with no position to protect, whose economic or social welfare was not dependent upon maintaining established ethnic or class ties. They had nothing to lose by the move.

Some of them, of course, may have hoped in time to become
rich, and all of them had the hope that they would never be poor.
But the dreams they held were the dreams of young people starting
out in life. The type of residence they had before their move to the
suburbs, the character of their occupation, the state of their finances,
or the nature of their primary associations were not such as to
develop on their part any strong ethnic or class feelings. There was
no seeking "a better address" when the address they had, very often
that of an apartment building on some main city street, had no

significance in terms of being good or bad; most of these young people, not long married, had not developed any concern about their credit standing; nor, with children little beyond the infancy stage, had they developed any concern about who were their neighbours. They suffered only from cramped living space. Thus the urge to "move up" was an urge to secure an improvement in type of residential accommodation, not an improvement in type of residential environment.

There is, of course, no easy way of establishing this lack of class, ethnic, or religious identification of the suburban population. From census figures, the British origin and predominantly Protestant religious affiliation of the population can be readily shown. Thus, in 1951, 83 per cent of the population of Scarborough was of British origin and 80.1 per cent belonged to one or other of the four major Protestant denominations—Baptist, Church of England, Presbyterian, and United Church of Canada. Of Etobicoke's population in that year, 83.6 per cent was of British origin and 81.4 per cent belonged to one or other of the four major Protestant denominations. In North York the invasion of the southern part of the township by ethnic minorities had already by 1951 made itself felt but even in this township there was no mistaking the preponderance of the British-Protestant population element: 77.2 per cent of North York's population was of British origin and precisely the same proportion of it belonged to one or other of the four major Protestant denominations. In contrast, in 1951, only 68.9 per cent of the population of the City of Toronto was of British origin and only 64.3 per cent belonged to one or other of the four major Protestant denominations.

By 1961 certain marked changes had taken place. The heavy infiltration of second-generation Jewish people into North York had given to the southern residential portions of this township a "packaged" character. Here now, while Canadian born comprised 70.7 per cent of the population, only 57.6 per cent was of British origin and 54.5 per cent affiliated with one of the four major Protestant religious denominations; 16.8 per cent of the population was Jewish (in census tracts 292 and 293 combined, 65.6 per cent) and 19.4 per cent of it was made up of people who had immigrated to Canada between 1946 and 1961. But Scarborough and Etobicoke were still predominantly of British origin and Protestant religious affiliation. In Scarborough, where 76.5 per cent were Canadian born, 74.6 per cent were of British origin and 71.2 per cent Protestant in religious affiliation; in Etobicoke, the proportions were 77.1, 70.9, and 68.5 per cent. Only 0.19 per cent of the population of Scarborough was Jewish, and only 0.34 per cent of that of Etobicoke.

Further out, where there had been a rapid growth of suburban population in the years 1956–61, the same preponderance prevailed of people of British origin and Protestant religious affiliation. In Vaughan Township, 80 per cent of the population in 1961 was Canadian born, 74.9 per cent of British origin, and 75.2 per cent of Protestant religious affiliation; in Markham Township, 79.2, 71.2, and 71.7 per cent; in Trafalgar Township, 75.3, 68.7, and 71.1 per cent; and in Pickering Township, 78.3, 77.4, and 77 per cent. In Richmond Hill, where the population had grown from 6,834 in 1956 to 16,446 in 1961, the proportions of Canadian born, British origin, and Protestant religious affiliation were 70.4, 72.2, and 72.4 per cent respectively.

In contrast, in the City of Toronto, in 1961, where 58.1 per cent of the population was Canadian born, only 51.7 per cent was of British origin and 47.6 per cent of Protestant religious affiliation. Near one-third, 29.1 per cent of the city's population, was made up of people who had immigrated to Canada in the 1946–61 period.

In terms of socio-economic background, the thing most clearly revealed by the census figures was the overwhelming preponderance among the suburban population of wage- and salary-earners in the $3,000–$10,000 range. Where, in the City of Toronto in 1961, 37 per cent of male wage-earners earned less than $3,000, only 14.1 per cent in Scarborough, 17.2 per cent in North York, 13.8 per cent in Etobicoke, and 14.2 per cent in Richmond Hill did. In the $3,000–6,000 range there was little difference between the city and the suburban municipalities; 54.1 per cent in the city, 61.6 per cent in Scarborough, 53.9 per cent in North York, 51.2 per cent in Etobicoke, and 57.5 per cent in Richmond Hill. Of wage-earners earning from $6,000 to $10,000, however, there were only 6.8 per cent in the city while there were 21.7 per cent in Scarborough, 21.4 per cent in North York, 25.4 per cent in Etobicoke, and 24.5 per cent in Richmond Hill. For those $10,000 and over, the proportions were 2.1 per cent in the city, 2.6 per cent in Scarborough, 7.5 per cent in North York, 9.6 per cent in Etobicoke, and 3.8 per cent in Richmond Hill. The City of Toronto was clearly the community of the poor (compared even with such neighbouring municipalities as Mimico and New Toronto). On the other hand, apart from Etobicoke which was on the way to becoming a community of the rich (its 9.6 per cent of the population with an income of $10,000 and over comparing with Forest Hill Village's 19.1 per cent), the suburbs were occupied predominantly by people in the middle income bracket. Although 14.1 per cent of Scarborough's population would have to be classified as poor, almost the whole of this 14.1 per cent was concentrated in the southwest and southeast corners of the township occupied long before 1951. Census tract 289, north of the Canadian National railway line, and extending east from Victoria Park to Birchmount, had 19.8 per cent males in receipt of wage and salary incomes of less than $3,000. Census tract 280, in contrast, made up almost wholly of a population settled less than five years, had only 6.9 per cent. Of the remainder 53.6 per cent were in the $3,000–6,000 bracket, 36.6 per cent in the $6,000–10,000, and 2.9 per cent in the $10,000 and over.

Clearly, in the migration to the suburbs, there tended to be a negative selection of population in terms of income, where the poor and rich remained in the city. The rich, of course, did not remain in the city proper. By 1961, 12,909 out of a total of 19,518 wage- and salary-earners in Metropolitan Toronto with incomes of $10,000 and more had located themselves outside the city limits. But they were located in areas immediately adjacent as in Forest Hill Village, or in areas not a great distance out where residential development was of a packaged character. In the vast expanse of the suburbs, the population which moved from the city was clearly neither rich nor poor. It was middle class in terms of income, as it was Canadian born, of British origin, and of Protestant religious affiliation.

It would, of course, be treacherous to conclude as a consequence of this middle-class, Anglo-Saxon, and Protestant affiliation of the population that those people the least closely identified with class, ethnic, or religious interests moved to the suburbs. But this in fact would appear to have been the case. There simply was no way in which the suburban population could identify itself in class, ethnic, or religious terms. To be of British origin and Protestant religious affiliation, and to have an income ranging from $3,000 to $10,000 a year, was to be just like everybody else, or so it seemed to the thousands of young families pouring into the suburbs. Among the people settling in the suburbs were certainly some who could not help but be made conscious of the fact that the move offered the promise of bringing them into association with persons of higher socio-economic standing. The plasterer who had become a plastering contractor, or the school teacher who had become a superintendent of schools, may have had reason to move to the suburbs as a way of establishing himself in an environment more becoming to his new station in life. But at best, all the suburbs could offer him was residence in an area where most people would have an income about the same as his own, for it was the price of the house, and little else, that determined who would locate in any particular residential area. The area in which to buy a home could not be chosen in terms of the type of people settled there. The community of the suburbs was a social leveller. People moved to wherever they could find the type of home they could afford and with large numbers of subdivisions offering homes for about the same price, it became almost a matter of indifference what particular area was chosen. It would have been hard, in terms of ethnic origin, religious affiliation, income, education, or type of occupation to discover any significant difference between suburban areas until, in the one direction, house prices rose somewhere above $20,000 or, in the other direction, fell somewhere below $12,000. Between these two levels, there was a general sameness in the population. What differences there were were between individual families, not residential areas.

In Lyons subdivision, where houses had sold in the price range $14,500–16,000, a sample of twenty-two heads of households revealed the following occupations: printer, fruit inspector, carpenter, chartered accountant, accountant, salesman, machinist, agricultural field representative, constructor, engineer, typographer, tool and die maker, high-school teacher, expeditor, store manager, credit collection clerk, policeman, welder, commercial artist, insurance agent, plumber, and aircraft fitter. In Crosby Heights, with houses selling in the same price range, the occupations of twelve heads of households were carpenter, fruit inspector, accountant, real estate agent, metal worker, engineer, chartered accountant, bricklayer, self employed, salesman, aircraft worker, and school principal. In Richmond Acres, where houses had sold for about $1,500 less, the occupations of fourteen heads of households were street-car operator, painter, factory worker, carpenter, metal worker, policeman, fireman, lawyer, supervisor, line manager, accountant, machinist, hydro linesman, and street-car superintendent. Incomes of the residents interviewed in Lyons subdivision ranged between $3,500 and $7,000, in Crosby Heights between $3,600 and $7,200, and in Richmond Acres between $3,000 and $5,000. Two persons in Lyons had a university education, three in Crosby Heights, and one in Richmond Acres; all had gone to high school except three in Lyons and one in Crosby Heights. All were of British origin except two in Lyons and one in Crosby Heights. The three residents of non-British origin were immigrants from Germany. Three of the families in Lyons, two in Crosby Heights, and two in Richmond Acres were British immigrants. All others, in the three areas, were raised in Canada and all but two, one in Lyons and one in Richmond Acres, were Canadian born.

It would be difficult to see how, in terms of type of people represented, any distinction could be made between these three areas. In education, occupation, and, to some extent, income, there were differences between the residents within any one area, but there was a remarkable sameness between the residents in one area and another. Comparison with other residential areas, where houses were sold within the same price range, would reveal an equal sameness.

Where the suburban residential area offered a very special social environment there did occur a selection of population in ethnic and class terms. Not just anybody was prepared to locate in an area like Thorncrest Village or Don Mills; they attracted only those who could feel socially comfortable in this type of community. Here, as a consequence, the almost solidly British origin, Protestant religious affiliation, and middle-class social standing of the population had a positive significance. Residents who were not of British origin, Protestant religious affiliation, or middle-class background were generally persons aspiring to the status which association with such residents offered.

There was, of course, no ready admission of sensitivity to ethnic or class values. Indeed, one of the distinguishing marks of a population such as located in Thorncrest Village or Don Mills was the heavy emphasis it placed, as a part of its social creed, upon values of social equality and ethnic tolerance. Much pride was taken in the fact that residence was open to people of widely varying incomes and different ethnic backgrounds. Good fellowship and neighbourhood friendliness were virtues built into the very structure of the community. There was a vigorous insistence that people taking up residence in these areas should feel "at home."

But this very creed of social equality and tolerance provided assurance that only "the right people" would locate in such an area. In a community where a heavy value was placed upon good fellowship and neighbourhood friendliness, it was people able to fit easily and comfortably into such relationships who were most prepared to take up residence there. People who had no regard who their neighbours were, who wanted to lead their own lives and not become a part of a tight little social group, were not likely to settle in such areas. Thus with very little deliberate effort, and no clear consciousness of what was involved, subtle pressures were brought to bear to secure the settlement in Thorncrest Village and Don Mills of "the right people." These residential areas were the creation of a social class and, to a high degree, ethnic group. They could scarcely be otherwise, considering the kind of attractions they held out to people locating in them.

There can be no certain way of knowing how conscious in class and ethnic terms this population was. But there was much, certainly, about the resident of Thorncrest Village or Don Mills which conformed to the character of Whyte's "organization man." These were people "on the make" who, if not yet enjoying an income greatly above average, could look forward to steady advancement and a considerable improvement in financial state. Of the 199 residents of Thorncrest Village, at the time they moved in, 23.5 per cent belonged to the professional class, 12.5 per cent were business executives, 20.5 per cent sales managers or buyers, 7.5 per cent accountants, 16 per cent managers or supervisors, 5.5 per cent owners of small businesses or contractors, 10 per cent skilled technicians, 2.5 per cent retired or widowed, and 2 per cent unclassified. In the 1958 survey of 1,932 home-owners in Don Mills, 22.7 per cent were described as professional, 33.6 per cent executives, 16.1 per cent skilled technicians, 5 per cent educational, 13.7 per cent salesmen, and 8.9 per cent miscellaneous. People with occupations such as these could not be unmindful of the advantages of a "good address," particularly if they took account of the good fortune the future might bring. Among the older age groups, it was people well established in their careers who settled in areas like Thorncrest Village and Don Mills. Among the younger age groups it was people, by and large, who had chosen the kind of career that promised almost certain advancement. A significantly large proportion of these younger people had university education. Indeed, of the sample of twenty-eight residents of Don Mills who were less than thirty-six years of age, seventeen or 60 per cent had such education. In financial terms such persons may have considered themselves poor, and they certainly would have denied having any strong class aspirations or feelings of ethnic exclusiveness, but they had a driving ambition to get ahead and to provide the best that was possible for their children. In this sense, very clearly, the people who located in Thorncrest Village or Don Mills were a status-conscious social group.

At the polar extreme to residential areas like Thorncrest Village and Don Mills, residential areas like Riverdrive Park and Wilcox Lake also tended to attract a status-conscious population. Here, as well, the predominantly British origin and Protestant religious affiliation of the population had a positive significance. Where this population had lived in the city there was no protection against the inroads of people of alien cultures. It was the "old Canadians" in the downtown, congested areas of the urban community who were attracted by the opportunity to secure a home for themselves in the country. There was among such people a strong sense of pride in nationality and, not at all curiously, in social class. The move out of the city represented an escape from a social world becoming dominated by "foreigners" and people of "lower-class" social standing.

Such a status consciousness was characteristic even of those people settling in areas like Riverdrive Park and Wilcox Lake who had only recently immigrated to Canada. One of the twenty-two families interviewed in Riverdrive Park were Dutch immigrants and two were immigrants from England; one of the twenty-one families in Wilcox Lake were English immigrants. What was striking was the absence of the southern or eastern European immigrant. Only nine residents of Riverdrive Park were designated as "aliens" on the assessment rolls out of a total of 268 and, of these nine, at least two were citizens of the United States. Not one recognizable Slavic name appeared among the 268. There were three or four names that were Italian and as many or more that were Dutch or German. It was overwhelmingly a community of British origin, and it was a community of Protestants. Only twenty-six residents, or 9.7 per cent, were assessed as Catholic taxpayers.

In education, occupation, and income, the people settling in Riverdrive Park and Wilcox Lake clearly belonged to the lower class. Only one of the twenty-two residents interviewed in Riverdrive Park had as much as a grade eleven education; eight had less than a grade eight education (one had not attended school at all); and fifteen, or 68 per cent, had only a public school education. In Wilcox Lake, only two of the twenty-one had as much as a grade eleven education; ten had less than a grade eight education, and fifteen, or 71.4 per cent, had only a public school education. Of the twenty-two residents interviewed in Riverdrive Park, three were carpenters, two were auto-body workers, three were living on old age pensions, one was unemployed, and the remainder had occupations ranging from factory worker and welder to radio mechanic and nursing orderly. In Wilcox Lake, two of the residents interviewed were unemployed, one was living on old age pension, and the remainder had such occupations as common labourer, truck driver, janitor, carpenter, and factory worker. The incomes of those working in Riverdrive Park ranged from $45.00 a week to $100; in Wilcox Lake from $45.00 a week to $130.

People with such lowly occupations and incomes would hardly be expected to be highly status conscious. Certainly they had none of the attributes considered characteristic of the middle class. Yet they did not lack a strong feeling of class pride. They were people able to make their own way, no part of that "riff-raff" crowding into the downtown areas of the urban community. This feeling of belonging to the respectable class of society, of being socially superior, was particularly characteristic of the population of Riverdrive Park. Here, it was people very much concerned about the social environment in which they had been living who made the move from the city. As in Thorncrest Village and Don Mills, there were in Riverdrive Park very real selective forces at work determining the character of the population in terms of its social class and ethnic identification.

Wherever a residential development offered a special kind of community environment, there tended to be a selection of population on an ethnic and class basis. The small residential development in the wooded hills south of Wilcocks Lake attracted almost exclusively German immigrants belonging to the class of skilled workers. The Sharon co-operative residential development was settled largely by working-class people. Bathurst Manor was occupied by a population predominantly Jewish in faith and strongly motivated in upper middle-class terms. Residential areas that developed with the move of large industrial firms to the suburbs were occupied by industrial workers.

To some extent, there was a selection of population in terms of social class in all suburban areas. In a residential development where all the houses were built to sell at the same price there could be no great mixing of people of different income groups; in such a development as a result people were assured that they would not find themselves living alongside other people with a very much lower income than themselves. Such a consideration unquestionably entered prominently in the decision to buy in areas of high-priced housing. Like the family locating in Thorncrest Village, the family locating in any area of high-priced homes, even if it was mass produced, was not unmindful of the advantages which their location offered.

In those areas where houses were sold near the bottom of the $11,000–$30,000 range, there also occurred a selection of population in terms of social class. Residential areas given over wholly to semi-detached houses, like Beverley Acres, attracted people on the fringe of the housing market. For them the alternative to buying a low-priced semi-detached house was renting a house in one of the older residential areas of the city. There was thus a sense of moving up, of escaping from the kind of undesirable neighbourhood association which residence in the city made inevitable.

Given the character of housing development which took place generally, however, the area given up to semi-detached housing was one offering a special kind of community environment. To live in an area such as this was to be different, as was to live in an area of high-priced homes. But to live in a subdivision of single-family dwellings selling in the price range $14,000–$20,000 could bring little mark of distinction. There were tens of thousands of people locating in subdivisions of this sort. Nothing in the social environment distinguished one residential area from another. Thus there was nothing to lead different classes of people to select different residential areas. What developed with large-scale residential building in the suburbs was a mass market for housing and it was this mass quality which was the distinguishing characteristic of the population seeking housing.

That is not to say that there were no families locating in mass-developed suburban areas who did not have a strong sense of identification with a social class or an ethnic or religious group. But such families were an exception and they did not bring with them into these suburban areas other families sharing the same sense of group identification. It was individual families not social groups who moved into the vast expanse of the suburbs, and, as individual families, everyone was different and everyone was the same.

Given its character of sameness, the suburban population could certainly appear to a David Riesman dull and uninteresting. It was on the streets of the big city that were to be found the social types which inspired the poet, the artist, and the novelist, and as well the social types which commanded the attention of the guardians of the laws and the morals of society. The city bred nonconformity; a condition of the mass housing market which developed in the suburbs was conformity. All houses were built alike and only people who were alike, in terms of income, work history, family state, and such were permitted to occupy them. In far-off corners of the countryside, where mortgage regulations were not made to apply and township councils knew nothing about principles of zoning, communities of the Riverdrive Park and Wilcox Lake sort could grow up, occupied by a population which, if troublesome to welfare, health, and police authorities, was at least unusual and interesting, while, in corners of the countryside not quite so far off, the efforts of a Mr. M. M. Foss or E. P. Taylor could bring into being a suburban community of a very special sort to be occupied by a population with very special characteristics. But the large-scale subdivision developer and builder could take little account of the idiosyncrasies which might appear in the housing market, especially when the pressures of the mass market were supported by the zoning regulations and building restrictions of municipal and mortgage authorities. The queer and the different could not be catered to in the mass-developed residential area of the suburbs. What only was demanded was the capacity to pay the price of the house offered for sale. It was the market which did the selecting. The consequence was a selection in terms of a common denominator which rigidly excluded certain elements of the urban population: those elements which gave to the urban community its character of diversity and heterogeneity.

Yet the very forces in the mass housing market which made for a character of sameness in the suburban population made also for a character of difference. If large-scale house-builders could not afford to take account of the particular demands of individual house-buyers, neither could they afford to take account of the particular demands of groups of house-buyers. The selection of population which took place was on a mass scale; in the individual subdivision, there was no selection. Whoever could afford the price of the house offered for sale was free to buy. The consequence was an almost complete lack of any sense of group identity on the part of people settling in any particular residential area. In truth, everyone was different from everyone else.

To conclude that the suburban population brought with it out of its past experience nothing that contributed to the building in the suburbs of a new society would, of course, be unwarranted. Even the least socially attached elements of this population were not without views and attitudes, prejudices and ideals, which went into their building of a new social world in the suburbs for themselves. But the new suburban population did not bring a great deal to the task of society building. Much of the effort which went into this task had to develop out of experience on the job. It was this lack of a clearly perceived view or "image" of what was the good society which was the distinguishing mark of the suburban population. What was sought in the suburbs, by the vast majority who settled there, was a home, not a new social world. When the new social world developed, its development was a consequence of seeking a home, not the reverse.

5 | The Deprivations of Suburban Living

THE POPULATION which took up residence in the new suburban community began with no large store of worldly, social, or cultural goods, and the effect of the move to the suburbs was to make it not richer but still poorer. What the new suburban resident brought with him, in the way of money, ties of friendship or community, ethnic, class, or associational attachments, or interests of a cultural sort, he largely lost in the struggle to establish himself in his new place of residence. Immediately, suburban living involved the acceptance of a number of very real deprivations. There could be the hope in the long-run of being better off, but it was not the prospect of gain—except in terms of family living—that led to the suburban move. What the family moving to the suburbs urgently required was a house, and to obtain a house it was prepared to make substantial sacrifices, of an economic, social, and cultural sort.

The economic sacrifice was the most obvious and the most readily measurable. The move to the suburbs involved a heavy capital outlay for the purchase of the house and its furnishing, and it left the people who had no great backlog of savings in a state of heavy indebtedness. The suburban was a debtor society. Its very character determined its state of economic impoverishment. To finance the down-payment on a house, and to secure what furnishings were urgently required, money was borrowed, instalment purchases were made, and heavy mortgage obligations were assumed. From the very moment of its taking up residence, the suburban population found itself faced with the task of trying to pay back what it had been forced to borrow in one form or another to make the move to the suburbs.

It made a difference, of course, whether the family already owned a house, and it also made a difference, in a direction the very opposite, whether there was an effort to "move up" to a class of house beyond the purchaser's financial means. When the purchase of a house in the suburbs involved selling a house already owned at a price almost as great as or even greater than the price of the house bought, the move to the suburbs (or from one suburb to another) could be made with little or no financial sacrifice. Indeed, among the residents of any suburban community could be found a number who had profited substantially from buying and selling a number of different homes. On the other hand, families that moved to the suburbs and bought houses far beyond their means courted the risk of financial disaster, and throughout the suburbs there were families that after a year or two lost their homes and moved back to the city. Where buying or selling property was involved there was always the possibility of substantial speculative gains or losses, and, in the suburbs as elsewhere, people could be made richer or poorer by the purchase of a house.

Of the people involved in the move to the suburbs, however, the number who profited greatly or lost heavily by the purchase of a house was inconsiderable. The vast majority of new suburbanites had not previously owned homes which could be sold at a profit. On the other hand, mortgage regulations, and the general prudence of young families seeking homes for themselves, meant that, except in areas where second mortgages were prevalent, not many people bought houses far beyond their financial means. Houses were built in the suburbs to sell at a price within general reach of that large middle-class segment of the urban population which in the years after the war was in need of housing. Buying these houses did not involve people's financial ruin. It did involve, however, the acceptance of a heavy financial burden. People were made poor by the move to the suburbs.

Since, in any particular area, virtually everybody purchased their homes and moved in at the same time, the whole population was made poor together. There was not a mixture of people struggling to get established and others now become financially secure. People who could afford more than the down-payment required in any particular area were likely to look elsewhere for a house. There was a selecting out of people by different residential areas in terms of their capacity to pay. People bought up to, or slightly beyond, what they could afford. Thus whatever the price of the house and the size of the down-payment, the effect of the house purchase in the suburbs was to tax to the limit the family's financial resources. Almost all new suburban residents were forced into debt before becoming fully settled in their new homes. They differed only in the extent of the indebtedness. This was so except for suburban residents in the upper income levels and, curiously enough, as well, suburban residents in the very low.

In an area like Beverley Acres, where second mortgages were readily available and $11,000 homes were sold for as little as $300 of a down-payment, the burden of debt assumed by the new residents could be exceedingly heavy. Of thirty home-owners interviewed in this area, only eight had sufficient savings to meet the down-payment and, of these, two previously owned homes, one selling his old home for more than he paid for the new. Only three of the thirty had been able to pay cash for their furniture and equipment as well as meet the down-payment. Ten were carrying second mortgages and two others third mortgages as well.

It was a population with no great earning power and with at best only a small backlog of savings which took up residence in Beverley Acres. With stricter enforcement of mortgage regulations, particularly those related to second mortgages, a substantial portion of this population would not have been able to enter the housing market at all. What many of the families moving to Beverley Acres had been offered was the choice between going on renting in the city or buying a house and assuming the burden of heavy mortgage payments. Since the actual purchase of the house was deceptively easy, and much of the burden of mortgage payments was hidden, the second choice had proved a highly attractive one. A considerable number of families settling in Beverley Acres were persuaded to buy suburban homes they could not afford. The consequence of the house purchase was to leave them in a state of almost abject poverty. Life in the suburbs was begun with a burden of debt which could be carried by many residents only by the greatest of effort. The following cases were not untypical:

Family number one was a young couple 28 and 25, with two children. The husband earned $65.00 a week when working but was laid off from his job during winter months. During this period he sought other work to supplement his income. The family had been living in a two-and-a-half-room flat in a semi-detached house in the city. The house they bought had been previously owned and they paid $13,000 for it. The down-payment was $250 which the husband's mother paid. "We didn't have a cent," the wife confessed; they had had two life insurance policies but had given them up when the husband had been laid off and they had just paid $200 for an appendix operation on the husband. Besides the N.H.A. mortgage, they took a second mortgage for $3,000. They bought all their furniture on time. "The kids are hard on furniture," the wife reported, "So we didn't buy much." At the time of the interview this family was still struggling to pay off the second mortgage. Their washing machine was broken but they couldn't afford the cost of repairing it.

Family number two was a couple, 31 and 28, with three children. At the time of the house purchase, and for three years after, the husband had two jobs, working 19 hours a day, and earning $140 a week. The family had been living in a rented house in the city but it was torn down to make way for an office building. They paid $11,900 for their new house. They borrowed the $500 required for the down-payment with interest at 12½ per cent and took a second mortgage of $1,500 which with the bonus of $1,000 amounted to $2,500. "We didn't save in advance," the wife admitted; "the children came and they cost too much." They had a life insurance policy but it lapsed. They had enough furniture and their car was paid for. It was paying off the loan of $500 and the second mortgage which presented the greatest difficulty. At the time of the interview the second mortgage was again coming due. The husband's mother was now living with them and the wife working to help meet the payments. The husband had given up his second job. "They should prevent people being able to buy at $500," the wife complained. "It is too hard."

Family number three was a couple 33 and 32 with two children. The husband earned $75.00 a week. They had been living in an apartment in the city. They paid $15,000 for the house (which had been previously owned), $1,600 cash with a second and third mortgage. "We were not very well off," the wife reported, "but we lived in an apartment and there was no place for the children so we just chanced it. We were glad for the children so that's why we went into the deal with our eyes closed." The family had no savings and no life insurance. Considerable difficulty was being faced in meeting the payments on the second and third mortgages.

Not all the families in Beverley Acres were faced with financial problems as great as these. It was families taking second, or second and third, mortgages who were most impoverished by the house purchase. But four out of ten of the total sample were families in this position. Not many of the remainder could boast of a condition of financial security. The following family was in what might be described as average circumstances:

The husband was 33, the wife 29. There were two children. The husband earned $4,400 a year. Before moving to this area the family had lived for seven years in a flat on the outskirts of Toronto. They paid $10,085 for the house, borrowing $1,000 from the husband's parents to help meet the down-payment of $1,500. The wife worked at nights to help pay off the $1,000 borrowed. "I'm the type," she explained, "that don't like to let my bills pile up." Their furniture was bought on time and a car with $1,000 to pay off, $50.00 a month. "We're all right financially," this family was able to report at the time of the field study. "We haven't any savings except life insurance."

Beverley Acres was an area offering homes to people on the very margin of the housing market. Only two of the thirty home-owners interviewed had incomes over $5,000 a year; one was a high-school teacher, the other an architect. Twenty of the thirty were earning $4,000 a year or less. Few had jobs that offered any advancement; typical were such occupations as carpenter, barber, truck driver, machinist, mechanic, painter, salesman. Seven of the wives worked to supplement their husbands' incomes.

It could be expected that people moving into more favoured residential areas would find themselves in less desperate financial circumstances. The incomes of such people were generally higher, and to a greater extent they were in types of occupations where income went up with age and promotion. What burden of debt was assumed thus could be more readily borne and, with more favourable credit standing, the conditions of the indebtedness were generally less onerous. Resort was had less frequently to second mortgages.

Yet whatever the income of the home-buyer, until it approached the upper levels, the purchase of a house in the suburbs involved a heavy financial commitment which only very rarely left the resident free of debt. They were young people buying homes in the suburbs, and few young people had any great backlog of savings. Nor had they advanced far in their careers even when in occupations where promotions and salary increases could be expected. The lawyer or architect could be poor at thirty though there might be the promise of financial security later in life.

Thus in Crosby Heights, Richmond Acres, and Lyons, where single-family dwellings were sold in the price range $14,000–$17,000, it was a population far from well off financially which undertook the task of establishing for itself a new suburban society. On one street in Richmond Acres, of fourteen residents, one-half lacked sufficient savings to meet the down-payment. Only five of the fourteen claimed not to be in debt after the house purchase and four of these five were families which previously owned homes. In Crosby Heights, where homes sold for about $2,000 more, of twelve residents on one street, three were unable to meet the down-payment. Seven of the twelve claimed not to have gone into debt, but one admitted having only $15.00 left in his pocket and a second admitted having used up all the family's savings for the down-payment and being left with nothing to equip the house with furniture. In Lyons, of twenty-three residents interviewed, eleven had to take second mortgages or borrow for the down-payment. Six others had gone into debt furnishing the house. Of the remaining six who claimed freedom from debt after the house purchase three had previously owned homes. The following were among families in these three areas experiencing the most financial difficulty in the purchase of the house:

Family number one was a couple 26 and 24 years of age with two children at the time of the house purchase. The husband earned about $5,000 a year. The wife worked as a clerk. They paid $14,200 for the house; $2,800 as a down-payment. By taking a second mortgage of $800 they were able to meet the down-payment and by selling some property they owned they had money to buy furniture. "We were not too well off," the wife reported their financial state. Three years after the house purchase, the second mortgage had been paid off. "We can manage as long as I'm working," was the way the wife described their financial situation at that time.

The second was a couple, both 28 at the time of the house purchase, with one child. Between them they earned about $6,000 a year. They paid $16,500 for the house, $3,000 of a down-payment. Their financial state they described as average. The down-payment was met from savings. Some things for the house were bought on time. When questioned about their financial state, the wife's reply was: "I'm not going dancing no more."

Family number three was a couple 23 and 21 at the time of the house purchase, without then any children. The husband was earning $85.00 a week, and the wife $50.00 a week. They paid $12,500 for the house, $2,500 down-payment. They were in a poor financial state when they bought the house, the wife reported. They had no savings. For the down-payment they sold their new car and borrowed the other half from her father. They had some furniture and bought what further they needed on time. "The first year, of course, was the hardest, paying back all the money we owed," the wife related. "We are not as nervy now as we were four years ago."

Family number four was a couple 24 and 22 at the time of the house purchase, then with two children. He was earning something less than $4,200, but he was able to secure a mortgage because of fringe benefits connected with his work. The wife worked part time. They paid $12,800 for the house with a down-payment of $2,500. "We went in up to our neck to get the place," the wife reported. "For two years we just existed. Outside of that it was rough. Most of our clothes were gifts from relatives." The down-payment had been financed from savings and a bank loan. "We may get a new washing machine but it won't be any trouble. We save for things."

Family number five was a couple 24 and 22 at the time of the house purchase, then with one child and another born soon after. He earned $50.00 a week. She had stopped working after the birth of the first child. They paid $12,800 for the house, $2,200 down. They had some savings and borrowed $1,000 from the husband's mother for the down-payment. They had very little furniture; they had to buy a refrigerator and stove on time and from then on a piece at a time, half cash and half on time. "Financially speaking, we came in blind really," the wife reported. "We couldn't hold the house on what my husband was earning so I took care of my sister's children for a while when she was sick and my husband held as many as three jobs, doing part-time work for a dry cleaner and managing a bowling alley. It was touch and go." But now, four years later, no great financial difficulty was being experienced. "We are in good solid shape now—I feel as though I can breathe." They had started subscribing to several bonds but had to quit.

It was no accident that the five cases selected to illustrate the problem of financing the house purchase were couples in the lower age group. The young, of course, were not the only ones in the suburbs who experienced financial hardship. Indeed, the greatest financial hardship was probably experienced by those middle-aged couples who were persuaded by the prospect of buying a home with a very low down-payment to enter the housing market when, given their financial circumstances, they would have been much better off to have gone on renting. In some of the areas studied, particularly those given up to semi-detached housing, there were to be found a number of middle-aged couples, often with large families, whose financial position was truly desperate. Many such couples, over-burdened with second mortgage payments, lost the homes they had purchased.

But it was the young not the middle-aged who occupied the suburbs in great numbers after the war, and, though most of them could be expected to overcome the financial difficulties involved in the purchase of a house and attain ultimately a degree of financial security, immediately they were the very people among the urban population who could least afford, generally speaking, the financial outlay involved in the purchase of a suburban home. These young people belonged socially to the property class, but few in fact had yet been earning long enough to acquire any property. They were not property-minded. For most of them, the purchase of a house in the suburbs represented the first substantial investment they had made in their lives. Whether it was a good investment or bad, few had any idea. All that they had known was that they were in need of a house, and with down-payments of not more than $3,000 or so, the purchase of a house in the suburbs was made deceptively easy. Throughout the suburbs were to be found new home-buyers who had been "taken in." It took a very honest real estate agent, indeed, to inform the prospective house-buyer of all the various costs of taking over a house that were not covered by the down-payment.

There were, of course, a considerable number of families moving to the suburbs who knew a good deal about what was involved in the purchase of a house. This was particularly true of families that had previously owned homes or where the husband, or the father or father-in-law, had experience in building or in real estate selling. But there were vast numbers who knew little or nothing about house-buying. Many were wise enough to consult lawyers or knowledgeable friends before making the purchase, but even those who took such precautions were seldom sufficiently well informed to be able to fully count the cost of the house they were buying. They could take account of the house plan and pass judgment upon the house's architectural style, but they might know nothing about the construction of the house, what the taxes were, or what were the costs of maintenance. Nor might they know what were some of the other hidden costs of living in the suburbs, such as that of getting to work.

The daily cost of getting to work, as many suburban residents discovered, could constitute a heavy drain upon the family's budget. Even more financially crippling, for many families, was the cost of buying a car, so necessary in the suburbs. Few new suburban communities were provided with bus services. A car thus had to be purchased, or, if one was owned, it very often had to be traded in for a better. Among the suburban residents interviewed, payments on the car and the costs of its maintenance were made to appear almost as financially burdensome as payments on borrowings to meet the down-payment on the house. "I guess the purchase of a car for commuting purposes has given us the most financial diffi- culty," one resident was forced to confess. "It is hard to get along if you don't have a decent car," another reported, "which we didn't have when we moved here. We had to buy a better one." Still two others reported: "The car is the biggest problem because of repair bills and unforeseen things like that"; "My husband's had the worst luck with his car since we came up here."

Where there was an effort to extend to the limit the family's capacity to secure credit in order to acquire all those things con- sidered necessary for suburban living, the financial consequences could be disastrous. There were families who after a year or two of residence in the suburbs found themselves hopelessly in debt. For the most part, however, it was not a financially irresponsible population which took up residence in the suburbs. The new suburban population had known very well what it wanted, and for what it wanted it had been prepared to make the sacrifices necessary. However little it might have known about the purchase of a house, and however misled it may have been by real estate agents over-anxious to make a sale, it was not on the whole a bad investment that it was persuaded to make. People in the suburbs did get good value for the houses they bought.

If there were disappointments on the part of many suburban residents in their new homes, the disappointments had to do largely with matters of detail in the construction of the house. "Poor plaster around windows and window hardware is poor," was the complaint of one resident; another that "the windows aren't plumb and the baseboards are cracked"; a third, "exterior paint was cheap"; "plumbing was poorly done," "floors are poor," "basement leaks," "walls crooked," "baseboard trim poorly finished," "cement work rough," "bad plaster cracks," "house hard to heat," were the complaints of still others. Not many suburban residents could feel that their new house came fully up to expectations. Yet the majority of those residents interviewed expressed themselves as well satisfied with the house they had bought. Indeed, the reaction of a good many was one almost of elation. "My husband says the quality of the house is not good at all—these houses were thrown up—but I am happy with it," could be the confession of one housewife. There was good reason to feel pleased with the house. It was the urge to secure a house which had led to the move to the suburbs for the vast majority and, though there might be much wanting in it, most suburban residents could nevertheless feel well off. "It was as good as we could expect for the money," was the way a considerable number of the residents expressed their feelings about the house. Certainly, for most suburban residents, they were much better housed than they had ever been before.

But, while the suburban move had brought for most people a vast improvement in their standard of housing, it had done so at the price of their accepting a substantially lower general standard of living. The house purchase meant for very large numbers the giving up of many things which they previously could afford. These things varied from family to family. There were some who reported having sold their car to raise enough money for the down-payment, or had changed from a late- to an old-model car. Great numbers talked in terms of giving up all forms of entertainment or of doing without holidays. Many took on second jobs in their spare time, or their wives worked. There were few residents interviewed who did not admit resorting to some means or other of cutting down on the size of the family budget. Baby sitters were done without, food costs reduced, less spent on clothing, and a hundred and one other small ways discovered to save money. "I'm not going dancing no more" gave expression certainly to the financial plight of more than one suburban housewife.

The financial pressure resulting from the purchase of a suburban home could have many salutary effects upon family living. People settling in the suburbs were suddenly turned from young persons, with no great sense of responsibility, to persons now faced with the cares of home-ownership. Much of what they had been compelled to give up were the pleasures and pastimes of an age group to which they no longer belonged. New satisfactions were to be found in forms of family life which under the conditions of residence in the city had not been possible.

Yet, whatever the compensations discovered, there could be no hiding the very real deprivations which resulted from the suburban move. The suburban was a population frantically striving to make ends meet. In the day or two before pay-day they could have no money in the house for anything but the barest essentials. The constant struggle to finance, in meeting debt charges and maintaining the home, often exacted a heavy psychological—and as well physical—toll. There was much, indeed, that was drab and hapless about family living in the year or two after people took up residence in the new suburban community. Considering the general financial circumstances of the population forced into the suburbs in search of housing, it could hardly be expected to be otherwise.

It was different, of course, with the population settling in residential areas like Thorncrest Village and Don Mills. They had not been forced into the suburbs in search of housing. Their move, from the city or from an older suburban residential area, had represented a move up in type of residential accommodation and environment. Far more of the residents of Thorncrest Village and Don Mills had previously owned homes and far more of them were middle-aged people with a substantial backlog of savings. This was particularly true of Thorncrest Village.

They were people near rich, if not rich, who located in this residential area. Few of the residents had incomes that were not above average and few were not of an age when they could be expected to have considerable savings. Of the twelve families interviewed in the village all but two had previously owned homes and only four reported incomes of less than $10,000 a year. The price of the houses bought by the twelve families ranged from $16,200 to $39,000. Down-payments between $7,000 and $12,000 were required. None of the twelve was unable to finance the down-payment. At least two paid the full cash price for the house, one of these being the purchaser of the $39,000 house. There was no indication from anyone that he had faced a problem of financing the move to the village.

Information relating to their financial circumstances provided by residents of an area like Thorncrest Village, it is true, has to be treated cautiously. A number of families unquestionably were much more pressed financially than they cared to admit. Here, on the part of many residents, there had been an effort to "move up" and families in straightened financial circumstances who found themselves neighbours of families who were well off financially were not likely to divulge their true financial state. In the field study, more difficulty was experienced in Thorncrest Village than anywhere else in securing answers to questions relating to income and financial state. Where there was financial hardship, vigorous efforts were made to hide it from public view.

Among the 199 residents of the village, however, there could not have been many who were in straightened financial circumstances, and there is no question that a great number of the residents were in a very secure financial position. This was the significant fact which distinguished Thorncrest Village so sharply from most suburban residential areas. Here, if there were people made poor by the effort to establish themselves in new homes, there were many others who were not. Settlement in the suburbs did not involve the impoverishment of the whole population.

The population which occupied Don Mills was not as well off financially. Here there were far more young couples embarking on a career of home-ownership for the first time in their lives and the experiences of these couples were not greatly different from young couples settling elsewhere in the suburbs. Of fifty-five home-owners interviewed in Don Mills, as many as twenty-one had been compelled to take a second mortgage or borrow money for the down-payment. All but two of these twenty-one were thirty-five years of age or less. Ten others had acquired debts as a result of the house purchase. Of the twenty-four who claimed to be free of debt, fourteen had previously owned homes. The experience of the following two families was fairly typical of those who, in the young age group, had not previously owned homes before moving to Don Mills:

Family number one was a couple, 35 and 32, with no children. The husband's income at the time of the house purchase was $5,500 a year, the wife's $3,000 a year. They previously lived in an apartment in Toronto. Price of the house purchased was $18,500, with a down-payment of $5,750. Its purchase involved, as the wife expressed it, "literally going in over our head." "We were in awful financial condition." They had $3,500 in cash and took a second mortgage of $2,200. No furniture was required but a refrigerator and electric stove were bought on the instalment plan. "We're just beginning to save now," the wife reported at the time of the field study, three years after the house purchase.

Family number two was a couple, 29 and 31, with two children. The husband earned $95.00 a week. They had been living in a rented house in a nearby city. They paid $17,500 for the house in Don Mills, $5,400 of a down-payment. Financially, they confessed, they were close to the line. The down-payment came to the husband through his mother's death. They had sufficient furniture but had to borrow money from the husband's employer to move and a home improvement loan was secured for landscaping. As well, a loan was needed to buy a car. At the time of the field study, two years after the house purchase, the wife described their financial condition as "still close to the line."

In terms of the financial circumstances of its residents, Don Mills stood about midway between the residential area of $35,000 homes being occupied by the near rich and the residential area of $11,000 homes being occupied by the near poor. It had characteristics that gave it the appearance of a "typical" suburb. It possessed something of the character of the mass-developed suburban residential area. Yet its "packaged" quality was apparent in the large proportion of its residents who had given up homes in less desirable areas of the city in order to take advantage of the residential environment it offered. Unlike the suburbs generally, in Don Mills a substantial element of the population experienced virtually no difficulty in financing the house purchase. As in Thorncrest Village, settlement in Don Mills did not involve the impoverishment of the whole population.

For very different reasons, the same was true of residential areas like Riverdrive Park and Wilcox Lake. The population locating in Riverdrive Park or Wilcox Lake was as poor as the population locating in Thorncrest Village or Don Mills was rich, but it was a population which began poor and was not made poorer by the move to the suburbs. Few of the residents in either Riverdrive Park or Wilcox Lake had paid more than $4,000 in total price for the homes they occupied; most of them, indeed, had paid a good deal less. When Riverdrive Park was first opened up for occupation in 1950, homes were sold for $1,900 with a $200 down-payment and the balance carried by payments of $25.00 a month without interest. Both price and down-payment edged up as houses were improved and changed hands, but the total capital outlay remained relatively small. Of the twenty-one residents interviewed in this area who replied to questions regarding the financing of the house purchase, only five bought houses at a price more than $2,800. The average price of the twenty-one houses was $2,620. Only one required a down-payment of more than $500. Three were sold without down-payment. Two of the residents paid the full cash price for their houses, $2,500 and $3,000. Only seven in all had to borrow for the down-payment.

There were few of these residents who talked in any terms other than being poor. If they had any savings, it was in the order of $500 or $600. Indeed, only one of the twenty-one claimed to have had any money left over after financing the down-payment. But with limited borrowing power, a population such as this was not likely to find itself heavily in debt. What indebtedness it did acquire was usually not of an onerous sort. Of the seven residents unable to finance the down-payment, two borrowed from their parents and two from their employers. Almost all made do with what furniture they had although only one was so fortunate as to possess two refrigerators, "one for food and one for beer." Only six of the twenty-one admitted having bought any furniture or other equipment for the house on the instalment plan. At the time of the field study, many of the residents talked about difficulties of financing but none of them attributed these difficulties to the house purchase. Several, indeed, claimed to have been better off financially with the move to the suburbs.

In Wilcox Lake, somewhat greater financial difficulties were faced by the population in the house purchase. This was a population, indeed, that was very poor. Few of the residents could boast steady employment and a number were on some sort of relief. Yet in the field interviews there was seldom mention of financial difficulties resulting from the house purchase. A greater number, it is true, reported having borrowed for the down-payment. But in no case was the down-payment more than $500. To be in debt to that extent was not something unusual for the class of people living in Wilcox Lake. Whenever any great demand was made upon the family budget, borrowing or buying on credit was resorted to. Few families were ever out of debt, but with limited borrowing capacity the debt was never very great. Certainly, not many of the people in this area were made poorer as a consequence of the move from the city.

As in Thorncrest Village and Don Mills, there was in Riverdrive Park and Wilcox Lake a great variation in people's financial state. One Wilcox Lake resident interviewed was the proud owner of a Cadillac! A number of residents, particularly in Riverdrive Park, owned fairly late model cars, though of a modest price. Here, unlike the suburbs generally, people did not buy a house always up to the price that could be afforded. Among the people attracted to a residential area of this type were some who had a desperate fear of debt. The fact, of course, that there was such a great range in the ages of the residents meant that there would be considerable variation in their financial circumstances. On the one side, there were young couples who could not boast of any financial security. On the other side, however, were middle-aged and retired couples who, given their modest style of life, were financially comfortable. Not always, in residential areas like Riverdrive Park and Wilcox Lake, could a man's financial worth be gauged by the kind of house in which he lived. If many residents were secretive about their financial state it was because, like certain residents in Thorn-crest Village and Don Mills, they were conscious of not being as well off as some of their neighbours.

In almost any suburban area, of course, whatever the type, there were to be found differences between residents in their financial state. But in the mass-developed residential area such differences tended to be minimal. In contrast to areas like Thorncrest Village and Don Mills or Riverdrive Park and Wilcox Lake, the mass-developed residential area became occupied all at once. There was no oppor-tunity for certain families to get well established before others made their appearance. The drapes on the front windows were being put up in all the houses in the area at the same time. So as well at the same time were being made the first mortgage payment, the first payment for hydro, oil, and, if yet available, the telephone, and the first substantial purchase for the house, usually a stove and a refrigerator. For those families who delayed the purchase of a house, until they had sufficient savings to take care of all the necessary costs, there was no financial hardship involved and in the early days, and months, of settling into the new residential area their more fortunate financial position was apparent. But in the mass-developed residential area there were not many such families. Families who had such savings were likely to look elsewhere for a house, where there were offered more amenities of community living and greater protection of house values. The house in the mass-developed residential area was seldom bought as an invest-ment. It might turn into an investment, but the immediate reason for acquiring it was the need for residential accommodation. Thus, in a very real sense, the new suburban home-owner was not made richer by the purchase of a house but poorer. What he was buying, and at a price he could scarcely afford, was a place for his family to live.

What people gave up to finance the purchase of a house repre-sented a very real price they paid for the suburban move. Just as real was the price they paid for being forced to settle in residential areas unable to offer the services normally provided in an old established urban community. People who moved to the suburbs were deprived not only of things which now they could not afford but also of things which the community in which they now lived could not afford.

For most of the young families making the move to the suburbs life in the city, apart from cramped living quarters, had been reasonably comfortable. Large and well-established stores provided for their shopping needs. Transportation facilities were available almost wherever they wished to go. Nearly every conceivable form of entertainment was offered. Doctors, hospitals, and other essential services were within reach and so as well were more frequently employed services such as barbers, dry cleaners, shoe repairmen, and plumbers. No one conceived of a telephone as something unobtainable, and paved streets, street lights, and sewerage were taken for granted. Schools had long been built ready to provide for the education of each new crop of youngsters. There was not much here, indeed, in the old well-established city which people could be left wanting, and particularly those very people who in greatest numbers were forced into the suburbs in search of housing.

These were not people who had come out of the most depressed areas of the urban community. On the other hand, they were people with modest needs and with no exacting or demanding tastes. The vast majority of them had grown up in the city. It was here they had gone to school, found work, married, and made their first homes. Everything about them seemed always to have been there. They had not been called upon to provide for the schools, churches, playgrounds, and other such services which now as young families they found they needed, nor had they, in any very real sense, been called upon to pay for such services. As tenants rather than property-owners, they had not yet become in a truly meaningful way a part of the urban tax-paying public. Almost all that they required from the community was there, already provided. Even friends and companions required no searching for; childhood and adolescent associations offered a firm basis on which to build the friendship ties of adulthood.

Compared thus with the city, the new suburban community was poor indeed. How poor it was depended, of course, upon the manner of its development. In the design of a community like Thorncrest

Village or Don Mills it was the intention that it should lack nothing, good and proper, which the city had to offer; and, though the intention was not fully realized and hardships of a sort were experienced, the move into such suburban areas for the most part was easy. So was it also for people locating in subdivisions situated near areas already developed residentially, where shopping centres, schools, churches, hospitals, and such had been established and where a township government, now long experienced in coping with the problems of suburban development, stood ready to expand its services to meet the needs of the new incoming population. It was not in areas like Edge Park in Scarborough, developing after much of the township had been built up, or Thorncrest Village or Don Mills, that the real deprivations of suburban life were faced, for they were, to only a modified degree, truly suburban communities. Here a good part of the structure of the urban society was carried over and made a part of the suburban society. People could move from the city into such areas without depriving themselves of much that the city had to offer. In Thorncrest Village and Don Mills the structure of the society came "ready made." In Edge Park it was built up in the older established suburban residential areas nearby and much that was needed in the new society was there now in the old.

But where new suburban residential areas developed far beyond the reach of old, the incoming population had immediately provided for it few indeed of those services which in the urban community were taken for granted. There were, of course, great differences between suburban areas. Some could boast, even before the arrival of the first residents, paved streets, street lights, sewerage, and shopping centres. Some began with schools and churches already established or at least with their building underway. A few were so located beside established and prospering small-town or village communities that their residents could share in the services already provided. But though there were differences in degree, the new suburban community by its very nature was a poor community. It began primarily as a housing project. What was built into it was only that which was necessary to sell the houses it had to offer. It was the competition in the market for houses within any particular price range which determined how much, or how little, could be built into the housing project besides the house.

In residential areas where houses were built to sell for $11,000 and even less, virtually nothing in fact was built into the housing project but the house. Such was certainly the case with East Gwillimbury Heights. This subdivision was studied "in the raw," so to speak. At the time of the field study the last available houses had just become occupied; the first residents had moved in not more than a year previously. In this short period of time, a suburban community of more than three hundred families had come into being.

Nothing more than a casual survey would have been required to have determined that this was a population adequately housed. Though there were already complaints of cracking plaster or leaking basements, there was about the houses and their furnishings an air of completeness. Truly, as far as the house was concerned, people had got good value for their money.

Outside the house, however, nothing much was offered. The streets were unpaved. There were no street lights. Only a few of the residents had yet acquired telephones. Gas mains had been promised and also a sewerage plant, but thus far dependence had to be placed upon propane gas for heating and a large septic tank for sewage. An inadequate well and tank provided an uncertain water supply, which at times of heavy demand completely failed. There were no schools in the area and the first residents had been required to send their children to a township school a mile and a half distant. Now some portables had been established, and the school was operating on a shift basis with each room used for two classes. A voluntary fire brigade at Holland Landing, two miles away, was the only fire protection offered. Policing was dependent upon a small township force. There were no stores in the area, but a small shopping centre had just become established across the main thoroughfare within the limits of Newmarket. There was no hospital or other medical facilities available within the area nor were there any recreational facilities. There was not even a park.

Newmarket was not far distant and a bus ran every hour; but what had been a town of 2,500 people had now become one of

8,000. The services a small-town community had to offer were far from adequate to meet the needs of the population the town itself now boasted, and there was not a great deal that could be made available to the residents of East Gwillimbury Heights outside the town limits. Unfriendly feelings on the part of the Newmarket town officials and the Newmarket population to this new residential development accentuated the lack of co-operation and intensified the feeling of isolation of the East Gwillimbury Heights inhabitants. Shopping, recreational, and medical facilities were made available but could be taken advantage of by only a small proportion of the population. A heavy dependence had to be placed upon services offered by the Toronto urban community, thirty miles distant.

For most families locating in East Gwillimbury Heights it was a rude shock to discover how little they were offered in the way of community services. For one resident it took a trip to his lawyer to learn that nothing in his contract with the builder provided for sidewalks. Less naïve were those residents who took the real estate agent at his word that the large new school across Davis Drive within the town limits of Newmarket was there available for the education of their children. Not many people who bought homes in East Gwillimbury Heights realized that, until reorganized, the subdivision was simply a part of a rural school district, that the fire protection offered by the town of Newmarket was not available to them, that the sewage from their homes ran into nothing but a large septic tank, and that the developer was not responsible for paving the streets or installing street lights. Even after several months' residence in the area there were a good many residents who had no idea who was responsible for providing essential services. Some still thought the fire department was in the town of Newmarket, others that it was in Aurora or Bradford. Scarcely any one knew where to telephone if their house got on fire. "Guess I would just let it burn," one resident confessed. "I don't know what I would do," another answered, "—that's how stupid we are here— that's how much we know." With a township government far removed (situated in the village of Sharon) and school administration in charge of three trustees elected by the surrounding farm population and unknown to them, several residents of East Gwillimbury Heights imagined that somehow its governance was the responsi-

bility of the local Ratepayers' Association which at the time of the
field study had only recently come into being.

Ignorance of the nature of community services and what authorities were responsible for their provision was not peculiar to the
residents of East Gwillimbury Heights though it may have been
greater here than in most places. There was a good deal of confusion in people's minds about the limits of jurisdiction of municipal
authorities and where redress of various grievances should be
sought. No one seemed to know for certain what rightly could be
expected from the developer, and confusion deepened when the
question at issue touched upon the powers of the provincial or
federal authorities.

People sought in the suburbs for a house, and in the short time
they gave to the quest there was more than enough to learn about
what was involved in the house purchase. Few enquiries had been
made about what services were provided. What was available had
been taken largely on faith. In a surprising number of cases, all that
residents knew about community services they had learnt from the
real estate agent who sold them the house.

As would be expected, there were not many residents of East
Gwillimbury Heights who did not express some disappointment with
the services offered. Complaints were most frequent with respect
to those services upon which people relied in their day-by-day
existence and found most vigorous expression from those people
who had been in the area longest. Many residents had lived in the
area such a short time that they had not yet learnt what to expect.
A considerable number at the time of the field study did not know
their neighbours and had formed no view about people in the area.
Some of the discomforts experienced could be related to the act
of moving and not judged a consequence of the shortcomings of the
residential area. But it took only a few months' residence to make
people aware of the serious inadequacy of certain community
services.

The uncertain supply of water aroused the greatest complaint.
A water tower had recently been built which had led to a considerable improvement, but there was still at the time of the field study
general dissatisfaction. As many as eight out of ten of those residents who commented on the water supply still complained about

it. "The water's always going off and on without warning," was the complaint of one housewife. "We went months without water in the summer in real hot weather," another asserted; "you'd turn on the tap and not get a drop." Still another complained: "The water supply is terrible—it turns off without warning and often when you are in the middle of a shower and all lathered up." One resident, on the day she was interviewed, had to wait until one P.M. before she could wash her breakfast dishes.

Next to the water, the greatest complaint was about the state of the streets. Almost all the residents felt they had been cheated. Though nothing had been written into their contracts, they had bought on the understanding the streets would be paved. Instead, they were left with gravelled roads which when dry produced clouds of dust and when wet became a sea of mud. "The roads were supposed to be paved by the time we moved out," one resident expressed his disappointment; "We now find that they won't be done for two years. We could pave them ourselves but then we would be responsible for future repairs." "The streets used to be so muddy," a second asserted, "that you couldn't even walk across them in the rain; they looked like excavating for the subway. We would bring our cars in at first when the roads were frozen but when it started to thaw we couldn't." A third commented: "The mud was really terrible. The roads were so bad we had to leave our cars over on the highway. Then we had the dust this summer." For one resident, the combination of bad roads and an inadequate supply of water led to the determination that if she ever moved she "would never go to a new house again."

The school situation was clearly unsatisfactory and might have been expected to arouse general complaint. But about half of the residents did not yet have children of school age (44 per cent of the residents were under thirty years of age), and, with the promise of a school building to come, they could be indifferent to the immediate problem. Thus, of the one hundred families interviewed, only about one-third had anything to say about the school situation and only about one-half of these expressed worry or dissatisfaction. Complaints had mostly to do with the shift system and the crowding of two classes in every room, but some concern was shown with respect to the quality of teaching, the discipline in the school, and the inadequate recreational facilities. The more discerning parents clearly recognized that a price was being paid in the education of their children. One resident asserted: "The schooling is bad. A half day is not enough. This is the only thing worrying us and we may have to move because of the school situation. They are getting more portables. Our son is behind in his schooling. My husband is giving him homework. The salespeople had told us that there would be a school."

Shopping was something that touched more on their daily lives and few residents were satisfied with what facilities were available in the area. Across Davis Drive, the street leading to the town, there was a local plaza but it had few stores and there was little variety. A number of residents reported they bought their groceries at the plaza but went into Newmarket for other shopping. The poor bus service into the town, and the unfriendly attitude of the town merchants, however, discouraged many from shopping there. A number still did most of their shopping in the City of Toronto. "I miss the shopping convenience of downtown stores," one resident expressed her feelings about shopping facilities in the area.

There was general ignorance on the part of the residents as to whether they had septic tanks or sewers, but this was one service about which they had no complaint. Nor was there any great concern about fire or police protection though few residents knew where to turn if such services were required. There was hydro; and while they were using propane gas for heating, which was very unpopular, there was general confidence that natural gas would be put in soon. All but a few of the residents at the time of the field study had mail service. The lack of street lighting aroused complaint from some of the residents but a surprisingly large number seemed little concerned. Those who were still without were much more concerned about telephone service.

East Gwillimbury Heights very much exemplified the problems and shortcomings of a subdivision development not yet a year old. There was a great deal that was wrong with it. On the other hand, however, by virtue of the very fact that it was new, it could be a reasonable expectation that many of those things now wrong would soon be corrected. The residents of this area lived in high hopes with regard to the future. It was only the most pessimistic of them who let their feelings about the immediate situation determine them in the resolve to move back to the city if the opportunity presented itself.

In subdivisions like Crosby Heights, Richmond Acres, and Beverley Acres in Richmond Hill or Lyons in Newmarket, there could not be such an indifference to the lack of community services in the easy confidence that improvement would soon come. These subdivisions were from three to four years old. In these three or four years much had been done to make living in them more congenial. Streets had been paved and, of course, there was street lighting. Everyone had telephones. Small shopping plazas had come into being, and schools and churches had been built. By being a part of Richmond Hill or Newmarket, they were provided with fire and police protection and also the various other kinds of services small towns had to offer—a library, a movie, and, in the case of Lyons, a hospital.

Yet it was evident that much still was lacking or inadequately provided for, particularly in the three Richmond Hill subdivisions of Crosby Heights, Richmond Acres, and Beverley Acres. Here complaints had to do with such things as the state of the access roads leading to Yonge Street, the lack of storm sewerage and dependence upon open ditches, the smell and taste of the water, the inadequacy of shopping facilities, the effect upon the children of being shifted from one school to another as new schools were built, the lack of parks and other recreational facilities and the lack of sidewalks, the cost of transportation into the city, and the infrequent collection of garbage. "There are better roads out in the bush than we have here," one resident could express his feelings regarding the state of the roads. "With the taxes we pay," another asserted, "we should have paved roads out to the main street—the roads were mud last Spring." "These blasted open ditches are not a healthy situation at all," was the complaint registered by a third resident. "The drainage seems to be a bit of a mess" and "no storm sewers—this is the biggest beef" were the way two other residents expressed their feelings about this service. "They should build a sidewalk to the shopping centre before someone gets killed," complained still another resident. Scarcely less emphatic were some of the remarks made about the water, the shopping facilities, the schools, the lack of recreational facilities, and the infrequent collection of garbage. "Boy, you should have been talking to my husband," one housewife asserted regarding the state of services in the area, "he'd have a thing or two to tell you."

In even the most well-to-do suburban residential developments there was some feeling of deprivation. However smart the house and however well planned the community, there was no escaping the fact that many of the comforts of life in the city were here not available. Inadequate transportation facilities was a complaint of almost every single resident interviewed in Don Mills. For the suburban housewife nearness to the big downtown city stores was the thing that seemed to be most sorely missed. Schools, medical facilities, libraries, and such were never adequate in residential areas growing rapidly in population. Even the residents of Thorncrest Village had some reason to be envious of friends they had left behind in the city.

But the very design of a residential area like Thorncrest Village or Don Mills was directed to the end of assuring that it should lack nothing which the old established urban community had to offer. Because of its size, of course, Thorncrest Village could not offer everything that was a part of a fully developed community. Schools, churches, and public libraries lay outside the village. Only the facilities of the residential neighbourhood became fully built into the development. But to a considerable extent the planning of Thorncrest Village took place in relation to what was available outside. In particular, the township was made a partner in the village's packaging. What could not be provided by the village was largely provided by the township authorities.

In the case of Don Mills, its size made it possible to build into the development all the various facilities of the community. For the early residents in the area, it is true, there was a period of waiting for certain services. However careful the planning, not everything could be provided at once. But of essential services, there was not much the Don Mills resident was left wanting. Paved streets, sewerage, police and fire protection, and schools were provided from the very beginning. Other services soon came. It was not long, indeed, before the community could boast a T. Eaton store!

Wherever houses in the suburbs were built to sell in the upper price ranges, the development usually provided for almost all required community services. Certainly, where house prices reached $35,000 or more, the prospective home-owner was not expected to do without much that was available to him in the city. On the other side, as the scale was descended to a point where, as in the case of residential areas like Riverdrive Park and Wilcox Lake, houses were built to sell for as little as $1,900, virtually no urban services were offered. There was no running water or sewerage, and, of course, no paved streets or street lights; and there was no promise that such services were on the way. For several years, the only school, in either area, was one outside, serving the rural district. Indeed, apart from a local store, there were no services provided except those available in the rural township of which these residential areas were a part.

Dissatisfaction of the residents in these areas about the state of services thus could occasion no surprise. In Riverdrive Park, two things were the subject of most general complaint: the state of the road leading out to the main highway and pollution of the river. "In winter, this place is real bad—all we want is one good hard road to the highway," was the way one resident expressed his feelings about the road. "They won't do nothing," another complained, "fix roads, no lights. The cars cost a lot because of bad roads. A lot of people here, they curse that road." A third asserted: "The chief problem is the people are paying taxes and not getting anything for it. The roads are terrible here. They won't do nothing about it." Over half the residents interviewed expressed strong dissatisfaction about the state of the roads. There was little less complaint about pollution of the river. "The biggest problem is the river," was the comment of one resident; "it's really deadly and too bad it couldn't be cleared up—we figure something should be done about it."

The distance children had to travel to school, the lack of recreational facilities, and the inadequacy of a water supply which depended upon private wells were other matters about which some of the residents of Riverdrive Park complained. Dissatisfaction was even more general in the Wilcox Lake area. Here complaints had to do with such things as the lack of a water supply, sewerage, street lights, shopping facilities, paved streets and sidewalks, recreational facilities (other than a lake that was shared with week-end crowds from the city) and any sort of bus service. "A daily existence rather than a life as I know it," was the way one resident described living in this residential area.

Yet, in both Riverdrive Park and Wilcox Lake, there was a general indifference of the population to the state of community services. In making the move to these areas, not too much was expected. Many of the residents had come from small towns or farm districts where few community services had been available. Those who had come from the city could boast little about the amenities of community life they had enjoyed there. The open spaces and pure air of the country went far to compensate for the loss of what the congested downtown urban residential area had to offer in the way of services. People could feel that they were as well off as they had been before making the move to the suburbs. The following were some of the replies to the question about community services:

We have no problems. We got everything we need up here.

I don't find any difference in this place and the city. We have all the conveniences here. It's all right if it would stay as it is, but every year people are coming up and building and wanting sidewalks and street lights and making taxes go up.

I like this district. We ain't got no problems here. When we came from Cosburn Avenue it was a rough place, no water, no nothing. Take a look at it now.

It was better than what I expected. I didn't build my hopes up too high and I wasn't disappointed.

The majority of the people have been satisfied once they knew what they were getting. Those who have stayed and weathered the storm have got to like it.

I just expected what we got.

I don't see no problems but ours—we have a lot of expense on the car.

I can't say there are problems—just home life. I have a lot of trouble with my husband—he drinks a lot—and the kids are very unruly.

It was not in suburban residential areas like Riverdrive Park and Wilcox Lake any more than, at the other end of the scale, in residential areas like Thorncrest Village and Don Mills, that were most fully exemplified the effects of the lack of community services in the impoverishment of the population. There was not much the population of these areas had given up in making the move from the city. Indeed, there were some things it was offered that had not been available to it in the city. The community swimming pool in Thorncrest Village (there almost from the time the first residents arrived) was a conspicuous example. But so as well was the river bordering Riverdrive Park, however polluted it may have been, and the lake bordering Wilcox Lake, however crowded with week-end visitors. There was here, in both types of residential development, something of a "moving up" not only in standard of house but in standard of community services as well. People, in certain important respects, were made richer, not poorer, by the kind of community into which they moved.

But not so people who moved into mass-developed subdivisions. There could, it is true, be the hope that the future would bring improvement. The construction of schools, churches, hospitals, libraries, recreational centres, and such, and the widening of main streets and establishment of regular and frequent bus service, represented ways in which the suburbs were making themselves over into a society much like an urban society. Indeed, in the end, with respect to community services as in other respects, the suburbs generally became no different from the city out of which they had grown. Immediately, however, they represented a step back rather than forward in the development of an urban society.

There were compensations, it is true, but they were not many. Where subdivision developments were interspersed with open country, something of a rural atmosphere obtained. It was possible to be persuaded that the suburbs offered the best of both the city and the country. Yet, in fact, in the large-scale subdivision development, nothing much of the country was left remaining, not even its trees, and the main urban feature established was the pattern of people living side by side on streets, often, indeed, crowded as close together as in heavily populated urban residential areas given up to semi-detached or single-family dwellings. The truth was the suburbs could not be made like the country if they were to provide housing on a scale required. The suburbs had to be made like the city. But to make them like the city required much more than the subdivision development could offer. Out of the physical structure of the suburban community had to be built a social structure.

Paved streets, sewers, telephones, shopping centres, schools, churches, bus service, public libraries, and the like were the essential equipment of a truly urban community. Without them the suburban community was incomplete. Its residents were required to make do with inadequate substitutes; conspicuous as examples were gravelled streets sprayed with oil, septic tanks, open drainage ditches, car pools, and school portables. In extreme cases, almost everything outside the house which the urban community provided had in the suburban community to find a substitute.

By itself, of course, no particular urban service was essential for urban living. Indeed, an urban way of life was not impossible even where there was absent almost everything a normal urban community provided in the way of services. The septic tank made the person who used it no less a city man! But the physical structure of a community was not something existing separate from the social. The amenities of urban life had an important social meaning. They made up the physical apparatus in which could be developed the community's social apparatus. Thus the lack of them in the suburban community reflected kinds of social deprivations which extended far beyond the physical discomforts of residing in an inadequately serviced housing development. In the end, what gives reality to a community are the social associations which make it up. A community is a place in which people know one another. The associations of friends and acquaintances, it is true, may extend little beyond the neighbourhood and even in the neighbourhood strangers can be living side by side. But in any true community there is a general feeling of social belonging. Not everyone feels himself a stranger to everyone else. The community possesses a character of social reality by giving people a sense of knowing one another. People living in an established urban area clearly had such a sense. In the new suburban area it was almost completely absent.

In no suburban residential area, of course, was everyone a stranger to everyone else. From the very first moment of settling in the new suburban home acquaintances could be made and friendships formed. As well, friends and acquaintances of the past could be persuaded to locate nearby. But the suburbs were settled not by social groups but individual families, and where particular families located was seldom determined by considerations that had anything to do with obligations of friendship. People settled where they found the house that they wanted. Friends and acquaintances might be found nearby, but if they were it was more likely to have been by accident than by design. House-buyers had been too interested in finding the type of house that they could afford to be concerned about the preservation of social associations of the past. That is not to say that it was an unfriendly population which made the move to the suburbs. Indeed, made up very largely of young married couples only just beginning to assume the responsibilities of raising a family, it was a population for which in the city friendship associations had been lively and highly meaningful. Most of the young people moving to the suburbs had been born and raised in the urban community. It was in the urban community that they had their friends and acquaintances, and probably most of their relatives as well. If the maintenance of friendship and kinship ties had been a dominant consideration, they would have had good reason to remain where they were. Talk of the "friendly atmosphere" of the suburbs, while it may have been used by the real estate agent in persuading the prospective house-buyer that it was there he should locate, could have had little meaning to most of those people who made the move from the city. Compared with the community that was known, the suburban community had little to offer in terms of associations of friendship and kinship. It began, indeed, very much as a community of strangers. The break of social ties of the past represented a price paid for suburban residence.

How large was the price depended upon the circumstances of the suburban move. It was possible to take up residence in the suburbs, if the distance from the city was not too great, with virtually no disturbance to established friendship associations. But as suburban residential developments moved further and further away from the built-up urban community, and took on more completely the character of mass housing projects, the more isolated became the family locating in them. For many people buying homes in such developments the only social contact could be with the real estate agent. Even the builder of the house was not likely to be known.

Thus only three of twelve residents interviewed in Crosby Heights, six of fifteen in Richmond Acres, eight of thirty-one in Beverley Acres, and seven of twenty-three in Lyons had known anyone in the area before they located there. "We didn't know a soul up here," was the way, with slight variations, the fifty-seven residents (out of a total of eighty-one) described their social state. For these fifty-seven residents, of course, past friendship ties were not completely severed, and in no great time new ties were formed. But the replies of most residents interviewed made it evident how lacking was the new suburban community in human companionship and forms of intimate social relationships.

Women in particular were likely to feel the loneliness of suburban life. With husbands going off to work early in the morning and returning late in the evening, with no sidewalks to encourage easy visiting or short strolls, and often without telephones, many women found themselves living in almost complete isolation. Even the return of the husband from work did little to relieve the monotony; after the long drive in rush-hour traffic, few husbands were willing to drive back into the city to visit friends or relatives or to make the effort even to visit neighbours nearby. "It was awful lonesome when we first came," was the way one housewife in East Gwillimbury Heights expressed her early feelings about living in the suburbs. "We had no phone at first. It was real nice when we got one. One of the reasons it was difficult to make friends at first was that it was winter when we came and people aren't out so much in the winter. At first my boy hated it." Another housewife of the same area expressed her feelings at greater length:

I definitely prefer city life. Here one is too tied down with children. It is so far to drag them to the plaza. In the city I never minded taking them shopping. It is very hard to keep in touch with friends or relatives. I really miss my mother and sister. We could visit back and forth in the city but we can't here. Also, my mother could mind the children and let me have a day off. This cannot happen here. People will not phone long distance to say they are coming out and when they do come they stay much too long.

In time the suburban community came to offer the kind of social satisfactions that could be offered by any established urban residential area. People got to know one another. Associations of various sorts were formed and among some of the residents warm friendships developed. But these developments came only after the suburban community began to lose some of its suburban character. It was when they were first settled that the suburbs displayed most completely the character of residential areas made up of isolated individual families, socially unrelated to one another. At this time, the suburban community came very close to being a community wholly of strangers.

This was so unless, of course, as in the packaged residential development, settlement was not of individual families but of social groups. Not everyone locating in residential areas like Thorncrest Village and Don Mills knew everyone else, but almost everyone knew a great number of others. Such was particularly the case in Thorncrest Village, but even in Don Mills a surprising number of residents knew people in the area before they themselves had located there. Only twenty-one of fifty-eight residents interviewed claimed not to have known anyone and a considerable proportion of these were young couples locating in one of the areas of semi-detached housing. What was perhaps still more significant, however, was the degree of intimacy which characterized the relations between most of the people who knew one another. It was a social class which occupied Don Mills, and even more Thorncrest Village. Ties of friendship were secured by the mutual interests of people who had much more in common than simply residence in the same area. People moved in much the same social circles in the larger community of which Don Mills and Thorncrest Village were a part. Thus even residents in the area who were not known could be counted associates if not friends, and where this was the case friendship ties were quickly formed.

Very much the same was true of residential areas like Riverdrive Park and Wilcox Lake, however socially disorganized might be their external appearance. In Riverdrive Park, only eight of twenty-two residents interviewed had known no one in the area before they made the move there. A number of the residents had close friends or relatives living in the area. In Wilcox Lake, a much greater degree of social anonymity prevailed. Here, with half the residents renting, the population was very much more transient. Only three of nine home-owners and two of nine tenants had known anyone in the area. Yet even in this area there was apparent a tendency for families who knew one another to settle together. A number of residents had relatives living nearby. Like Thorncrest Village and Don Mills, Riverdrive Park and Wilcox Lake were largely the creation of a social class. If people in the area began as strangers to one another, there was nevertheless something about them that was familiar. Their social background was much the same; indeed, for most of their lives, they had lived in the same kinds of residential areas and been engaged in the same types of occupations. They began at least with some sense of being a social group.

Throughout the suburbs, there was enough of a sense of social identity among the population to make possible the development from the very beginning of some form of neighbourhood social life. Negatively, at least, social class offered support to such a development. In residential areas where there were no great differences in house prices there could be no great differences in people's social circumstances. The rich certainly were not compelled to associate with the poor for there to develop within the suburban community the social relationships of neighbourhood.

But the very sameness of the population made difficult the development of forms of social relationships of a more discriminating sort. Everyone was too much like everyone else. Where there were no means of discerning who among the neighbours could be claimed a good friend, neighbourhood associations necessarily assumed a character of casualness and ephemerality. There were few with whom secrets could be shared or intimacies exchanged. What appeared thus as conditions favouring sociability went far to destroy the basis upon which such sociability could develop. It was an atmosphere only superficially friendly that the new suburban community offered.

The loneliness of suburban life, in the end, did nothing more perhaps than accentuate more directly felt physical discomforts of residence in a community which socially was yet far from complete. The effect of a society's shortcomings upon the psychological and social well-being of the people who make it up can be very easily exaggerated. It was tough human material out of which the suburbs were built. But however incalculable and subject to exaggeration were the social costs of suburban living, their reality and consequences cannot be questioned. They extended certainly far beyond giving up sewers, neighbourhood movies, or even libraries and concert halls. In the end, they touched man's intellectual—and spiritual—development. People were made into different beings by the demands of suburban living, with tastes that were inevitably simpler, standards of judgment that were lower, and social interests that were narrower and more self-centred. The sociologist, of course, cannot judge what is good or desirable. Human society may take a multitude of shapes and forms and only he who is a part of no society has truly a right to say which is best. But given what suburban development was intended to accomplish—the making of an urban society out of that which had not been urban—the social consequences of this development clearly can be assessed and judged. The mass movement of population from the city to the country provided a new dimension of urban life and a new form of urban society, but not without payment of a price. That price was the deterioration if not destruction of a way of urban life and a form of urban society that had been known. For what was to be gained, in this new social world, very real social costs were involved.

6 | The Repudiation of the Urban Society

THE MOVE BACK to the city of many people who had taken up residence in the suburbs was an inevitable consequence of the character of the development which had led in the first instance to their move from the city. There had been no counting fully the costs of life in a community far distant from the city and devoid of much that the city had to offer. Great numbers of people had rushed almost blindly into the suburbs, the victim in no small degree of a propaganda organized in the interests of the home-appliance, house-building, and other such industries. Values of home-ownership and country living, like that of child rearing, were built into the cult of the new boom society of the post-war world. People were persuaded to marry when perhaps they still should have remained single, to have children when they were not yet ready to rear them, and to buy a house in the suburbs when rented quarters in the city would have much better suited their circumstances. Feelings of disappointment, disillusionment, frustration, and despair were the result for a great many.

Fortunately an active real estate market throughout most of the nineteen-fifties made possible the ready re-sale of the new suburban home, and a considerable number of suburban residents took advantage of the opportunities thus offered to abandon suburban life and return to residence in the city. To the things said and written about the evils of suburban life were added now the plaints of persons who had tried such a life and found it wanting. The big city daily, and the magazine with a national circulation, always right with the fashion, eagerly found space for the publication of anything the ex-suburbanite cared to affirm about the society of which he had once been a part. The flight back to the city, it appeared, offered convincing proof of the folly of people seeking to escape the demands of urban life by moving beyond the bounds of the urban community into the new residential areas growing up in the suburbs.

A wide range of reasons led to the move of people back to the city. There were some who were simply evicted from suburban homes they could not afford, while there were others who, through change of circumstances, now found residence in the city more suited to their personal needs. Still others made the move because they could not be satisfied wherever they were. Probably few suburban residents returned to the city only because of their dislike for the suburbs.

In any mass movement of population there occurs, and particularly in its earlier phases, a turning back of people. Hopes are built too high; much that was promised is found not to be. Persons who would have been better off to remain where they were become caught up in the wave of general enthusiasm built up by the movement of population into new and strange parts of the world. So it was in the settlement of the Western Canadian Prairies in the early years of the century and so it was as well in the settlement of the suburbs in the years after the Second World War.

There were people moving to the suburbs because this was where they thought they wanted to live, and for such people what they found could come as a rude shock. The suburbs were not as the real estate advertisements had pictured them. Residence in even some of the most favoured suburban areas could bring disappointment and disillusionment. Long distances to travel to work, the inadequacies of shopping facilities, the lack of a rich and meaningful social life, and the constant strain of family budgeting in the face of heavy mortgage and other payments exacted their toll. Upon the suburban housewife in particular the deprivations of suburban life could make their effects felt. "I spent five unhappy years in a suburb," one such housewife (now returned to the city) wrote. "As far as I am concerned, they can keep their suburbs," another wrote. "The suburbs are for the birds," wrote still another. Expressions such as these of people who had found life in the suburban community unbearable and had now again taken up residence in the city could be multiplied manyfold.

Although the movement of population back into the city reached considerable proportions, yet, no more than in the case of the Western Canadian Prairies, did the suburbs fail to become settled as a consequence. Those who remained may have found much reason for being disgruntled and dissatisfied, but the same compelling forces which had dictated their move to the suburbs dictated that there they should remain. For such people, the question of liking or disliking the suburbs had no great meaning. They had here found what they had been seeking—a home—and the hardships experienced were largely accepted as part of the price which had to be paid.

Thus, of twelve residents on one street in Crosby Heights and fourteen on one street in Richmond Acres, a total of twenty-six, only seven indicated that they were prepared to sell their homes if the opportunity presented itself and move back to the city or the city's outskirts, and, of these, one admitted that if he bought a house in Toronto as good as the one he now owned his wife would have to take in boarders. Four others expressed a readiness to sell but only if they could buy a larger house and with no thought of moving back to the city. "You could give me a house down there," one of these residents asserted; "I wouldn't live in it. Anyway you wouldn't find a house like this in the city." The other fourteen residents interviewed were united in the view that they would not sell the homes they now owned. "We'd have to start all over again," one of these answered; "we just don't have the money." "It would be no sense at all," another asserted, "would have to pay it again for another house." One housewife admitted that when she and her husband had bought their suburban home it had been with the intention of selling it in three years. "Our plans have changed though," this resident asserted, "we had wanted to move back to the city but we don't now."

It might have been expected that the residents of Beverley Acres, owning homes that were semi-detached, would have been more prepared to sell if they had the opportunity. There was less satisfaction expressed in the house. But of thirty residents interviewed living on two different streets, only five indicated that they were prepared to sell their homes and move back to the city. One other admitted his wife would sell, but he would not. "I couldn't get anything better or closer to the city for the same price," this resident asserted. Five others were prepared to sell but had no desire to live nearer the city. Indeed, one wanted to live still further out in the country. "I would sell and buy a frame house away out in the woods somewhere—away out in the sticks," was the answer he gave. The other nineteen residents expressed themselves as not being prepared to sell. "I used to like the city very much," one answered, "until I moved out here." "We couldn't sell and get our money out of the house," a second replied. "I sell the house now I only can lose," was the reply of a third.

In none of the other residential areas examined was there expressed by the families interviewed any greater readiness to sell and move back to the city. As a whole, the suburban was not a madly happy population but neither was it a population that was intensely unhappy. Talk of the "sickness of the suburbs" made good popular reading and could on occasion serve the cause of city and small-town politicians anxious about the shifting balance of power in municipal jurisdictions. Truly, the suburbs were not as one might have liked them. Far distant from the city, the row upon row of new and largely similar houses, situated on treeless lots, with streets filled with playing children, presented a picture of dreariness, sameness, and, to the more demanding, boredom and aimlessness. The long drive by husbands to and from work, the lack among the wives of any social activity except the morning coffee party and backyard visiting, the paucity of community services and amenities, and the concentration of almost the whole population upon such elementary objectives of life as keeping up mortgage payments and financing the expenses of the household appeared to produce a society that could be described as dull. There was in this society no mixing of age groups, of people of different cultures, religions, and races, of the poor and the rich. Everyone seemed alike and bent upon the same ends. But characteristics such as these of the suburban way of life were what was to be expected. There was nothing "sick" about this society. If anything, it would have to be described as disturbingly healthy.

It was easy enough for the outsider, particularly if he was one accustomed to the comforts of an established urban district, to deplore the way of life of the new suburban resident and to see as intolerable the kind of deprivations he suffered. Yet what appeared so intolerable was very often to the suburban resident not intolerable at all. The long drive to work might well have taxed the nerves of a fifty-year-old and led him, had he tried suburban residence, to give up quickly in despair. So as well might the absence of any rich social life in the suburbs, the endless grind financially to make ends meet, the shortcomings of community services, the hazards of child rearing. But to the young families moving into the suburbs, these were the very stuff of life, the things that gave meaning to the struggle to establish for themselves a home and place in the community.

The tendency to treat lightly what had the appearance of hardships was evident in the views expressed by most suburban residents about the problem of getting to and from work. Many residents complained about the state of access roads and about the inadequacy of bus service, but only a very small number about the difficulties of driving to work. When pressed, they recognized the costs involved and some mentioned the time involved, particularly during the winter months when traffic tie-ups became more frequent. But these were people for the most part who liked to drive cars and people who were not highly conscious of the value of time. What hardships were involved were considered by most a small price to pay for the advantage of being able to own a home.

There were differences in attitude in different suburban areas, depending upon their location and the state of well-being of their residents. To the residents of Lyons and East Gwillimbury Heights who worked in Toronto, the problem of getting to work was clearly of more concern than it was to the residents of such subdivisions as Crosby Heights, Richmond Acres, and Beverley Acres. The twelve additional miles to travel could make a considerable difference. So as well could the suburban resident's financial state. Residents of East Gwillimbury Heights and Beverley Acres more often expressed concern about the condition of their car than did residents of areas like Lyons and Crosby Heights. Where financing the house purchase was taxing to the limit the resources of the suburban resident, getting to and from work could loom as a formidable problem.

It was not in areas such as these, however, except for the most financially insecure, that transportation assumed such dimensions as to make suburban living almost intolerable. Few residents in these areas indicated that they would like to move back to the city because of the difficulty of getting to work. At most was expressed the hope that work might be found nearer their place of residence.

In areas, however, like Don Mills and Thorncrest Village, on the one side, and Riverdrive Park and Wilcox Lake on the other, there was more likely to be expressed a determination to abandon suburban living because of the difficulty of getting to and from work. For the residents of Don Mills and Thorncrest Village, of course, the difficulty was not really considerable. Distances were not great and few of these residents were without a late-model car. But they were older people, more likely to feel the strains of driving in heavy traffic, and they placed a much higher value on their time. Thus the problem of transportation assumed larger dimensions. How much larger cannot be readily shown by the attitudes expressed in the field study. But from the tenor of the answers given there would seem to be little question but that the residents of Don Mills and Thorncrest Village were less indifferent to the problem of getting to and from work, more anxious about it, than were the residents of such areas as Crosby Heights, Lyons, and even Beverley Acres and East Gwillimbury Heights.

At the other end of the scale, the residents of areas like Riverdrive Park and Wilcox Lake had good reason to be concerned about the problem of getting to and from work. The distances were great —the residents of Riverdrive Park if they worked in Toronto had as much as forty miles to drive—the road leading to the main highway was seldom in good repair, and not many people had good cars. Again, they were older people, often in a poor state of health, and on the very margin of the labour market, poorly paid for the most part and threatened with unemployment. Some worked nearby, of course, and some were retired or unemployed. But these residential areas grew up in isolated parts of the country where there existed few employment opportunities, and as a consequence most of the residents, if they were to work at all, had to travel great distances. For such people the cost of getting to work came close to making it impossible for them to continue residence in the suburbs—or to continue to work. Certainly, it was this cost which was singled out by most of the residents interviewed as the one giving the most financial difficulty. The hold of many of these people on jobs was tenuous indeed, and the long distance and cost of travelling to work seriously limited their mobility in the labour market. The result could either be periodic unemployment or else the abandonment of residence in the suburbs.

To some extent, the suburban population generally was placed in such a position of disadvantage in the labour market by its being separated a considerable distance from where it was employed. People and industry did not move together to the suburbs. The people employed in activities—sales, financial, insurance, and such—concentrated in the down-town areas of the city were the very people who moved in such vast numbers to the suburbs. Industries locating in the suburbs continued to rely heavily upon workers resident in the city or near the city (or, in Alice in Wonderland fashion, came to recruit their workers from areas on the opposite side of the city). Worker met worker on their way to and from their place of employment, in this strange tangle of industrial and residential development. There could be no questioning the increased costs involved.

But it was easy to exaggerate these costs. The suburban population went to work by car, and, with improvements in cars and in the roads cars travelled, probably no greater effort and time were involved in getting to work than had been the case a generation ago. People had come to live differently, taking advantage of new facilities of travel, and in ways that brought little less discomfort than the ways people once lived.

Indeed, for many suburban residents, the drive to and from work could be the most pleasant experience of their day. For those joined in car pools, there was offered the opportunity to visit with neighbours; for those travelling alone, seclusion in the car provided a means of relaxation and contemplation. And, considering the fact that the majority of the people involved were young in years, there was to be derived the sheer pleasure of driving a car. It would, of course, be an exaggeration of an opposite sort to the one usually made, to suggest that the distance from place of work was a positive advantage of suburban residence. Yet it is not without significance that few of the men interviewed in the field study expressed any concern about the problem. Marriage and the responsibility of rearing children had imposed upon those young men who took up residence in the suburbs burdens that confined them, when not at work, largely to the society of their families. In the city, it had not been easy to escape from such confinement. At the very least, delays in arriving home from work called for elaborate explanations and oft-repeated excuses. These were not men long settled down to the comforts of home and the companionship of a wife and children. A very large number of them were less than thirty years of age, and less than five years married. The long drive to and from work brought for such men a break from the routine of family living. In a very real sense, it was a means of escaping the demands and obligations of a settled urban society.

For the suburban housewife, in contrast, there were few compensations in a pattern of family living which witnessed the early departure of the husband for work and his late arrival home, and it was not surprising, therefore, that it was the women rather than the men who not only expressed the greater concern about this problem but who were the more likely to indicate a determination to abandon suburban life at the first opportunity. For a few suburban housewives there was a feeling of being caught in a net from which escape was impossible. They could not afford to move back to the city and often they found themselves opposed in such a wish by their husbands and children. "I have two young children," one housewife asserted with feeling, "who love the suburbs and one of those devoted homey husbands who thinks I have something wrong with me to even entertain the thought of leaving this little green paradise." "I would move back to the city tomorrow if my husband and two boys would agree," another asserted. For some of these women, it was the loneliness that made suburban life unpleasant, for others, it was being caught in a web of neighbourhood and community relationships which appeared largely meaningless and time-consuming. But however expressed, there could be no doubting on the part of such women the feeling of dislike for everything the suburbs had to offer. One housewife, a nurse whose husband was a university graduate in engineering, asserted:

I am not disappointed in the house. For what we paid it is as good as we could expect. But I am disappointed in the district, very much. It is too far away—nothing to do—no social groups. Other residents are working class and not our type—boring for wives—travel to work is tiring for husbands—shopping is poor—dumpy stores. It is better for children, I guess. Most of the wives find it boring. If we lived in the city we would join more clubs and have more friends in. There is greater freedom here I'd say in dress—too much. People don't dress up at all —no one ever appears here in high heels. There are too many women around—not enough men. I realized how it was when I took sick and my doctor said bluntly it was due to boredom and loneliness up here. He told us to move. We will be gone before the year is up.

Yet, among the suburban residents interviewed, the number of housewives who expressed a dislike for the suburban way of life was an exceedingly small minority. For the most part, they were older women, or women who it could be suspected had strong class feelings or were suffering from emotional or nervous disorders of some sort. It would be a curious society indeed which had among its numbers no persons who did not fit in and who were not without feelings of estrangement or even hostility.

The general absence among suburban housewives, and among their husbands, of any strong dislike for the suburban way of life did not mean, however, as has so often been supposed, that there was a widespread and enthusiastic love for the associations of neighbour-hoods, an urge for "togetherness," and a desire to build a new and better society. Motivations such as these could be found governing the lives of some of the residents scattered throughout the suburbs. There were people who moved to the suburbs in search of a richer or fuller neighbourhood and community life. But motivations of almost exactly the opposite sort governed the lives of most suburban residents. The young family moving to the suburbs, struggling to make a living and rear children, and assuming now the burden of purchasing and maintaining a home, wanted no vigorous or demand-ing neighbourhood or community life. In large part, it wanted nothing more than to be left alone. Involvement in the life of the neighbourhood and community could cost money and time, and the new suburban resident had little of either to spare. He was thus not likely to deplore the absence in the suburbs of a rich and meaningful social life. The social life the suburbs offered, involving few obligations of any sort, to the neighbourhood, community, or world at large, was almost precisely the social life the new resident wanted.

Such certainly would appear to have been the case in such residential areas as Beverley Acres, Crosby Heights, Richmond Acres, Lyons, and East Gwillimbury Heights. There was, in the responses of the residents interviewed, no indication that they wanted to become involved in neighbourhood associations, or in the life of the community, to organize or become organized. Such forms of social activity were not completely rejected. These were not an unfriendly people nor were they a people whose financial plight was so desperate that they could tolerate no social ties that imposed upon them some obligation. Of the 253 residents interviewed in these five housing areas regarding the character of their social life, few admitted to having no friends in their area or of failing to participate to some extent in the life of the neighbourhood and community. They did not resist the less demanding of the social ties of neighbourhood and community. But it was clear that they were not anxious to seek in such ties a new purpose in life. Few residents gave any indication that it was the social life there offered that had brought them to the suburbs.

Upon the new suburban resident the ties of neighbourhood imposed the least obligation and these were the ties that were most readily accepted. Though some of the residents interviewed expressed hostility to any type of neighbourhood association—"I have a definite policy of not associating too closely with my neighbours," one such resident asserted—for the most part there was a generous if not eager acceptance of neighbourhood obligations. People living next door became acquainted, favours were exchanged, and some visiting took place, particularly by women during the day. But no amount of probing, or searching for a detailed account of the daily round of activities of suburban residents, was able to reveal a neighbourhood social life in any way approaching in character that associated with what in the literature has been called suburbia.

As would be expected, there was a flurry of neighbourhood

association during the first few months of settlement in the new suburban residential area. This was a period of intense excitement, of exploring what was to be found inside the new house and what was to be found outside. Neighbours rushed to one another's assistance, partly because at this time such assistance was urgently needed and partly because it offered an occasion to become acquainted. There developed among people living on the street some feeling of being a group. One East Gwillimbury Heights resident reported: "We are closer to our neighbours here than we were in Mimico. Mud caused so much trouble but also much fun. Through it, we got to know everyone else—laughing at and with others struggling through the mud. There were no neighbours here to help us when we moved in. We helped our neighbours move in though. But most people bring their own help to move in." Another in the same area replied to the same question: "We have formed close friendships with our neighbours. We all have the same problems and so a close feeling exists. There are about four families in this group, each of whom has a party about once a month."

At the time of the field study, the residents of East Gwillimbury Heights were just settling in. Curtains in many houses had yet to be hung. There was about the area an air of newness and rawness. The effect, on the one side, was to generate a general feeling of friendliness. People were made to laugh at and with one another in "struggling through the mud."

On the other side, however, the effect of this air of newness and rawness was to generate a feeling of people living socially outside the residential area. Of the 101 residents interviewed in East Gwillimbury Heights, almost all reported that most of their visiting was with friends back in the residential areas from which they had moved. If they had close friends in East Gwillimbury Heights almost invariably these were people they had known previously. Neighbourhood associations were not shunned, but, on the other hand, people did not seek such associations to satisfy the need for fellowship and companionship. One resident reported:

We have no close friends in the area. We have friends in Scarborough and Oakville as well as in Toronto and we visit just as often as we did while we were still in the city. The only friends we have acquired in the neighbourhood are the people next door. This friendship is based on a relationship of mutual help. Our neighbours take in our milk for us. At first they let us use their washing machine but we now have our own. We baby-sat for them in return.

Another resident reported:

We have no close friends or relatives living in the area, but we keep in close touch with our friends outside the area. There is an open and standing invitation for them to come and visit us. Someone comes almost every week-end. Neighbours drop back and forth a few times every week but none has become a friend really. Apart from people on the street I don't know anyone in the area.

East Gwillimbury Heights was a suburban society scarcely yet born. Physically, it had the character of a self-contained residential community. Its boundaries were more sharply defined than those of most subdivisions. All houses were semi-detached and built close together on small lots. People were thrown in close physical contact. Yet, at the time it was studied, there was little about the community that gave it the character of a society. People lived their lives largely outside the area, at work and in social activities. There was here no "packaging" of the associations of neighbourhood or community. Nothing came ready-made to the residents of East Gwillimbury Heights. Settlement was not planned so that people on the same street would be socially congenial, nor was there anywhere in the area a natural "meeting-place," some sort of centre about which the associations of community could develop. The area boasted no park, school, church, or other such community institution. The name of the subdivision appeared only over a small, temporary building which housed the sales office. It would have been difficult to imagine, under such circumstances, the existence of any feeling of community.

To a considerable extent, these people remained a part of the society to which they had belonged. Highway Eleven ran almost by their front doors. Few of the residents at the time of the field study had yet spent a winter in the area, and during summer months there appeared nothing forbidding about the drive down to the city. They visited friends regularly and kept in touch with relatives; indeed, much shopping and seeking of entertainment was still done in Toronto.

Yet there was revealed in the responses of many residents an indication of the development of patterns of behaviour which were no part of the society to which they had belonged. The maintenance of previous friendship associations had offered a means of avoiding the social obligations involved in any too close association with fellow suburban residents, but there were obligations involved as well in the previous associations of friendship. Long distances had to be travelled for visiting, a show of affluence was called for when entertaining, even the long-distance telephone call could become a burden. Almost all residents reported a falling off of contacts with friends and relatives outside.

We visit our Mimico friends but not too frequently because my husband drives so much anyway to work. Our friends come here more often; they do not mind the drive at all.

My husband doesn't like going into the city but I do so—we go in about once a month and our friends come out.

We have friends in Toronto and Oak Ridges. Get to see them sometimes but not too often.

We are still friends with people we knew but have pretty much broken with them. You know how it is, even after a month when you don't see people very often you stop thinking about them. We have not been here long enough to make any friends but everyone is very friendly and pitched in to put up fences.

We keep in close touch with our Toronto friends; go into Toronto several times a week. Phone calls are too expensive—thirty-five cents for three minutes. You always have to figure on six minutes because the children don't realize it is long distance. Our friends come out here too, but they find it far to drive.

Occasionally our friends come up for dinner but not many though. Meals are expensive and also you have to dress up. Some of our friends were appalled at the 30-minute drive from Toronto.

Our friends live in Willowdale but we haven't seen them since August, principally because we and they have small babies to take care of. In addition, my husband does not like to drive around on the week-ends because of all the driving he does during the week.

We had a lot of company at first. People came out to see why we were so crazy in moving away up here.

The weakening of ties with friends and relatives outside the area was accompanied by a strengthening of ties with friends and neighbours within, but not to any great degree. East Gwillimbury

Heights was yet too new a suburban community to be certain what was happening. It was in areas like Crosby Heights, Richmond Acres, Beverley Acres, and Lyons that the new patterns of behaviour emerging were more apparent. These were residential areas now about three years old. The excitement that had come from taking up residence in a new suburban community had long since passed. So as well had passed any dependence upon social ties which had been formed before settlement in the suburbs. It was apparent that the residents of these areas were far less isolated socially than were the residents of East Gwillimbury Heights. Visiting with friends and relatives outside the area was not as frequent. On the other hand, almost all those interviewed reported seeing a fair amount of their neighbours and most of them could boast acquaintances if not friends living in different parts of the area. People had become "settled in" and had accepted at least the obligations of being a tax-paying member of the community.

Yet what had emerged over these two or three years was not a form of neighbourhood life making constant and heavy demands upon the residents or a form of community life exacting a rigorous conformity to common values. Indeed, there was almost general agreement that after the first flush of excitement in taking up residence in the area there was a growing tendency to restrict contacts with other people on the street. One Crosby Heights resident reported:

We got to know a lot of the neighbours all at once; all moving in together with no roads. The men got together first. We have made a few close friends. We play bridge and just visit and chat. The fellows have a poker club; we girls a court whist club. There is quite a bit of visiting. I didn't really expect more neighbourhood life here; I hoped that we would be friendly. I don't think there is as much visiting now because I guess when we first moved in we were all thrown together and we all had a lot in common. We don't know too many people other than neighbours.

A resident of Richmond Acres responded in similar vein:

We got to know the neighbours just talking to them. About three or four have become close friends. There is not visiting like there used to be when we moved up; visiting drops off as newness drops off. At first everybody was more friendly, more sociable, but now they more or less keep to themselves. We don't know anybody off the street.

What interfered with neighbourhood social life may have been, as one male resident asserted, that "wives seem to be pregnant every year," or it may have been, as in the view of one housewife, that "people haven't got much time—most of the mothers here work," but, whatever the reasons, there was evident a general reluctance to become too closely involved in this form of social life. "There isn't much visiting," one resident asserted; "here maybe it's more friendly than in the city, but on the other hand everybody is interested in his own life." "We didn't move here because we wanted neighbourhod life," was the response of another resident; "that's what we intended to keep away from. I think the neighbourhood life here is about ideal, friendly but don't bother each other." Still another resident reported: "There is no visiting. I moved out here for privacy not for sociability. It's no good having a neighbour sitting on your house steps all the time."

The neighbourhood was a part of the social life of the established urban community. That is not to say that the urban neighbourhood associations were characterized by close in-group feelings and involved the full and active participation of all the residents on the street. It was possible to live in the city without knowing one's next-door neighbour and sociability appeared no requirement for the maintenance of satisfactory relations between urban residents. Compared with the new suburban community, where neighbour got to know neighbour in sharing the exciting experience of settling in a new home and community, the urban neighbourhood, indeed, appeared cold and friendless. But it imposed upon the resident social obligations of a very real and exacting sort. The family living on an urban residential street had a position to maintain. It made a difference, of course, whether residence was in areas where real estate values and zoning restrictions created residential exclusiveness or in areas where continuous population movement made difficult the maintenance of stable forms of community life, or somewhere in between. But wherever family lived beside family in the urban community it was impossible to wholly escape the obligation of acting in a manner that took account of the fact of neighbourhood.

Residence in the suburban community, by contrast, made it possible to ignore the fact of neighbourhood. The very physical character of the suburban community, with its row upon row of streets all alike, operated to discourage the development of any tight neighbourhood groupings. It was easy to get to know people here but it was anything but easy to make social distinctions between them. The neighbourhood in this kind of community had no boundaries. Streets continued on as though never coming to an end. No sorting out in advance of people settling on different streets brought to them a distinctive quality. Some subdividers had introduced in their plans streets that curved and wound about in apparently senseless fashion in the fond belief that closer forms of neighbourhood life would thereby be developed, and the effect had been perhaps to limit slightly the character of physical openness of the suburban community; but the forces making for this openness in the mass-developed residential area were too strong to be overcome in this manner. Every person was made to appear alike in a community where every house and street were in fact alike. The lack of a physical character to the suburban neighbourhood reinforced and gave support to its lack of a social character.

In truth, of course, it was only in appearance that everyone in the suburban community was alike; everyone seemed alike because everyone was different. But a social state where everyone seemed alike was the very social state the new suburban resident favoured. The new suburban resident was not anxious to make known the manner in which he was different. He could do this only by identifying himself with those other people in the community who were different in the same way he was, and paying the price of conformity which such identification exacted. The spirit of friendliness characteristic of the new suburban community thus did not develop out of any sense of group identity or common purpose; it offered itself as a natural response to a social situation of anonymity and acted to preserve such anonymity in social relations where the establishment of ties on the basis of a feeling of belonging involved obligations the suburban resident was anxious to avoid.

In a very real sense, it was not a new social state which the suburban resident had entered with his move from the city. As a city dweller, not long married and moving from one place of residence to another, he already possessed a character of anonymity and it was this character of anonymity that he sought, in the suburbs, to preserve. Here he had become, in a way that he had not been in the city, a resident of a particular street and, to the extent that it had determinable boundaries, a particular community. Yet the circumstance which had brought about the change—the purchase of a house—was the very circumstance compelling the suburban resident to preserve his character of anonymity. Relations with neighbours—with other people on the street—could not be avoided, but the obligations assumed thereby could be so diffused that they went scarcely felt. It was not a "tight little social group" which developed out of the suburban neighbourhood but a social group as indeterminate in its boundaries as was the neighbourhood itself. Such would be expected given the character of the forces leading to the mass movement of population out of the city into the suburbs.

If the circumstance of his taking up residence in the suburbs offered the new suburban dweller reason to avoid the costly entanglements of neighbourhood association, it offered him even more reason to avoid the costly entanglements of organized community activity. They were not "organization men" who moved into the vast expanse of the suburbs, and, contrary to the stereotype of suburbia, they did not become organization men. Indeed, the field study revealed people the very opposite in character. The evidence was overwhelming of a general social apathy among the population, of an unwillingness to become in any way involved in forms of organized activity demanding time, effort, and money. Here clearly was expressed the urge of the suburban resident to be left alone.

It was perhaps not surprising that the most active participation of the residents in the organized life of the community was found in East Gwillimbury Heights. Like the neighbourhood, the community to the residents of East Gwillimbury Heights was yet largely something to be explored. There were many residents who literally had no idea in what municipal or school district they were living, who was responsible for the administration of the affairs of the community, what were the jurisdictional limits of different agencies of government. To find themselves within their new place of residence—to cope with some of the most elementary problems of settling in—involved reaching out and making contact with what forms of organized group activity existed. There was a feeling of excitement over involvement in new associations of the community as in new associations of the neighbourhood.

There were, of course, a good many residents who were so new to the community that they had yet made no contact whatsoever with its organized life. Of seventy-five residents who responded, thirty-nine, or slightly more than one-half, reported that they belonged to no organized group in the residential area. Most of these indicated a knowledge of the existence of community organizations and a number suggested that it was their intention to join as soon as circumstances permitted, but there were some residents who confessed having no idea what organizations existed in the area. They were people who yet had not in any sense become settled in.

What was significant about East Gwillimbury Heights, however, was not the fact that there were, among those reporting, thirty-nine residents who belonged to no organized group but the fact that there were thirty-six residents who did. This was, indeed, an impressive record. Almost all these thirty-six residents belonged to the rate payers' association. No other organizational affiliation was mentioned except by a few Catholic families who belonged to a home and school association attached to the separate school in Newmarket. Within the area a bowling league had been established and a number of residents belonged. Few residents indicated any affiliation with organizations outside the area (apart from the Catholic home and school association). One family which previously had resided in Newmarket reported maintaining its connections in the town but in a way that involved no active participation. No other participation in the organized life of Newmarket was revealed. A number of residents occasionally attended church services and went to movies there, as well as shopped, but they belonged to no organizations. "It isn't exactly the friendliest place for newcomers" was the reason given by one resident for avoiding fuller involvement. Unfriendly remarks made about the area by the mayor of Newmarket in a radio talk served to strengthen the feeling among the population that it was no part of the Newmarket community. Among those residents expressing a view, there was unanimous opposition to the suggestion that East Gwillimbury Heights should be incorporated in the town. Such incorporation, it was felt, would result in a substantial increase in taxation.

Formidable social as well as physical barriers separated the East Gwillimbury Heights residential development from the town of Newmarket. Old established class lines still remained fairly intact in the town. The newcomers to the area clearly were not welcomed by the small, but politically and socially powerful, élite made up of old families in the town, and it was the voice of this élite which was heard, across the store counters, in church gatherings, and at any social functions the East Gwillimbury Heights resident may have attended.

Though East Gwillimbury Heights was a part of the Township of East Gwillimbury, the residents felt even less a part of the township than of the town of Newmarket. Of sixty-four residents responding, forty-nine indicated that they had no interest in or knowledge of township affairs. Many did not even know where the township offices were situated. Some believed that the ratepayers' association was responsible for the government of the area. Of the fifteen expressing an interest in township affairs, not one professed having any knowledge about what was going on. Generally, nothing more was indicated than a determination to vote at the next municipal election. "We are interested in township government," one of these fifteen residents responded, "we read about it in the papers. We're very interested in the fire hazards. We all talk a lot about these problems, about the problem of what is East Gwillimbury. I guess we're not very progressive." Another resident, perhaps the most knowledgeable of those responding, indicated his interest in township affairs:

There is a wall between Newmarket and East Gwillimbury Heights. Newmarket thinks this will become a slum. The township government isn't very good. It is just a matter of farmers looking after farmers. They don't realize what is happening. There are now 500 houses in East Gwillimbury Heights and 450 more are going up. They will soon have a metropolis on their hands and don't know it. But the ratepayers' organization is working and is handling the local affairs effectively. The ratepayers' organization is the most important organization which the community has.

As would be expected, the population of East Gwillimbury Heights participated more in the social affairs of Toronto. Many of the residents still thought of themselves as Toronto people. Yet there was scarcely any indication of an attachment to organizations centred in the city. One resident belonged to a concert and art society and a few belonged to organizations connected with their work, trade unions and such. Several attended church services in the Toronto area. But these people clearly had not been active in organized community affairs before their move to the suburbs and they carried with them into their new place of residence few previously established associational attachments. Contacts with friends and relatives in the Toronto community could for a time be vigorously maintained but with the life of the larger community there never had been much contact. Associational ties that had existed were quickly broken when residence was taken up in the suburbs.

What this meant was that virtually the whole of the organized community life of East Gwillimbury Heights centred about the ratepayers' association. It was a narrow base on which to build a feeling of community belonging or identity, but during this early stage of development of the suburban community there was perhaps no other type of association which could more effectively secure the involvement of the population. The new suburban resident urgently needed to be informed. He suddenly found himself with countless questions to which he needed answers, relating to such things as faulty construction of the house he had bought, the location of the school and the administration of school affairs, the responsibility for the repair of streets, the acquisition of telephones, the disposal of garbage. Some of the questions were answered for him by the neighbour next door, settled here before him: where the school was located, what was the best area in which to shop, where the mail was delivered, and so on. The neighbourhood in the new suburban community quickly gained importance as a repository of the collective knowledge of the street. But it was a knowledge severely limited in dimensions: there was much the neighbourhood did not know and had no means of getting to know. Beyond the neighbourhood there was no social agency, no person or group of persons, to turn to for information. The real estate agent, so knowledgeable about the house and all that pertained to the house before its sale was consummated, had passed from the scene, his responsibility discharged. There was no mayor, alderman, school trustee, or chief of police. There were no old residents, except the scattered farm families in the countryside beyond who lacked any interest in or understanding of the problems of these new suburban residents. Information did not come ready assembled for the residents of this area— there was no "packaging" done here—and, if questions were to find an answer, it was only through the establishment by the residents themselves of an organization like the ratepayers' association.

The ratepayers' association did more than act as a repository of information. In a very real sense, it served as a means of extending the boundaries of the neighbourhood to include the whole residential area. What neighbour sought with neighbour, in associations of the street, was sought beyond the street in the association of the ratepayers: a forum in which to air grievances and a meeting-place for human fellowship. It may well have been, as one resident of the area asserted, that the first ratepayers' meetings showed that "90 per cent of the people here are complete morons—they talked about things that had nothing to do with ratepayers, complaints about builder, front windows, kitchen cupboards, silly things, rather than about communal things that ratepayers could deal with such as roads and schools." But the fact was that the new suburban resident carried into the meeting of the ratepayers the same worries, anxieties, and longings that found expression on an only slightly more elementary level in his associations with other residents on the street. The resident of East Gwillimbury Heights could not for long reside in the area while socially living outside it. The same compelling forces that brought him into association with his neighbours brought him into association with his fellow residents at large. Involvement in the ratepayers' association was a part of the process of settling into the new suburban community.

Like the warm fellowship of the neighbourhood, the warm fellowship of the community began to disappear once the settling in had taken place. The residents of Crosby Heights, Richmond Acres, and Beverley Acres, though not Lyons, at the time of the field study, were less involved in forms of organized group activity than were the residents of East Gwillimbury Heights. Of sixty-six residents in Crosby Heights and Richmond Acres responding, forty-three or 65 per cent indicated that they belonged to no organizations; in Beverley Acres, of sixty-eight residents responding, fifty-three or 78 per cent so indicated. As would be expected, in Lyons, where a considerable proportion of the residents worked in the Newmarket area or had previously lived in the town, the number not participating in organizations was much less, nine out of twenty-two, or 41 per cent. Comparison with East Gwillimbury Heights in terms simply of these figures, it is true, can be misleading; it was easy enough for the resident of East Gwillimbury Heights to recall that he had joined or had attended some meetings of the recently formed ratepayers' association, not so easy for the resident of these other, longer settled, areas to recall his attachment to or participation in organizations which now had come to be taken for granted. Certainly, in the community at large as within the neighbourhood, the resident of Crosby Heights, Richmond Acres, Beverley Acres, or Lyons was less socially isolated than the resident of East Gwillimbury Heights. Everyone in these areas was aware in what municipality he resided and who was responsible for the administering of the affairs of the community. The population had become settled in. But the very act of settling in had led to a weakening of those ties with the community that very early had developed. The hydro was now connected, the telephone installed, the time for the collection of garbage determined, the children enrolled in school. There was thus no longer the same urgent need to know what was going on in the community. The ratepayers' association had lost its importance as a repository of community information. The population had no reason to concern itself with anything much that was happening beyond the street on which it lived.

By now, the residents of Crosby Heights, Richmond Acres, Beverley Acres, or Lyons had ceased in any sense to be a part of the community of Toronto. Few residents interviewed reported belonging to organizations centred in the city. At most, they drove down to the city occasionally to shop or attend a movie. What other ties they had had with the city were now largely broken.

On the other hand, the residents of these areas had not developed any real feeling of belonging to the community into which they had moved. This was especially true of the residents of Crosby Heights, Richmond Acres, and Beverley Acres, situated within the town limits of Richmond Hill. The services for these areas were provided by the town. Yet, except for a few residents who worked in the town, the population was largely indifferent to town affairs. Indeed, out of a sample of sixty-four residents interviewed in these three areas, only twelve expressed the feeling that they were in any way a part of Richmond Hill. Most of the residents saw the town as a completely different community—a place in which they had no interest. Typical were such responses: "don't feel a part," "feel very little a part," "feel we're kind of separate here," "don't actually feel a part—we just live here," "the people here don't seem to associate this subdivision with Richmond Hill at all," "don't feel a part—just that they collect our garbage every week," "don't feel a part of the town—haven't been there since I went to get the water hooked up," "don't feel a part of the town, nothing at all—this district could just as well be out in Port Credit," "never even go down there, to the town." The separation of these three areas from the town by the Canadian National Railway and by a belt of land zoned for industrial purposes accentuated the feeling of the residents of not being a part of Richmond Hill. To get to the town, it was necesary to take the access road out to the highway south of the town, and once the highway was reached it was almost as easy to drive into the city. One resident, active in community affairs, commented on the division between the new residential developments and the town:

Richmond Hill was not on the whole very aware of what was happening with this new residential development. They were not too anxious to see the town grow this way. The real old timers still regard us as newcomers. They accept us almost on sufferance. In the subdivisions, there is a general lack of interest in the affairs of the town. I don't really know why. A group of us put in a lot of time before the last municipal election knocking on doors in Beverley Acres. We met great ignorance and apathy. We were disappointed that the vote from Beverley Acres was not better than it was. There is a feeling of separation between the old town and the subdivision. There's a physical separation—railroad and creek—you cannot ignore it. Then there's the industrial belt. And then some want the distinction. There is no ward system and this seems to foster division. Sometimes I feel the people over there (in Beverley Acres and the other subdivisions) don't care about the separation. They aren't integrated at all—just another patch of 200 or 300 houses go up and then we have to step in and make it work. They have very limited resources within themselves. Some will come to meetings, but take office—no.

The residents interviewed were generally apathetic regarding municipal affairs. Of fifty-two residents responding (out of sixty-four interviewed) in Crosby Heights, Richmond Acres, and Beverley Acres, twenty-eight or 54 per cent indicated that they had very little if any interest in municipal politics. The replies of three of these residents were typical:

We used to go to the Home and School when we lived in the city. We don't take part in local government. We haven't voted. We're not too interested. We just read the papers to see what's going on. I don't belong to the Ratepayers'.

We didn't vote in the first municipal election after we moved here. I didn't know then and I have never voted because I didn't know who I was voting for. I picked up some information from a fellow who goes into the Anglican Church in Richmond Hill—this is the old established church in Richmond Hill where the mayor and other important people go.

I definitely voted in the first election. We weren't too well informed, I'll say that. I take no interest in municipal affairs, not even in the Ratepayers'. I'm maybe dissatisfied with the local government at times —the tax differential.

Unlike the residents of East Gwillimbury Heights, the residents of Crosby Heights, Richmond Acres, and Beverley Acres were not unaware of what was going on in their community. They were necessarily involved in certain activities. But like the ties of neighbourhood, the ties of community had become so diffused that the demands on individual suburban residents were scarcely felt. Within the community at large they had succeeded largely in loosing themselves by avoiding any too close identification with particular organizations.

The ratepayers' association had been the first casualty in this search of the suburban resident for a cloak of anonymity in the community. Unless it became reorganized on a very different basis, an association such as this had a life expectancy of about two years. Already in East Gwillimbury Heights, at the time of the field study and only six months after it had been formed, the association was beginning to show signs of change: new officers had been elected to replace those responsible for bringing the organization into being. Associations formed in Crosby Heights, Richmond Acres, and Beverley Acres had ceased to exist. In Lyons the ratepayers' association had been transformed into a community association.

By this time, it is true, other associations had come into existence. Conspicuous in most suburban areas was a home and school or parent-teachers association. Organizations associated with the church, politics, social service, and recreation had also made an appearance. A housewives' recreational association called Take a Break, or TAB, was to be found in a number of residential areas. Service clubs were being formed.

The suburban community was becoming more organized. Indeed, the listing of the different associations existing in an area like Crosby Heights would give the impression of a community very much caught up in forms of organized group activity. But no great amount of probing was required to reveal the fact that by far the majority of residents—perhaps as many as 65 per cent in Crosby Heights and Richmond Acres and 78 per cent in Beverley Acres— participated in none of these organizations.

After the first flurry of excitement and anxiety, interest in community affairs had dropped off, and clear lines had now formed between those people who were organization-minded and those people who were not. Whyte's "organization men" (and "organization women") could be found in all suburban residential areas. They were the people who became prominent in the management of the affairs of the ratepayers' association and they were the people who brought into being such organizations as the home and school association. For the ratepayers' association this narrowing of the constituency upon which it depended for support signalled the beginning of its disintegration. Charges that it was being run by a small clique found justification in face of the association's claim that it spoke for the whole community. In the case of the other associations that developed in the suburban residential area, however, no claim was made to speak for the whole community and their dependence upon a narrow constituency for support was as a consequence no threat to their survival. There could develop the distinction, to the satisfaction of the one group and the indifference of the other, between those people interested in the affairs of the community and those people who were not.

That is not to say that persons active in community organizations made no effort to arouse the interest of persons not active. Rather, the very cause they served was that of arousing such an interest. The "good society" was conceived as the society in which people were actively involved. Apathy was considered a social fault. The purpose of the community organization was to strengthen in the population a feeling of community identity—to make people better citizens.

Yet a condition of successful establishment of residence in the suburbs was an avoidance of any great involvement in forms of organized group activity. Associations acted in effect either as tax-imposing bodies themselves or as organizations acting in support of tax-imposing bodies, and taxation, in whatever guise it appeared, was something the new suburban resident was determined to resist. The "good society" for most suburban residents was the society that made no demands upon them. Associations like the Home and School could hold out the promise of building a "better" community: a community boasting not only sewers, paved streets, and street lights, but also well-staffed schools, recreational centres, libraries, and a population informed about and alive to the affairs of the world at large. But building such a community could not be done without expenditure of time and money, and intent upon the main purpose which had led him to make the move to the suburbs —the establishment of a home for his family—the new suburban resident was in no mood to undertake such an expenditure.

Few suburban residents, of course, saw the problem in such broad general terms as these. It could be a canvasser at the door seeking a donation to some cause, or a telephone call urging attendance at some meeting, which compelled the suburban resident to make up his mind whether he was going to be active in community affairs or not. Closing the door or hanging up the telephone receiver with a polite "I'm sorry" could result from the simple consideration that nowhere in the house was to be found any spare money or nowhere in the daily schedule of work and of household care was to be found a free evening.

The past president of a home and school association in one of the suburban areas commented:

It requires missionary work to get people out to things. I think many stayed away from organizations because they couldn't afford them. Many of them simply couldn't afford to do anything—they just sat. A club has to be very careful what it plans up here; they can't hold dinners, say, because people couldn't afford to go. They can't have fund-raising campaigns because there is little money and you can't sell tickets for something and hold it in the public school. You can charge a silver collection, but they don't even like that.

Another resident active in organizations of the community was less sympathetic in her explanation of the lack of response from the population:

People here are in hock up to their ears. They have no money for baby-sitters. And many of the husbands work long hours and shifts and the women are tied in. These people don't want to make the effort to get out. Why, I don't know. Most of them come from the city. There were no buses here at first, and these people don't want to walk, even if it's just a couple of blocks. I don't know how you can capture their interest. They are much too self-centred. They don't want to make this a community. They don't want to put forth the effort to do something for someone else. If there is something in it for them then O.K.

A third community organization leader responded:

Most of the people have to be coaxed to join organizations. They're afraid they might be asked for money. They can't be bothered. If they want to join they will. There is no community spirit here. Last night over at the school they had the candidates speak and there were only 15–20 from this area. And there were only 60–70 from the whole area east of the tracks. I can't figure it out. They just won't come. They're afraid if they do they'll be asked to do some work. And there's no sense in pleading with people to come out, because if they don't want to then they're no good when they do. They won't come out because they are afraid someone will say "will you do something?"

Community leaders interviewed were almost unanimous in the view that only a small proportion of the suburban residents were prepared to lend support to forms of organized group activity. There was much scolding about the general lack of interest and very seldom an expression of a favourable judgment. To most persons active in organizations, the suburban community lacked a sense of pride and spirit of enterprise. It was made up of an apathetic population, intent only upon individual ends with no concern for the welfare of the whole.

Persons involved in organizational activity tend always to exaggerate the lack of community interest of those persons not so involved. The suburban population was probably not as lacking in community-mindedness as it was made out to be. Yet the field study revealed certainly a general lack of interest in community affairs. In the response of some of the residents interviewed there entered a note of apology—few said that community organizations were not a good thing—but whatever the explanation offered there was clearly a reluctance to become drawn very far into the affairs of the community. One Crosby Heights resident asserted:

When people have just got married they have more time. I used to go out more in the city. Up here we are just young couples. We have showers here and other activities. We get together quite often in the summer. Now that it is winter we stay home more often and watch T.V. In fact we can't go anywhere. When people have just started working, see, with the mortgage payments, oil bill, and everything there is not much to do—we can't spend money so we do not join anything.

Another resident of the same area replied:

I am not a member of any organizations in Richmond Hill. It is difficult right now—you see people are just getting settled. They cannot be interested in organizations. Added to that there is the problem of baby-sitters, we cannot get any around here. None of my friends is interested in organizations. They can't go out as they too have small children. We do not even go to movies. We sit and watch T.V. Husbands are tired too. I don't think I am going to join any organizations. I can't say I am. Most of us here have to work hard in the house. We are poor. Before we came here we had less space to look after and no children. Now we are here we have more space and children to look after. So I can't say I will join any organization. I know my husband won't be able to join any organizations.

Not everywhere in the suburbs was the repudiation of the ties of community carried the same distance. It made a difference how close to the line financially was the suburban resident; and it also made a difference what were the cultural values he brought with him to the suburbs. The residents of Beverley Acres were a good deal less well off financially than were the residents of Crosby Heights, Richmond Acres, or Lyons, a larger number of the wives worked, and there was a much larger turnover of population. The effects showed up in the highly unstable character of organizations in this area and in the almost complete lack of participation by the population in community affairs. Very few of the Beverley Acres residents had belonged to organizations before moving to the suburbs and very few of them now were prepared to develop such attachments. Interest in the affairs of the community was almost completely lacking. Typical was the reply of one resident:

I don't belong to any organizations. I suppose there are some here I could belong to if I wanted. I look after my neighbour's children while she works from 7:45 a.m. to 6:00 p.m. And then I go home and get meals and look after my own place—there's no time left over. My husband doesn't belong to any organizations either. He works shifts. We're both too tied up. I didn't belong to any organizations before we came up here. I worked there too. I have heard of the "Y" T-A-B in Beverley Acres. I think it is good but I haven't got any time.

The residents of Beverley Acres were far from being organization-minded. On the other side, however, their financial state and cultural values made them much more dependent upon the ties of neighbourhood than were the residents of areas like Crosby Heights, Richmond Acres, and Lyons. As well, there could not occur to the same extent a break with friends and relatives of the past. More of the old society as these people had known it was carried over and maintained intact in the new, and there was a more desperate striving to reconstruct the patterns of behaviour, such as those built around the neighbourhood association, that the move to the suburbs had disturbed. There was more neighbourhood visiting, more borrowing and lending, and more neighbourhood parties in Beverley Acres than in areas like Crosby Heights, Richmond Acres, or Lyons; and there was more clinging to associations of the past, with friends and relatives. Social ties such as these involved obligations less onerous than similar ties did for the middle-class resident of these other areas. A bottle of beer in the backyard or a cup of tea in the kitchen was a more accepted form of entertainment. In time and money, it was less demanding to maintain or build up ties of social group.

One resident reported:

We knew the family living on the other side of this house before moving here. I didn't get to know many people when I was working—I got to know the family across the driveway. Nine other women and I meet every two weeks for coffee. We used to take the children but it got too noisy. Now we meet every Friday night—we collect 25 cents from each person and spend one night in Toronto. Our husbands baby-sit. Most visiting is during the day on account of the children. When we visit the talk is about children. I have got to know almost all the people on the street since I stopped working a year ago.

Another answered in similar vein:

We knew one family here reasonably well before moving. I got to know the neighbour over the back fence through putting out the laundry. It took quite a long time to get chatty. I haven't got too many friends, about three or four. I see them roughly every day. We talk. There's visiting among the mothers with small children. The women just talk and keep one another company—those with young children.

It was not in Beverley Acres, however, that were to be found patterns of behaviour sharply at variance with those characteristic of the suburbs generally. The people of Beverley Acres were not greatly different from the people of Crosby Heights, Richmond Acres, or Lyons. Much the same forces were at work, weakening the ties of the past with friends and relatives, and discouraging close ties of neighbourhood as well as community. "There is very little community life here," one Beverley Acres resident could assert, "it is easy to make friends if you want to but my husband is too busy at night school and is away on week-ends." Another responded to the question about social life in the area: "I like the neighbourhood—people are friendly but not too so." At least one resident reported living in almost complete social isolation, cut off from contact with the neighbourhood as well as with the community at large.

I don't belong to any organizations. I don't know of any. You see I do not go out. I do not even know my neighbour. I know that she has red hair that's all. The kids go out and meet people though; they like it here. I can't say much about the community. I do not go anywhere. I don't even know what is happening. I do not know whether other people belong to organizations. But I believe they will become more active when the community grows older. At present people are too busy paying off debts.

Where differences in patterns of behaviour showed up in clear form was between areas like Crosby Heights, Richmond Acres, Lyons, and Beverley Acres on the one side and areas like Thorncrest Village and Don Mills or, at the other extreme, Riverdrive Park and Wilcox Lake, on the other. Beverley Acres in certain respects was like Riverdrive Park as, indeed, in other respects, Crosby Heights or Lyons was like Don Mills, if not Thorncrest Village. But there was no mistaking the differences.

In Thorncrest Village and Don Mills the demands of neighbourhood and community, and the world at large, could not easily be escaped. A readiness to fit into the social life of the community was virtually a condition of settlement in these areas. What was offered was a "friendly atmosphere." The atmosphere could scarcely have been kept friendly if people had determined to live apart from their fellow residents. The very planning of the physical structure of the community was directed to the end of cultivating the close associations of neighbourhood and community. In Thorncrest Village even the building of fences around lots was prohibited, a prohibition which had the effect of protecting certain social as well as aesthetic values. What was distinctive about Thorncrest Village and Don Mills depended upon a structure of social life fostering a spirit of good fellowship and togetherness.

References made by some of the residents interviewed in Thorncrest Village to other residents who refused to enter into the village's social life were an indication of a failure to secure complete conformity to the values underlying the community's social structure. How strong were the pressures to conformity were evident, however, by the harshness of the disapproval of the conduct of these residents. To seek to live apart from other persons in the community was to court the risk of social ostracism. People were made into a close social group.

But this was precisely what had been sought by people taking up residence in Thorncrest Village or Don Mills. These were people who had risen in the social scale and fled the urban neighbourhood because there they could not avoid association with people of different social class, cultural values, and tastes. What was sought was an escape from the type of neighbourhood the city had to offer, but there was no attempt to escape from the associations of neighbourhood and community as they could be reconstructed free from the disturbing and disintegrating forces of the urban environment. Rather, the very opposite was the case. For the men, associations of a business, professional, or leisure-time character offered support within the urban community to values of social class, but for the women and children it was in the associations of neighbourhood that the supports of values of social class had to be found. To obtain a "wholesome family atmosphere" it was necessary to build, whether within the urban community or outside, a tightly structured form of neighbourhood life.

Given the age and financial circumstances of the people who located in Thorncrest Village and Don Mills (young and middle-aged people "on the make" but not yet for the most part with any great amount of savings) it was not easy to buy a home in a "good" urban residential district. Houses available in the city in the price range of houses in Thorncrest Village and Don Mills were in areas where the exclusive character of the neighbourhood had broken down. What residential developments like Thorncrest Village and Don Mills offered were neighbourhoods as socially acceptable as were those offered by areas of very expensive housing in the city.

Thus it was in their highly urban character that areas such as Thorncrest Village and Don Mills secured distinctiveness. They were made more urban than the urban community itself in the sense that in them could be realized that social exclusiveness of the urban neighbourhood which in the city was being threatened. Feelings of togetherness, of being a tight social group, cultivated in the associations of the neighbourhood and the community at large, offered an important support to values of social class which no longer could be successfully protected in the urban environment.

This is not to say that the residents of Thorncrest Village and Don Mills were wholly occupied with local affairs. These were people who moved about a great deal, had many friends beyond the community, and were heavily involved in activities related to their work, politics, and other interests. They had no great need of neighbours, for fellowship or mutual help. Many families had two cars, and wives as well as husbands (and older children) maintained close and continuous contact with the world outside.

But like the associations of the outside world—professional, business, political, or other—the associations of neighbourhood and community were considered something valuable to foster and preserve. A certain, carefully calculated, amount of time, money, and effort was directed to the support of such associations. Means were allocated to a great number of different ends, of which support of the local community was one. Thus if the demands of neighbourhood and community were not wholly consuming, they were nevertheless exacting. There were things people were expected to do: attend at least occasionally community affairs, share in driving children to school, entertain neighbours and other friends in the area, and generally behave sociably. There developed a characteristic pattern of neighbourhood and community activity.

As would be expected, there was a difference in the degree of involvement in neighbourhood and community affairs between Thorncrest Village and Don Mills. Thorncrest Village, when fully settled, had a population of two hundred families. It was easy to walk from one end of the village to the other. Identification of people with the community was readily maintained, through the activities of the village club house and through the physical compactness of the area. Almost, everyone came to know everyone else. There was scarcely anyone interviewed in the area who did not indicate considerable involvement in the life of the neighbourhood and the affairs of the community. All of them, of course, belonged to the Thorncrest Village Association and to all there was sent a monthly news letter. No one in the village could plead ignorance of what was going on. The means of disseminating information were built into the structure of the community. So as well were the means of securing the active participation of the population in community affairs. At the informal level of the neighbourhood and the formal level of the community there developed highly effective techniques to bring people together, make them acquainted, and weld them into a social group. One resident reported:

We have Red Cross meetings and social gatherings to meet newcomers. They gave a tea for me. We have a bridge tournament so that all the people in the village get a chance to play with all the other couples. We have neighbours here that are just tops. I would say that there is a great deal of visiting—very often just dropping around in the evening or morning. I got to know most people through the Red Cross, bridge tournaments, and meetings at the club house.

Another resident responded to the same query:

We didn't know anyone when we moved here. Our neighbours came and called on us. There was a tea for all the neighbours. We went to the next club dance. We didn't really know what to expect in a planned community. We never had much neighbourhood life before. Neighbours go swimming together to the village pool—go back to a house for cards—on Sunday barbecue dinners together—a lot of card playing and some drinking too. Bridge, dances, and swimming at the pool are the more important activities in the community.

Still another resident reported:

Our neighbours came to see us when we moved in. One neighbour had a luncheon for a number of us. There is a good deal of visiting among neighbours. In summer the girls get together and go to the pool. If I accepted all the invitations I get I would be out every other day. We have each other's children to lunch—take each other's children to the pool. We have got to know the people in the village through going to club dances and house parties.

People in Thorncrest Village were kept busy attending to their neighbourhood duties and their duties as residents of the village. But they did not neglect their obligations to the world outside. Only two of the residents interviewed indicated that they did not belong to organizations of any sort. There were a number of others, of course, whose organizational attachments were parochial, church groups, the home and school association, and such. But important people lived in Thorncrest Village and their importance was made apparent by the organizations to which they belonged: the Toronto Board of Trade, the Progressive Conservative Association, the Rotary Club, and the like. Ties such as these posed no threat to ties within the village of neighbourhood and community. The social exclusiveness secured within the village social structure derived from and reinforced the social exclusiveness secured in associations of the outside world.

Don Mills, of course, could not be made into such a tight social group. This was a residential area with a much greater population, spread over a larger territory. In spite of the efforts to plan its growth, it acquired from the beginning something of a mass quality. There were people who sought to lose themselves in Don Mills as in the suburbs at large. "Neighbourhood life was one of the things that nearly frightened us off Don Mills," one resident asserted. "We don't want to become involved in the social life of Don Mills or neighbours—too narrow and boring," said another. Of fifty-seven residents responding, twenty-five or about 44 per cent indicated that they belonged to no organizations in the area. A considerable proportion of the residents of Don Mills were young families, undertaking for the first time the responsibilities of home ownership. They could scarcely escape the same pressures that in the suburbs generally compelled people to avoid involvement in neighbourhood and community affairs.

Yet there was a great difference between Don Mills and the ordinary suburban community and this difference showed up in the considerably larger proportion of the residents who did belong to organizations, 56 per cent. What was important was the general, over-all character of the area, and in terms of this general, over-all character Don Mills was much more like Thorncrest Village than it was like the ordinary suburban community. No planned suburban residential area could fully realize the ideals upon which it was built. Thorncrest Village was not the perfect neighbourhood and community that it was designed to be. Indeed, in certain important respects, Don Mills came closer to realizing the ideals of its promoters than did Thorncrest Village. Thorncrest Village was too small to become a self-contained residential area. People had to go out of the village too much to do the things they wanted to do: the village had no schools, churches, or adequate shopping. Even the boundaries of the neighbourhood could not be maintained wholly successfully. Residents living on the outskirts of the village (and such residents made up a substantial proportion of the whole) reported that the people living across the street outside the village were as much their neighbours as the people living within. The areas surrounding Thorncrest Village had attracted a class of residents not greatly different from the class locating in the village. Under these circumstances the exclusiveness of the village as a residential area was difficult to maintain. As houses changed in ownership, and new people moved in, the sense of group identity weakened. Thorncrest Village began to approach in character other residential areas offering housing within the same price range.

In contrast, Don Mills as a community was highly self-contained. People could live complete lives within Don Mills, going outside only to earn a living. The community lacked its own municipal government—and this was a serious lack—but it had almost everything else: schools, churches, a shopping centre, medical services, recreational facilities, a community newspaper, and the like. The whole area was built around a single centre where all community services were located, with local services—notably the elementary school—centred in clearly defined neighbourhood areas. Such a design gave to the community, and the neighbourhood, very much a viable character. People could feel they were a part of a neighbourhood and community.

But differences such as these between Don Mills and Thorncrest Village only pointed up the fact that the strengths—and the weaknesses—of the two areas in terms of the structure of their neighbourhood and community life were not the same. Both areas, for different reasons, were unable to escape some of the pressures resulting from the mass overrunning of the countryside by an urban population. On balance, the structure of the planned neighbourhood and community was probably maintained more intact in Thorncrest Village than in Don Mills. Thorncrest Village attempted to "package" less, but what it did package, it did more thoroughly. There was, however, no mistaking the "packaged" character of both areas.

This was apparent in the extent to which the structuring of the neighbourhood and the community did secure considerable involvement of the population in local affairs. Even the most superficial observation pointed up the difference between Don Mills and the suburbs generally. In the suburbs generally, residents who were active in the life of the community clearly were a minority. In Don Mills, in contrast, everyone seemed to be active; everyone, that is to say, except a small group of residents, mostly young in years, who successfully resisted efforts to be drawn into neighbourhood and community affairs. A good deal of the activity centred around children in efforts made to provide for their better education and for their recreational needs, but a wide range of informal and formal group activities developed to bring people together, within the neighbourhood and community. Of a purely social nature were such organizations as a square-dance club, a bowling club, and a bridge club. Service clubs were well represented by such organizations as the Lions, the Kiwanis, the Knights of Columbus, Civitan, and the Masonic Lodge. Conspicuous in relation to the affairs of the school was, of course, the Home and School Association. Business, professional, and church organizations were active, the Junior Chamber of Commerce, the Canadian Association of Consumers, the Catholic Women's League, and such; and political interests found expression in such organizations as the Don Mills Progressive Conservative Club. Active in community affairs was the Don Mills Horticultural Association and the Don Mills Community Association.

It was not difficult, living in Don Mills, to become informed about what was going on, within the community and the world at large. A Don Mills newspaper provided news about local affairs; Toronto morning and evening papers were delivered at every doorstep. People were made to feel that it was a duty to be concerned about the welfare of their community. Of fifty-seven residents responding, only fifteen or 26 per cent expressed themselves as not interested in the government of the township. A number indicated considerable involvement in municipal politics. There was a lively consciousness of the identity of Don Mills as a community. People were made to feel proud of being a part of the community. A variety of social mechanisms operated to fit the resident into the neighbourhood and secure his identification with the larger residential area. One resident reported:

When we moved in some of the neighbours came to see us and we introduced ourselves to the neighbour next door. We met a number more at a meeting to put up fences. We have made other friends through the church, clubs, and work. There is visiting among the women during the daytime especially in winter and on rainy days. The Dominion store brings people together—it's almost like the main street of a small town. The neighbourhood life of Don Mills was a reason for moving here; we wanted a friendly, young community, especially for the children. We belong to the Home and School Association and the Don Mills Community Association. My husband belongs to the Lawyers Club, the

Canadian Mental Health Association, and he hopes to get into the Lions Club and the Yonge Street Business Men's Association.

Another resident responded:

We got to know the neighbours through the children and street parties. Every day or every second day we play bridge, listen to records, go to dances, and go out to dinner. There is little visiting except for bridge; we don't do running in and out. We moved here because we liked the kind of neighbourhood life—there are more people our own age. There are barbecues and bridge. I belong to the Women's Auxiliary of the Church. My husband coaches baseball. That's the only thing we belong to.

A third answered:

Had coffee with next door neighbour soon after moving in. My husband and I worked on the campaign for the Progressive Conservative candidate in the last federal election. I think there is quite a bit of visiting on the street. But we don't have much to do with that group. Since we don't have any children we're not encouraged. When we moved here we couldn't have cared less for the kind of neighbourhood this was. We belong to a good many clubs. My husband is a member of Civitan. We belong to the Don Mills Progressive Conservative Club. We didn't belong to any organizations before we came to Don Mills. It is pretty much the same sort of life here as a small town. You make your own fun.

A great deal of variety characterized the social life of Don Mills. This was a community with a population of several thousand families. There was a mixture of detached and semi-detached housing, and as well there was a substantial development of apartment dwellings, duplexes, and some row housing. Divisions of the population along class lines were built into the structure of the community. There was no thought that the whole Don Mills population would be made into "one big happy family." From the very beginning, social life in the neighbourhood and the community at large tended to develop around the interests of different groups of people. "You form little groups and play bridge," was the way one resident described how neighbourhood associations in the area came into being. "There are all sorts of groups here—music, discussion and so on," another resident described the neighbourhood. Where the community was as large as Don Mills, the physical location of people offered in itself an exceedingly narrow and crude base upon which to erect the structure of a society. Neighbourhood associations were reinforced by associations built up on the basis of interests cutting across and extending beyond neighbourhood lines.

Such divisions of the population along the lines of different social and cultural interests, however, did not mean a weakening of the ties of neighbourhood or community as a consequence. Because people were less enclosed within the physical bounds of the neighbourhood they were drawn more fully into the life of the community. The Don Mills neighbourhood was very much like an urban neighbourhood. People moved out of the city to secure in Don Mills that urban kind of society, and urban way of life, which in the city was unattainable given their financial means. It was a society less exclusive, easier to fit into, than the one offered in Thorncrest Village, but it was not that much less exclusive that any but the right people would choose to become a part of it.

In the development of residential areas like Riverdrive Park and Wilcox Lake the same kind of selective forces were at work securing the reconstruction of forms of neighbourhood and community life carried over from the urban society. Here was a population which in the urban society had placed a heavy dependence upon kinship and neighbourhood associations. In the downtown areas of the city (or in small towns or farm communities), the population had been little involved in the affairs of the wider community. But in the warm and intimate associations of the kinship group and the neighbourhood the lives of these people were deeply imbedded. The society that they had known was the society that they reconstructed for themselves in the suburbs. The ways of life of the society of the past were built into the very structure of the community.

In order to build such a society no planning consultants or rigid zoning regulations were required. The structure of the society could be transferred almost intact from city to country through reliance upon the deeply rooted ties of the informal group. The people of Riverdrive Park and Wilcox Lake went on living much as they had been living. There was a difference, but the difference was not in a weakening but instead a strengthening of the ties of the kinship group and the neighbourhood. In downtown areas of the city the pouring in of immigrant peoples and the expansion of the commercial district had broken down established forms of community life.

"Old" Canadians found themselves living alongside "New" Canadians or next door to parking lots or commercial establishments. In their move from the city they had no urge to escape urban patterns of neighbourhood and community life. Rather, they desperately strove to preserve such patterns.

Of twenty-two families interviewed in Riverdrive Park only two claimed not to be involved in the life of the neighbourhood or community. One was an old couple, seventy-six and seventy-four, who had moved to the area because their son was living there. "They don't come near me and I don't go near them," the wife asserted with regard to her neighbours. The other was a young couple, both twenty-nine with two small children. They had given as the reason for moving to Riverdrive Park that they had been unable to find residential accommodation anywhere else. This couple clearly had no wish to be identified with the community. The only family they knew was the one living next door. They belonged to no organizations in the area. "It isn't hard to mix up if you want to," the wife asserted, "but I wouldn't want to." The interest of this couple was centred in the home and the family.

There were other families in the area who had no strong feeling of being a part of the community. Riverdrive Park did not escape (as neither did Don Mills nor Thorncrest Village) the effects of the mass push of population out of the city into the suburbs. But it was only a small minority of the residents who sought to avoid involvement in the life of the neighbourhood and community. Exactly one-half of the residents interviewed declared that they belonged to one or more organizations in the area: the Home and School Association, the Ladies' Auxiliary, the Ratepayers' Association, the Boy Scouts. "It's like all small communities," one resident could assert, "you get to know everybody."

A housewife, fifty years of age, described neighbourhood life:

I didn't know a soul when I came here. I got to know the woman two doors down the street I guess because she has a child of the same age and we're the same age. And then I joined the Ladies' Auxiliary and got to know some people. I see some of the neighbours once or twice a day. There is a lot of visiting. Some of the women are never home. I got to know some more people through going to the Post Office. There are showers. I get invited to all of them. Now they've started a plastic demonstration. I belong to the Ladies' Auxiliary and the Home and School.

Another housewife, seventy-five years of age, reported:

I did know one or two people here but not very well. The people across the street were the first I met. You push yourself in and get to know people. Quite a few are good friends. We see them every day. You can't help it. People are always outside and around. There is good neighbourhood life here. They all help you with your car, with anything. I would say it's a good place to live. There's bingo, dances, the men have a baseball pool. This is a sociable place. They're always doing things.

A retired man, sixty-seven years old, reported:

My daughter was the only person I knew here. Other than that I was a complete stranger. I got to know a lot of people through my son-in-law. We go fishing, play cards, and of course we have our beer. The neighbours just visit one another and talk. Last month we had a party here and people came from all over and brought their own drinks. The fellow down the end of the street he brought a bath-tub full of beer and we didn't know him. People here are good and friendly. There's bingo, cards, parties. Last Saturday friends invited us over to a party. They said come over you and the wife.

It was a social life rich in the associations of neighbourhood and community which characterized Riverdrive Park. Everybody seemed to know everybody else. Children played unattended on the street, to be directed or scolded by whatever adult was nearby. Housewives dropped in and out of one another's homes, or visited on the street or in one or other of the two small grocery stores in the area. The large number of men around, retired or temporarily out of work, gave to the community a certain completeness. There was a "leisure class" to assume responsibility for the management of local affairs. Though the community could boast no shopping centre, park, church, library, place of amusement, or, for a long time, local school, there was a crudely furnished wooden hall and with few facilities there developed an active social life both in the neighbourhood and the community. People became caught up and involved in social groups.

There was, of course, another side to the social life of Riverdrive Park. Not all social relations between people in the community were pleasant. There was general agreement that as homes had changed hands and new people had moved in the character of the area had improved. "We have nicer and cleaner people moving in here," one resident asserted, "before we had the scruff from the city." Another replied in similar vein: "I think the area is improving, a better class of people are moving in on a better financial footing." "When I first moved here," another reported, "there was an awful lot of bickering and fighting." Still another responded: "We used to have some tough kids here; two years ago they had nineteen kids in the house next door and only one room—the husband got put into jail." Stable forms of neighbourhood and community life were not established without difficulty. In Wilcox Lake the population brought with it so few social ties of any sort—family, kinship, neighbourhood, or community—and there occurred such a rapid turnover of home-owners and tenants, that no really stable neighbourhood or community life developed, but Riverdrive Park as well suffered from the drifting in and out of people who had no secure place in a social world built up about the family, the kinship group, and the neighbourhood. For people so close to the margin, economically and socially, as were most of the residents of an area such as this, the distinction between the respectable and the disreputable at certain points became narrow indeed. The whole community existed in almost complete isolation from the outside world. It was "they"—persons unknown in the world outside—who provided the police protection, the education, the jobs and whatever else was needed that could not be provided within the community. Almost the whole population constantly faced the threat of unemployment. These people had no secure place in the world of work nor did they have much of a place in the outside social, political, religious, or cultural world. They knew few people outside Riverdrive Park and they belonged to few outside organizations. Of twenty-two residents interviewed, one belonged to a kennel and a collie club and another to the Progressive Conservative party, an international union, and the Legion. The other twenty had no institutional attachments whatsoever outside Riverdrive Park, not even to a church.

It was a fragile base on which to erect a community. How fragile was made evident by the fate of a similar residential area in eastern Scarborough, the Willows, destroyed by the fury of a hurricane and the dictates of a township council. There were not resources in this type of residential area to make it possible to withstand any severe pressure from the outside. Indeed, Wilcox Lake never acquired in any real sense the shape of a community. This area was too near the city—too attractive to the week-end visitor—to make possible the preservation of what family and neighbourhood ties the people settling here may have carried with them. "Don't ask me about my neighbours," one resident in this area said: "we were here a year before there was a neighbour in the house. My son did tell me who some of them were. There's hardly anybody living around here was living here when we came." Another responded: "There is only one neighbour with whom I'm friendly. As I said we've been living here for fifteen months and all those we saw at the time have moved out." There was, of course, particularly among the home-owners as distinguished from the tenants, an effort to develop some sort of social life in the area. There were reports from some residents that they did a good deal of visiting and partying, and, indeed, from a few, that they participated in social activities in the nearby village. But for a very large proportion of the residents, this area was nothing more than a place to live—a temporary haven, offering cheap shelter.

Riverdrive Park did not wholly escape the effects of forces that in Wilcox Lake came near to making impossible the establishment of forms of community life. But this area was forty miles from the City of Toronto and eight miles from the nearest town, Newmarket. The small village of Holland Landing five miles distant was the only disturbing influence in the life of the community. Riverdrive Park had no voice in the affairs of the larger society—no ties with the outside world—but, on the other hand, so completely was it cut off from the world outside that nothing that happened there affected it much. Indeed, to a degree, the people of Riverdrive Park had even escaped from the economic vicissitudes of the outside world; it did not cost much to live in an area such as this and a few dollars earned now and then could keep the family going. There could develop here as a consequence, without too much difficulty, the forms of social life and patterns of social relations which many of the residents had known where they had previously lived. Riverdrive Park had almost no urban characteristics; it seemed much more like a country village than a part of a large city. Yet in a very real sense it represented not an effort to escape urban society but an effort to preserve certain forms of urban life, in particular those built around the associations of kinship and neighbourhood, which in the urban community were being destroyed. Riverdrive Park was almost as much a creation of an urban social class as was Thorncrest Village.

Throughout the suburbs, people carried with them from the city the forms of social life they had known. They went on living much as they had been living. This was as true of the people moving into mass-developed residential areas as into, on the one side, areas like Thorncrest Village or, on the other side, Riverdrive Park. But the people moving into mass-developed residential areas had not been, while living in the city, greatly dependent upon ties of neighbour-hood and community, and now, in face of pressures developing out of buying a house, they were even less dependent upon such ties. In contrast, the people moving into areas like Thorncrest Village or Riverdrive Park had been highly dependent upon neighbourhood and community ties and now in their new place of residence they found conditions that made possible the strengthening of such ties.

The difference between these types of residential areas were not in actuality as clear-cut as is here suggested. All suburban resi-dential areas were to some degree packaged and all had something of a mass-developed character. Nevertheless, there was a difference, and this difference was made evident by the extent to which there had been an effort to build into the structure of the new suburban community urban forms of social life. If differentiation is considered a characteristic of the urban society, the more highly differentiated the society is the more highly urban it must be. Within the urban society people are sorted out in terms of their socio-economic posi-tion into different areas and into different formal and informal social groupings. But the lines that form are never firmly secured. Forces of urban growth lead to a continuous mixing of people and to a breaking down of the boundaries between different social groups, particularly as they have become formed along residential lines. The different residential areas in the urban community begin to lose their distinctive character. With urban growth the highly differentiated urban society moves in the direction of becoming an undifferentiated social mass.

The opening up of unoccupied countryside for urban settlement offered an opportunity for strengthening the lines setting off different social groupings of the urban population from one another. In the great number of little, carefully nourished—"packaged"—residential areas which grew up in the countryside surrounding Toronto people could be sorted out to an extent that was no longer possible in much of the built-up urban community. Catholic worker could live alongside Catholic worker in the Sharon co-operative development, German tradesman alongside German tradesman in the Bayview development south of Wilcocks Lake, middle-class Jew alongside middle-class Jew in Bathurst Manor, and remain secure, at least for a time, in their association. Suburban development of this sort carried forward the process of differentiation in urban society. It was in this sense that residential areas of the packaged type were more urban than the urban community itself.

It was not, of course, only outside the built-up area of the urban community that there was offered an opportunity for strengthening the lines setting off different social groupings in the urban population. The post-war community of Toronto became studded with small residential islands—little Italys, Germanys, Polands, and such; and, of course, a number of big residential islands remained, still secure in their exclusiveness—Rosedale, Forest Hill Village, North Toronto, Leaside, and others. But there was a sharp limit to the extent to which such residential differentiation could take place within the built-up urban community, particularly where there were involved people who inherently—in physical appearance, language, religion, and such—had no distinctive characteristics. It was easy enough for the Italian to form himself into a tight little society in the urban community but not so easy for the person whose only distinguishing characteristic was his social standing. For such people, settlement in the suburbs, where their distinctive ways of urban living were built into the structure of the community, offered a means of preserving their identity. The "packaged" residential development strengthened the differentiated character of the urban society.

But in the struggle for space with urban growth the differentiated character of the urban society was continuously threatened and nowhere more than in that vast unoccupied area surrounding the urban community which, at a certain point in residential development, could be penetrated so easily. In the mass overrunning of the countryside there occurred no sorting out of people but the very opposite. The struggle here was one for space and in the indiscriminate occupation of the country no groups of people could attempt to preserve their distinctive ways of urban life. It was people who were just becoming a part of the urban society— characteristically young married couples with one or two children —who were pitched most fully into the struggle for space. Such people carried with them into the suburbs no very distinctive urban way of life, and here, in the effort to establish themselves in homes, what urban way of life they had was largely lost. People in the vast expanse of the suburbs became less "urban" than they had been in the urban community. That is to say, they became more detached from urban cultural values, less given to urban manners, less involved in urban types of activities, than before the move to the suburbs. What emerged here was not the "solitary" individual but the "solitary" family. Suburban residents began as strangers to one another, and, though they could not remain so for long—suburban people had to get to know one another in the very effort to establish themselves in their new suburban homes—it was the fact that people were strangers to one another which was the distinctive quality of the suburban society. As the strangeness disappeared, and people got to know one another to the point where the differences between them became identifiable, the suburban society began to take on the character of an urban society.

Building the New Society

THE SUBURBAN was a society built around the family group. What was different about this society from the old established urban society was the extent to which the energies of the whole population were concentrated upon the single interest of establishing a home for the family. This interest was uppermost in determining the structure of social life that developed. Almost everything the new suburban resident found himself doing, within the suburban setting and in the world outside, was related to the needs of the family—sodding the front lawn, fencing in the backyard, building a recreation room, shopping for furniture, kitchen appliances, and other household accessories, attending to the needs of children, and, taking precedence before all, earning sufficient income to pay off the mortgage and other debts and to meet the recurring charges of the home. Obligations such as these, it is true, were faced by all young couples, with children, embarking on a career of home-ownership, wherever they may have located; but the new suburban community was almost entirely made up of such young couples. Within the new suburban community thus it was scarcely possible to speak of a society outside that of the family. People lived the whole of their lives—almost—within the family group.

The suburban population in actual fact, of course, could never become wholly family centred. There were obligations owing to the society of which this population had been a part which could not be completely ignored; relatives, old friends, the church of the home community, and social groups of various kinds continued to make demands. As well, the new society came sufficiently ready-made, even in the most mass-developed suburban residential area, that its presence was felt from the very first moment of residence. The tax-gatherer was soon on the doorstep of every new home-owner. The arm of the law reached out to assure that certain civic duties were attended to. Municipal and school officials made their voices heard. Even the dog-catcher attracted attention if nearby were to be found old established residents proud of their green shrubs and gardens. The suburban dweller was made a citizen of the community by virtue of the very act of taking up residence in it.

But this society which made demands upon him was a society he sought to avoid rather than become a part of. Representatives of the outside world required him to pay property taxes, wrap his garbage properly, confine his dog to the backyard, fill out forms indicating how many children of pre-school age were in his home, and perform various other acts of good citizenship. The suburban resident could not wholly retreat into the confines of the family, but it was this retreat which represented the first important step in building the new society. Out of efforts to resist the obligations of the world outside there developed the consciousness of being suburban; the consciousness, that is to say, of being part of a family which had problems peculiar to itself. The demands of the "they" outside gave meaning to the interests of the "we" within—the suburban family group.

The very physical character of the suburban community offered support to the sense of distinctiveness of the suburban family. The picture window became in a very real sense a suburban symbol, though one which had little to do with striving for a higher social status. The style of the suburban house (not all suburban houses, of course, had picture windows), its location far out from the city, its very newness when all houses about it were also new, served to distinguish very clearly the family which occupied it from the urban family. The ecological conditions of residence alone were sufficient to make the suburban family different from the urban. Given its physical setting, it was not possible to live in a suburban house without being made conscious of being suburban.

But the identity of the suburban family did not depend only on its physical location. What was different about this family developed out of the social conditions of suburban residence. People in the suburbs were forced to live differently from people in the old established urban community. There developed a consciousness of a suburban way of life.

In this consciousness there was certainly some feeling of self-satisfaction. The very acquisition of a house gave to many a suburban dweller a sense of having moved up socially. The people he knew and left behind in the city by and large did not own houses. The disadvantages of urban living—the smoke-laden air, the houses crowded together on the street, the unfriendliness of neighbours, the noise and confusion—were seized upon and used to build a picture of an urban way of life that was clearly inferior to the suburban. In residential areas of the packaged type, this feeling of superiority was rooted strongly in the consciousness of being suburban, but the feeling was there in the suburban population generally. Many people moving to the suburbs believed that here was to be found a better way of life.

For most new suburban residents, however, the consciousness of being suburban developed out of a feeling not of satisfaction but of dissatisfaction with the suburban way of life. The advantages of suburban living may have been played up in the effort to rationalize the move to the suburbs but there could be no overlooking the disadvantages. It was more often a sense of deprivation than a sense of superiority that led the suburban dweller to recognize his identity as a suburban dweller. The suburban population became a population with a strong sense of grievance.

Withdrawal from the world outside, and isolation within the family group, offered the most effective means by which the suburban resident could meet the kinds of problems he faced. The world outside made demands upon him and seemed to offer in return nothing that he wanted. Only by apathy—by avoiding the obligations of the good citizen—could he find protection for his interests. The effort to organize him—to develop in him a pride of community—represented an effort in effect to make him not suburban but urban. He was called upon to assume outside responsibilities (to his church, political party, social class, the community at large) which he could discharge only by neglecting that greater responsibility he owed his family—the responsibility to establish it in a new home.

What developed was a society of families turned in toward themselves. It was not a society in which people were alert to the important issues of the world. How the recreation room should be finished, when the baby should be fed, or where was the best place to shop were the kinds of problems which came to occupy the attention of the population. Activities reaching beyond the family, in relations with neighbours and other residents, were of a sort that seemed to have little social meaning. The social world of the new suburban resident was exceedingly small. In the daily round of activities, of adults and children alike, it extended no great distance beyond the family.

But the suburban society could not remain for long wholly family-centred. There was much the suburban resident needed which he could get only from the world outside. He was prepared to do without recreational centres (really only required for teen-age children which he did not have), community halls, libraries, even churches. But he had to have his garbage collected, his streets lighted, the flood waters about his house drained away, and he wanted badly such things as a good road out to the main highway and a properly staffed school to educate his children now approaching school age. These were things which, for a time, he assumed were on the way and required on his part nothing more than patient waiting. Much could be read into the promises of real estate salesmen or township reeves by a people full of hope, ready to take on faith whatever they were told. And, indeed, many things were provided without his doing anything about it. Subdivision developers, however anxious they may have been to profit from the house-building projects they had promoted, did not wholly lack a concern about public goodwill, and no township government was unaware of the fact that the new suburban resident, in becoming a property-owner, was made a citizen possessing the power of voting. There was considerable justification for the apathy of the new suburban resident. Much came to him without his asking, and the more he avoided involvement in the affairs of the community the more he escaped the costs which resulted from residence in the suburbs. Immediately, the people with the strongest sense of grievance were those who were there before the suburban resident arrived. It was they at first who bore the costs of residential growth in the suburbs.

But the suburban resident soon had grievances of his own. His garbage may have been collected (at a heavy cost to the old residents of the area) but it was collected only once in every two weeks when it needed to be collected every few days. The school which had been built at a cost of many thousands of dollars was still far from adequate for his needs; so as well were the storm drainage, the streets and roads leading out from his place of residence, the water supply, police and fire protection, the shopping facilities. Where suburban development had involved the movement of an urban population into areas long occupied by a population that was non-urban, there developed inevitably sharp conflicts of interest between the new and old residents. The new residents demanded services approaching the standard of urban services and the old residents were determined that such demands should not be met. In circumstances such as these, a struggle for power was inevitable.

The struggle ensued at that point where there occurred a shift of a sense of grievance from the old to the new population. At first, it was the old population which felt overwhelmed by forces beyond its control. There seemed little that it could do to prevent the invasion of its world by an urban population. Farm fields over night disappeared, and where wheat crops had ripened or cattle grazed hundreds of suburban homes now stood. Mounting taxes made apparent the costs involved. The mayor of Newmarket with some justification could bitterly lash out at the folly of planting a community of urban dwellers—East Gwillimbury Heights—thirty miles north of the city in an area that yet seemed only suitable for occupation by a farm people.

But the movement of an urban population into the country brought with it important compensations. The price of land soared as speculators moved in ahead of developers, and farmers and other real estate holders were put in the position where they could reap a substantial profit. Every small-town or village shopkeeper counted the gains that a greatly increased population would bring him; and so as well did the doctor, the dentist, the lawyer, the plumber, the barber. Even the school trustee, or the township councillor, unmindful of the problems that would result from rapid residential development, saw his importance vastly enhanced by the increase in the number of his constituents. There was much that was indeed fallacious in the association of growth with progress, but the association had some basis in fact. People were made rich by the opportunities for gain that suburban development offered them.

A sense of grievance might have developed slowly among suburban residents had there not come the realization that the very people who were gaining most from their presence were the ones most responsible for their deprivations. There were few communities in which the established power structure did not remain intact for a long time after the arrival of the first suburban residents. In the rural township it was the farmers, long after they had been outnumbered by suburban residents, who continued to control the township government and determine the character of the services that the township provided. In similar manner, in the small town, the old residents continued to hold on to the administration of affairs long after new residential subdivisions within the town borders had come into being. Local government was not so democratic that powerful interests were without means of maintaining a large measure of control.

Clamorous demands of newly organized ratepayers' associations, petitions to the municipal government, attendance at council meetings of delegations of angry, shouting residents, and the nomination of candidates to oppose councillors and school trustees thought to represent the interests of the old residents were means seized upon by the new suburban population to make its voice heard. The growing realization by suburban residents that their interests were different from those of the old established residents did much to give them a sense of identity, a feeling of belonging together. In almost every suburban residential area the population was stirred to action in protest against the established power structure of the local community.

Yet the sharp clashes between opposing factions and the struggles for office that took place within an organization like the ratepayers' association made apparent the limitations of any movement of protest by suburban residents. In the suburban community differences inevitably developed when what residents wanted depended very much on how long they had been settled. The difference in time of settlement might only be six months or a year, but it was sufficient to bring to the fore sharp differences of interests. So long as the ratepayers' association acted only as a forum for the airing of grievances, it could successfully bring suburban residents together and give them a sense of identity. The moment, however, it endeavoured to take action, its disintegration began.

The trouble with an association such as this was that it was too bound by the physical limits of the local residential area. The population of a particular residential area had grievances that were peculiar to itself—the state of its access roads, the smell of its water, its open drainage ditches—but many of its grievances were of a sort that extended far beyond its boundaries. Indeed, at a point quickly reached, they made meaningless any distinction between the new and the old population. For its bad roads, smelling water, or open drainage ditches the new population might hold the old population responsible, but it could scarcely hold this population responsible for the burden of heavy mortgage payments, for mounting property taxes, or for general economic and social hardships. The old population was almost as much a victim as the new of those forces of rapid growth and development in which the suburban community was caught up.

Who or what was to blame for his lot, the suburban resident could have no very clear idea. It was the world outside, a world made up in some vague fashion out of such disparate materials as the builder who had built his house, the developer who had developed his subdivision, Central Mortgage and Housing which had something to do with his mortgage, the City of Toronto which threatened him with amalgamation and taxation still higher, a provincial government which talked grandly about its support of education but denied the grants that were necessary for the proper schooling of his children, and a federal government so concerned about such matters as the Gross National Product that it seemed to be completely unaware of his existence. There could be no easy airing of grievances directed at bodies such as these in a movement or organization committed to action within the confines of the local community; endless talk and violent disagreement were the almost inevitable result. An association like that of the ratepayers quickly acquired, with some justification, a reputation for being an organization of cranks.

The suburban resident was not yet fully ready to identify himself with something as clearly defined as a local community, whether it was a local community made up only of his subdivision—a Crosby

Heights, Richmond Acres, or Beverley Acres—or one comprising a complex of residential and other kinds of areas—a Richmond Hill or Newmarket. Such an identification involved accepting a too specific and sharply focused responsibility. So long as he could maintain his anonymity, with no concern about a social position to protect, he could belong to an organization like the ratepayers' association, and such an organization could thrive. But from the very beginning an organization like the home and school association or a service club placed upon him a responsibility that he was not yet prepared to accept; unless, of course, he was one of that small number who, arriving in the suburbs with a clear sense of status or position, proceeded to take his responsibilities as a citizen of the community seriously by undertaking to organize and arouse to action his fellow citizens. The suburban residential area divided quickly between those people concerned about local community issues and those people largely indifferent; and under the conditions of mass development it was the indifferent who were more truly characteristic of the population.

Yet the vigour of the debate that went on over almost every backyard fence made it evident that the suburban resident was far from indifferent to those issues (exceedingly vague and ill-defined though they may have been) that seemed to touch closely upon his welfare and the welfare of his family. Some of these issues may have been highly trivial or have lacked any clear basis in reality, but they had an importance nevertheless in giving the suburban resident a sense of having something in common with his fellow suburban residents, of being a part of a social world extending beyond himself and his family. The suburban resident was ready to identify himself with that large, amorphous group, composed of suburban residents like himself, but having no boundaries, no clear-cut definition, before he was ready to identify himself with his local community. Here he could lose himself, avoid any direct and specific responsibility, and yet be made to feel that he was not alone, that he was joined by other people with grievances and grudges the same as his own. The suburban world came to be set over against the world outside with the growing conviction of suburban residents that they were not as well off as other people and that for this the outside world was in some way to blame.

Grumblings and complaints may have been the most that could develop out of the grievances and grudges that had no greater basis in reality than the belief of suburban residents that they were being badly done by. With no clear notion of what was wrong or who was to blame, there was a striking out in all directions. Much of the action that resulted was of a purely random sort, its shape depending upon the particular situation or mood of the moment. In the end, a good deal of the dissatisfaction of suburban residents blew itself out as the social supports of the local community structure were strengthened.

Even where movements of dissatisfaction assumed so little shape that they could scarcely be recognized as movements, they were not wholly lacking significance in the development among suburban people of a consciousness of being suburban. Almost every rate-payers' association began with some of the characteristics of a mass protest movement. It was where, however, movements of dissatisfaction of suburban residents were given a sense of direction and purpose that they gained very considerable importance as a force in the creation of the suburban society. With vigorous leadership, the vague and ill-defined feelings of uneasiness, unrest, and disturbance of the suburban population could be channelled into a movement of protest—a mass crusade—built around a few appealing issues and directed at a clearly recognizable and vulnerable adversary. Out of such a movement of protest of suburban residents came a very quickened sense of social belonging, a consciousness of their identity as a people different from the people of the outside world.

It required persons with exceptional gifts of mass appeal to arouse the support of a suburban population which extended over a great number of different residential areas, particularly if it was made up of both new and old residents. Mr. A. N. Belugin, who became mayor of Newmarket in 1958 at the height of its over-running by a suburban population, was such a person. Though Mr. Belugin, soon after his election as mayor, antagonized the residents of East Gwillimbury Heights, these people were not among his constituents, and within the Newmarket community he succeeded in uniting old and new residents in opposition to forces from outside that threatened the small-town character of the community:

Metropolitan Toronto, which seemed to be reaching out to control the development taking place beyond its borders, the mortgage trusts exacting their tolls upon the home-owner, the financial houses responsible for the rates of interest paid by the municipal borrower, the real estate promoters tearing up good farm land to bring into being such residential developments as East Gwillimbury Heights, and a provincial government insensitive to the problems faced by a small town growing rapidly in population. If Newmarket now suffered a problem of overcrowded schools and hospitals, of inadequate sewerage and police protection, of unemployment and labour unrest, of hoodlumism and crime, there seemed little doubt where the blame lay. The problems of the city had been dumped onto the town but the town shared in none of the city's prosperity. A Metropolitan Toronto Home for the Aged located in the town offered, in the eyes of the residents, a striking example of the way in which they were being made to bear burdens imposed on them by the city.

No one perhaps could have been more suited than Mr. Belugin to appeal to the sense of grievance of the Newmarket population of 1958–60. A Russian immigrant, successful in business, Mr. Belugin could neither be identified with the old residents of the town nor with the new suburban residents. He was able thus to become a spokesman as much for the new suburban community as for the old community of the town. He made the two communities into one. The people to whom he appealed were a people without a sense of identity. For the old residents, the town of Newmarket as they had known it had virtually ceased to exist. For the new residents, there had been no community of which they had felt a part. What Mr. Belugin brought into being, or stirred to greater strength, was a patriotism directed to the Newmarket of old and new resident alike. The people of Newmarket were given a sense of belonging when their community was set against the world outside and in particular Toronto.

The term of office of Mr. Oliver Crockford as reeve of the Township of Scarborough offers an even more striking example of the way in which a population made up of old farm and new suburban residents could be given a sense of common purpose and identity. Mr. Crockford held office from 1948 to 1955, the very period that witnessed the most rapid growth of the township. When he became reeve there was much that ailed the area. The local government was still largely controlled by the farm population. The township's financial position was highly precarious, while the desperate striving to keep taxes down had resulted in a far from adequate provision of essential community services. A form of government that had proved satisfactory for the needs of a farm community was badly suited to a community being overrun by a suburban population.

For much that ailed it, the new suburban population of Scarborough could hold the old residents responsible, and Mr. Crockford's rise to power was aided to some extent by this hostility of the new population to the old. But that was not a firm basis on which to build a political following. New and old could not be so clearly distinguished. The settlement of urban people in the township had by now been going on for a very long time. When Mr. Crockford became reeve much of the political power of the old farm population had already disappeared. Indeed, the farmers who remained in the township were not without grievances of their own. Their taxes were going up, and unless they took advantage of the rising value of land and sold, there were few compensations. Rural and suburban population alike was faced with the problem of bearing the heavy costs involved in transforming what had been a rural community into an urban.

For these heavy costs, the township government was more than a little to blame. Though an effort was made to encourage industrial development, residential development was permitted to proceed without halt and in an almost wholly uncontrolled fashion. The solution to the problem of over-rapid residential development was sought in the encouragement of even more rapid residential development. Great stretches of open countryside lying between residential subdivisions made it almost impossible to provide services. Mounting taxes and inadequate services were the inevitable result.

As would be expected, there was much grumbling and complaint, a mounting wave of dissatisfaction, and a growth of movements directed against the township administration. But, while isolated groups of residents, incensed by flooding basements or by schools too crowded for their children, could of a sudden become aroused to action, for problems of a more general nature there was no clear notion of just how the township administration was to blame. Everybody liked growth, and the reeve could mount an impressive array of statistics to demonstrate the success of his administration in promoting growth. Much of the opposition to the government that developed was dissipated in struggles over petty issues and in disagreements between warring factions within the council and the community at large.

But for his hold on office, it was not upon such a situation of social anomie that Mr. Crockford depended. In the move to secure the amalgamation of the City of Toronto and the surrounding municipalities into one metropolitan area was found an issue that united the great mass of township residents in his support. It was perhaps ironic that concern about the financial state of townships like Scarborough had led to the interest in amalgamation. An enquiry headed up by a Toronto planning consultant had done much to fasten attention upon the precariousness of Scarborough's financial position.[1] But the proposal of the City of Toronto that it be permitted to annex the built-up areas that adjoined it (including a part of the township of Scarborough) aroused the opposition of the township residents. It was not difficult to picture the city as suffering from bad government and mismanagement and now seeking to impose on the suburbs a part of the resulting burden.

In terms of the kind of situation the Scarborough population found itself in during the years 1948–54, such an appeal could be a highly effective one. What developed under Mr. Crockford's leadership was something of a mass crusade directed at saving the suburbs from the city. The picture he presented was one of himself leading the people into battle. Though he was not in office long before he had many bitter foes, there could be no doubting the strength of the attachment to him of vast numbers of Scarborough residents. Being neither a part of the old farm population of the township nor a part of the new suburban population, he was able to appeal to all sections of the population however diversified their interests, class dispositions, or tastes, and there was no group of residents in the township who could not identify themselves with

[1]Civic Advisory Council of Toronto, Committee on Metropolitan Problems, *Final Report* (1951).

him and with the cause that he represented. An attachment to him was made into an attachment to the township of which he was head. Violent attacks upon him by Toronto newspapers and certain outside parties served only to strengthen the feeling of identification of the people of the township with him. Aspersions cast upon their reeve were viewed as aspersions cast upon their township. People were made by Mr. Crockford proud to be a part of Scarborough.

It was certainly a highly tenuous social tie that developed out of such an appeal as that made by Mr. Crockford, but at the time the suburban population was yet ready for no other. Within the general movement of protest the suburban resident could acquire a sense of status but avoid obligations of a very specific and compelling character. Nothing much was asked of him, in time, money, or effort. Within the social world about him he could maintain his anonymity. Yet caught up in the support of a cause, he was given a sense of importance, made to feel that he was a part of something outside himself and his family. It was in these terms that the Crockford movement in Scarborough gained significance in the building of the new society in the suburbs.

But the very forces which had led to the growth of this movement acted, in the end, to destroy it. The Scarborough to which Mr. Crockford appealed was the Scarborough of pre-Korean war days. Amalgamation was a real issue. The township still was sharply cut off from the city. Many of the problems it faced appeared to have some relation to efforts of Toronto to transfer to the surrounding suburbs burdens which were properly its own; indeed, in the very heart of Scarborough were several hundred low-income families which the city, unable to accommodate after the war, had moved into war manufacturing buildings. But the residential development that took place in the township after 1952 was a kind that made increasingly meaningless the distinction between city and suburbs. The ills the suburban population of Scarborough came now to suffer could not easily be ascribed to the City of Toronto. In a very real sense, even a whole township like Scarborough became too restricted in its physical boundaries to make possible the identification with it of the suburban population. The Crockford movement was not so greatly different from the movements which, in still more restricted areas, had led to the establishment of ratepayers' associations. For a time there could be a feeding upon grievances within the local area and the turning to a scapegoat not so far removed, but, if the ratepayers' association collapsed quickly because so many of the grievances of the population were of a sort extending beyond the bounds of the local residential area, in the end the same limitations developed in a movement like that of Mr. Crockford's in Scarborough—or of Mr. Belugin's in Newmarket.

What was required, if the sense of grievance of the suburban population was to be fully exploited, was an appeal which cut across local boundaries, of the town, the township and, indeed, the metropolitan area. The villain had to be something more than the neighbouring city or even such an institution as Central Mortgage and Housing. Charges directed at such a villain had too specific a character. The suburban population needed to be angered. But to be given force, its anger had to be directed at something vague and far off.

It was an anger of this sort that Mr. Diefenbaker succeeded in generating in his election appeal of 1957 and 1958. The sweeping victories secured by Mr. Diefenbaker's Conservative party in 1957 and 1958 extended, of course, far beyond the suburbs. In no part of the country, in 1958, did the party not make substantial gains. But it was in the suburbs that Mr. Diefenbaker achieved his greatest successes.

It cannot be argued that these successes were entirely owing to Mr. Diefenbaker's skill in arousing among suburban people a sense of grievance. There was, indeed, a "drift" to conservatism in 1957–58, and nowhere more than in such well-to-do suburban areas as those in Etobicoke Township, west of Toronto. Where economic conditions had brought prosperity there resulted a growing sense of conservatism. People in well-to-do suburban areas had come to have a status to preserve. In Thorncrest Village the population voted overwhelmingly in 1957–58 for the Conservative party.

But in the suburbs generally it was a people with no strong sense of status who supported the Conservative cause in 1957–58. Here there was no drift to conservatism. Rather, there was what almost could be described as a headlong plunge in a direction the very opposite. What the great mass of suburban residents voted for in 1957–58 was not the Conservative party but the party of Mr.

Diefenbaker. It was not without significance that the most sweeping victory secured by a Conservative candidate in the country in 1958 was in York-Scarborough, a constituency made up of a suburban population of widely varying socio-economic circumstances.

The appeal by Mr. Diefenbaker to the residents of this constituency could not be as simple and direct as that which had been made by Mr. Crockford to the residents of Scarborough five years or so earlier. Mr. Diefenbaker was the leader of an old and established national party and what clearly was of first importance was the maintenance of that solid core of Conservative support which could be counted upon to return across the country a substantial number of members of Parliament. So small in numbers had the party faithful become, however, that there was in 1957–58 little hope of attaining power by a conventional kind of appeal. If the hold of the Liberal Administration in Ottawa was to be broken it could only be done by arousing across the country a great mass movement of protest against it. It was this that Mr. Diefenbaker succeeded in doing and nowhere more than in the new suburban areas.

In terms of their class interests (or what class interests they may have been thought to have had), it is not easy to see what suburban residents had against the Liberal party and the way it had governed the country. Not many of the ills they suffered from could in any clear way be attributed to what the Government in Ottawa had done. Indeed, their very ability to move into the suburbs and buy a home for themselves was largely owing to those conditions of economic prosperity closely associated with the long rule of the Liberal party. Certainly, if any social class had been slighted by the Government that class was not to be found in the suburbs. The kind of government offered by the Liberals was precisely the kind of government suburban residents might have been expected to favour.

On the other hand, there was little Mr. Diefenbaker had to offer that could have been expected to appeal to a suburban population. The campaign promises made by Mr. Diefenbaker meant spending great sums of public money for the development of projects, such as the South Saskatchewan River dam, the causeway to Prince Edward Island, and roads into the Arctic, about which suburban residents had little concern. Mr. Diefenbaker was too much the visionary and crusader to inspire among those suburban residents influenced by middle-class interests any strong feelings of confidence. It was not suburban residents highly conscious of their status as persons of Anglo-Saxon origin, Protestant religious affiliation, and middle-class social position who gave Mr. Diefenbaker the huge majorities he obtained in suburban areas. The appeal of Mr. Diefenbaker was to suburban residents of a very different sort.

If the suburban residents who voted for Mr. Diefenbaker had any one set of social characteristics in common it was that they were almost all young, had only recently become home-owners and settled members of a community, and were being called upon to vote in 1957 and 1958 for the first or second time in their lives. Thus in York-Scarborough the number of voters doubled between the election of 1953 and that of 1958. In 1953 the Liberal candidate in this constituency had won by a narrow majority. In 1958 the size of the Conservative majority almost exactly equalled the size of the increase in the electorate. About one-half of the electorate fell in the age-group 21–34. It could not be concluded, of course, that the whole of this new electorate supported the Conservatives in 1958 but there would seem little doubt that most of it did. The Conservatives polled their heaviest votes in those residential areas which had developed after 1953. Here probably as many as 70 per cent of all who voted fell in the age-group 21–34. In no constituency in Canada had there been such an intrusion of new voters as in York-Scarborough.

Voters such as these did not have strong party loyalties. Nor did they have strong loyalties of any other sort. What they were seeking was a meaning or purpose in their lives, a sense of social belonging or mission, and this they found in identification with Mr. Diefenbaker and the campaign to defeat the Liberal Government. Though as a person very different from the suburban resident, Mr. Diefenbaker as a political leader possessed those very qualities that made such identification possible. A Saskatchewan criminal lawyer, of German descent, with none of the easy informality and sophistication of the Ottawa politician or senior administrator, he could pose in 1957–58 as the underdog, despised by the men of power because he knew and spoke the language of the common man. It was this play upon people's sense of grievance, their need to be given a feeling of being important, which made so effective his appeal to suburban residents. There was among them much of the feeling which they could share with Mr. Diefenbaker of being underdogs. They had no important place in the outside world of affairs. If they had voted previously in federal elections, their votes had not appeared to count for much. It was the men of power in far-off places who had determined how the country should be governed. Until Mr. Diefenbaker appeared. Now suddenly, in joining forces in the attack upon the Liberal Administration in Ottawa, the suburban resident was given a sense of possession of enormous power. Momentarily at least, he was turned from being an unknown and seemingly forgotten person to becoming somebody of importance. The society of which he was made a part was widened to include the whole of that vast constituency which united to drive the Liberal party out of office.

It cannot be pretended, of course, that all of the support of the suburban population for the Conservative party in the elections of 1957 and 1958 developed out of such simple social forces as these. What was confusing about these elections was that there were two very different types of appeal made by the Conservatives: one in terms of the traditional image of the party, another in terms of an image of the party created by Mr. Diefenbaker. No certain distinction can be made between the people attracted by the one appeal and the other. Even the most traditionally minded Conservative was probably not unmoved by the image of the party placed before him by Mr. Diefenbaker and particularly as there developed the awareness that in the public acceptance of this image victory for the party was promised. But there was a vast difference nevertheless between the forces that led the population of well-established suburban residential areas (and residential areas of the urban community) to support the Conservative party in 1957–58 and the forces that led to the support of this party by the great mass of new suburban residents. In the smart new residential suburbs—the suburbs of the packaged sort—the population was not searching for a sense of social belonging. The residents of these areas had come to the suburbs with their society already largely built for them. They knew very clearly who they were and to what they belonged. They were people with interests to protect. Their very choice of a place of residence had grown out of a lively consciousness of what these interests were. Affiliation with business or professional groups, membership in the church and active participation in local community affairs had offered means of consolidating their social position and strengthening their social influence. Not all such people were Conservatives; prominent in the ranks of the Liberal party were a number of residents of the more well-to-do suburban areas. But whether Conservative or Liberal, these were people for the most part with strong party attachments. They belonged to a political party or they joined one. They did not become converted to a political cause. It was this which distinguished the political behaviour of the residents of the more well-to-do or well-established suburban areas from the residents of the suburbs generally.

It can be no part of the task undertaken here to attempt to account for the sweeping shift of support away from the Conservative party among suburban residents which took place in the elections of 1962 and 1963. People who had voted for Mr. Diefenbaker in 1957–58 out of the conviction that the party he led was best fitted to govern the country certainly found good reason to change their view four years later. But if the victory of 1957–58, in the suburbs, cannot be explained simply in terms of the drift to conservatism of people taking up suburban residence, neither can the defeats of 1962 and 1963 be explained simply in terms of the disillusionment with conservatism of such people. In 1962–63 Mr. Diefenbaker was attempting to appeal to a very different population in the suburbs. The great mass movement of population from the city to the country had come almost to an end by 1958. This was certainly true of the large suburban townships: Etobicoke, North York, and Scarborough. Here further development after 1958 involved mostly building apartment dwellings. The population of Etobicoke, North York, and Scarborough was fast becoming an urban population. By 1962–63 it possessed a character of sophistication that made it no longer receptive to the sort of appeal to which it had responded in 1957–58. The kind of forces in the suburbs that quickly shattered an organization like the ratepayers' association acted in the end to shatter as well such a movement as that of Mr. Diefenbaker's.

What the repudiation of the leadership of Mr. Diefenbaker—and on a smaller canvas that of Mr. Belugin in Newmarket and Mr. Crockford in Scarborough—by suburban residents would appear to demonstrate is that, while people can be made a part of a general social movement before they can be brought into a highly structured order of social relationships, there is no lasting strength in such an attachment, except only where there persists, for an indefinite time, a condition of population instability. There was no settling down in a residential area like Wilcox Lake. In Wilcox Lake people were as little integrated into the larger urban society ten years after the area was settled as in the first year. But it was not a population like that in Wilcox Lake which located in the suburbs generally. Though the suburban population at large began with no other social resource than the family, this was a resource of very great importance. It rooted the suburban dweller in the home and ultimately rooted him in the local community. People, in very large numbers, once settled in the suburbs, stopped moving.

Though the average length of time suburban families occupied the same house may have been, as certain students of urban life or urban planning have maintained, about five years, such a statistical average offers an exceedingly exaggerated measure of the extent of residential mobility in the suburbs. There were some people in the suburbs who moved about a great deal. Except, however, in those areas where second and third mortgages had led to the purchase by great numbers of families of houses they could not afford, a surprisingly large proportion of suburban residents went on living year after year in the house in which they had first located. Certainly, if what is revealed by a number of different samples can be relied upon, the proportion over a five-year period ranged from two-thirds to three-quarters.

Thus in one Scarborough Township residential area, Dorset Park, of 469 families who appeared on the voters' lists in the 1958 federal election, 354 were the voters' lists with the same address in the 1963 federal election, slightly more than 75 per cent. In Yorkminster, a residential area in North York of more expensive homes, of 398 families, 259 had the same address in 1963 as in 1958, 65 per cent. Field study samples revealed about the same amount of movement on the part of suburban residents. In Beverley Acres, where second and third mortgages were common, only sixteen out of twenty-seven residents, 59 per cent, were original home-owners, but in Crosby Heights and Richmond Acres, areas of single-family dwellings, twenty-four of twenty-seven residents, 89 per cent, were original home-owners. Dorset Park in Scarborough Township, an area five years old at the time of the field study, had, out of forty-four residents interviewed, thirty-three or 75 per cent original home-owners, and Wexford, in the same township, eight years old, had twenty-one out of thirty residents, or 70 per cent who either were the first owners of the homes they occupied or had owned their homes for at least five years.

The suburban population, once it had invested in the purchase of a home, became to a high degree a settled population. In the end, there was no escaping the consequences of such settlement, within the community at large as within the family.

The change came with the recognition that the house represented an investment as well as a place to live. So long as people were concerned mainly with paying back what had been borrowed for the down-payment on the house, and for its furnishing, they could not give serious thought to the house's value as an investment. In areas where residents were burdened with second mortgages there could be for many no end to the struggle of financing the purchase. But in the suburbs generally time brought a marked change in people's financial condition. Continued inflation and rising prices during the nineteen-fifties exacted their toll, but for people who had embarked on a career of home-ownership there were important compensations. Wages, salaries, and, even more, commission incomes rose and the burden of debt associated with the purchase of the house significantly lightened. The suburban population became, in a highly meaningful way, a propertied class. It could now begin to count the gains made from the house purchase.

The effect was evident in a new and very different attitude toward the local residential area. The residential area now became—as to people in areas like Thorncrest Village it had been from the beginning—an important consideration in terms of the protection of the house investment. A substantial proportion of residents, made increasingly conscious of the effect of the community environment upon the value of their house, abandoned the area in which they had first located and went off in search of a better. It was, indeed, people such as these in considerable numbers, now for four or five years suburban residents, who located in areas like Thorncrest Village and Don Mills. There was as well some movement in the opposite direction, though economic prosperity through the nineteen-fifties made the moving up much more noticeable than the moving down. After about five years, not more than three-quarters of the original home-owners remained within any residential area. Conversely, more than one-half of those people buying homes in a residential area now five years old were people previously owning homes.

Such a movement out and in (except where it assumed proportions as great as in areas like Beverley Acres) did not make for a condition of community instability but for the very opposite. The people who remained had a stake in the community. As well, the people who moved in for the most part had made the choice of a place of residence in terms of the character of the residential environment, and they too had a stake in the community. Where at the beginning there had been little concern about who one's neighbours were and how the residential area was regarded from outside, these now became considerations of very great importance. The movement in and out helped to bring together, within the same residential area and to some extent on the same street, persons of similar interests, tastes, and social aspirations; in a word, people of the same social class.

Thus in subdivisions four or five years old was found a pride in the area manifested by the comparison of it with other residential areas. For a time, the distinction may have had reference to nothing more than the possession of such community amenities as paved streets, sewers, nearby shopping facilities, or good bus connections with the city. But it was not a long step from making a distinction in these terms and making one in terms of class of people. The housing market had sorted people out by the price of house they could afford. There may have been a difference of only a thousand or so dollars between the price of the houses in one subdivision and in another, but this difference became significant, particularly as houses changed hands and the population became more homogeneous in character. It made an area of $15,000 homes "better" than one of $13,000 homes, and it made both of these "better" than one of $11,000 homes. A new significance came to be attached to the name of the subdivision. People became anxious not to have their place of residence confused with a nearby and less desirable place of residence. Only two of a sample of twenty-five residents interviewed in Crosby Heights and Richmond Acres failed to point out what they considered was the superiority of their residential area to Beverley Acres. "Take a ride around that area," one of these residents urged the interviewer, "and you'll see how much better this one is. Houses selling for $500 down just didn't make for as good a class of people." Another replied: "It's the type of people that's important. You get grades of people and grades of homes they were built for." Still a third replied: "It's the type of people and houses too that is important in determining whether an area is good—those houses over there are not up to much." Five of the residents interviewed in Crosby Heights compared their subdivision favourably not only to Beverley Acres but to Richmond Acres as well. There was no resident of Lyons who did not consider this area superior to East Gwillimbury Heights. The residents of Beverley Acres made comparisons with Wilcox Lake, where a number had formerly lived.

What developed was a social hierarchy of suburban residents based upon distinctions between residential areas. The more socially homogeneous the population of the residential area became, the more easily could a social distinction be made between it and other areas. Distinctions thus made were seldom if ever seen in terms of social class. They were seen rather as an expression of local patriotism. There was nothing socially unbecoming about pride in one's residential area. People could profess the superiority of the place where they lived without doing violence to their creed of social equality. Thus it was those very people who most disclaimed any feelings of social class who gave most vigorous expression to feelings of pride in the local residential area. In a residential area like Thorncrest Village from the very beginning it was easy for the residents to profess a complete indifference to class distinctions. There was no concern here on the part of particular residents to differentiate themselves socially from other residents. The important differentiation was between themselves and the residents of other areas and this was secured by the character of exclusiveness built into the social structure of the village.

In the mass-developed residential area the growth of a sense of being socially different was more halting and uncertain. Where there had been less discrimination in people's choice of a place of residence, marked social differences inevitably appeared between people living within the same area, and these differences made less readily discernible the differences between people living in one residential area and another. But a social hierarchy within the residential area was a long way from developing when there was made possible the development of such a hierarchy based upon distinctions between residential areas. There was a sufficient movement of people out of and into different residential areas to produce within particular areas in a period of a few years some degree of social homogeneity. People began to make distinctions, not between themselves and their neighbours, but between themselves and the people living in other residential areas.

There was a great difference in this regard between an area like East Gwillimbury Heights and areas like Crosby Heights and Richmond Acres, and, even more, areas like Dorset Park and Wexford, subdivisions in the Township of Scarborough which at the time of the field study had been settled for from five to eight years. The people of East Gwillimbury Heights had no way of seeing themselves in relationship to people in other residential areas. Settled in this area for less than a year, they had still very much the character of an undifferentiated social mass. But three years had brought a change to areas like Crosby Heights and Richmond Acres and five to eight years had come near to transforming areas like Dorset Park and Wexford. After five to eight years the suburban residential area began to take on much of the character of an old established urban residential area.

What certainly was found in Dorset Park and Wexford was a settled population. Here there were few people who did not socially belong. By now, a number of young families who found they could not afford the houses they bought had moved out, often to settle in new residential subdivisions more distant from the city, families who had prospered had found a more expensive home in a better district, and new people had moved in who seemed to fit better, in age and financial status, with those who remained. It was no longer possible to live in these areas without being conscious of their identity. The people of Dorset Park and Wexford saw themselves in unmistakable fashion in relationship to people living in other nearby areas. They compared their area socially favourably or unfavourably to these other areas.

But by now the lines of social differentiation cut across residential lines to give identity to social groups forming more subtly on the basis of common interests, tastes, and social aspirations. There was evident in Dorset Park and Wexford a social hierarchy of residents within and extending beyond the local area. People had begun to compare themselves with other people, on the same street, the next street, and streets beyond. Cliques had formed and the neighbourhood had taken on a new and different meaning. That is not to say that when interviewed the residents of Dorset Park or Wexford gave any greater expression to social class feelings than had the residents of Crosby Heights, Richmond Acres or even East Gwillimbury Heights. Social class remained something not talked about. The significant distinction still was between the people active in community affairs (including affairs of the wider community) and the people largely indifferent, but by now the balance had shifted so far in favour of the people active in community affairs (or at least alive to community issues) that the people who were not became a socially disapproved class if not one considered disreputable.

In a word, there were more organizations active in Dorset Park and Wexford, of a community-wide as well as local character, than in more recently developed residential areas (except those of a "packaged" type), and there was a larger proportion of the residents involved in such organizations. Indeed, there were to be found here many of the characteristics associated in the literature with what has been called "suburbia." With all their children in school, many housewives were found heavily involved in the work of the church and in such community organizations as the home and school association, the Women's Institute, and welfare groups. Men, home from work, and now no longer faced with such tasks as building a recreation room or fencing in a backyard, and with more money to spend, were in considerable numbers caught up in the activities of service clubs, the Boy Scout movement, the church, politics, and such. It was not as easy now to escape from the responsibilities owing the neighbourhood, the local community, and the world at large. The pressures towards conformity were very much greater.

The total picture that emerged, however, was of a society not like that of "suburbia" but like that of any "normal" urban residential area. No one in "suburbia"—that is to say in a packaged residential area such as Thorncrest Village—was permitted to be without an interest in community affairs. Thorncrest Village began as the creation of a social class, and there was a very vigorous effort to maintain in the population a character of social homogeneity. Instruments securing comformity were built into the structure of the village society. It would have taken more than time to have created out of a mass-developed residential area like Dorset Park or Wexford a population with such a character of social homogeneity. A number of residents who were interviewed in these areas confessed to having no interest in community affairs and no knowledge of what was going on about them. There were many others who indicated that while they were active in the affairs of the wider community they took no part in the life of the local community. The varied interests of the population not only cut across local community boundaries but attached some people almost exclusively to associations outside the local community. For many persons the residential area was nothing much more than a place to live. It was not the society of suburbia that was to be found in Dorset Park or Wexford.

Yet developments taking place in a residential area like Don Mills—or, indeed, Thorncrest Village—would suggest that in the end there could be no great difference between the packaged and the mass-developed residential area. The packaged residential area in time began to become "unpackaged." That is to say, people began to identify themselves less with the residential area and more with associations of people with similar interests wherever they lived. The tendency of the population to break up into small social groups or cliques within the residential area, and even more to identify themselves with associations outside rather than within the residential area, was apparent very early in Don Mills, but such a tendency could not be wholly arrested in Thorncrest Village either. In both areas the effect of the turnover of population was to weaken identification with the local community. The people who settled originally in Don Mills and Thorncrest Village looked for support of their class position. They tended to be heavily dependent upon identification with the local residential area. Such was less true of people moving in later. These were not to the same extent people "on the make." They had established social positions and were attracted to areas like Don Mills or Thorncrest Village because they were good places to live but good only in the same way as many other residential areas offering houses in the same price range. Increasing concern on the part of some of the older residents of Thorncrest Village that the newer residents had no feeling for the values and ideals of the village revealed the changing character of this area. Thorncrest Village and Don Mills were becoming increasingly like other urban residential areas, dependent simply upon property values to distinguish them from "better" or "poorer" areas. Such could scarcely fail to be the case as the open spaces separating them from the built-up areas of the urban community disappeared.

What distinctiveness the suburban community possessed— whether "packaged" or not—depended upon its location outside the built-up areas of the urban community. When packaged, the suburban community could attract a population in search of a very special kind of residential environment; when not packaged, its chief attraction was to a population in such sore need of housing that it was prepared to accept residence in an area that had nothing to offer except houses at a price it could afford. With the passing of time, however, these distinctive qualities were largely lost by both the packaged and non-packaged residential area. As the land surrounding them became built up, and the same sort of services came to be provided within the one type of area as the other, there ceased any longer to be anything much that distinguished either area from the old established urban residential area. The mass-developed residential area became more selective in the class of people it attracted as the packaged residential area became less selective. Both became increasingly subject to forces of residential mobility operating throughout the urban community. They were on the way to losing what distinctive character they had as suburban communities.

For suburban residential areas offering housing to the urban poor, the consequences of the general pushing out of the boundaries of the urban community were very different. The very existence of such areas depended in large part upon their isolation from the urban community. As open spaces in between were built up, and land values rose, a point could be reached where re-development of such areas became financially attractive. Land occupied by the poor was not usually good farm country, but, for this very reason, it often had a scenic quality that made it attractive for development as an exclusive residential area when it came near enough to the city; such, for example, was the residential development of Guild-wood Village in Scarborough Township, in an area which for long had been given over to a type of housing suitable for the very poor. Industry as well could move into such an area and bring about its complete transformation.

But farther out in the country havens for the urban poor could exist for a very long time before the urban community came near. Only far distant from the city or in out-of-the-way places could land be found that the urban poor could afford. Riverdrive Park was forty miles from the City of Toronto. Residential communities growing out of summer colonies on Lake Simcoe were nearly sixty miles from the City. The urban community did not crowd in upon such residential areas within the first ten or, indeed, twenty years of their development. Vast open spaces remained unoccupied between them and the city long after most suburban residential areas had become indistinguishable from urban. After ten years Riverdrive Park was as isolated almost as it was when first occupied.

It is true, there was much of the urban society built into River-drive Park from the very beginning. The population carried with it from the city the close primary group associations of the family and neighbourhood. The local community developed a clear and unmistakable identity. Almost everyone living in Riverdrive Park had a strong sense of belonging. They did not confuse themselves with people living outside. Beyond the community's borders were many miles of woods or scattered farmsteads.

But while the society of Riverdrive Park could develop quickly to a certain point there was practically no development beyond. This was a society based upon primary group relationships and such it largely remained. There was some settling down of the population. Many of the social misfits moved out and among an increasing number of the inhabitants there developed a strong sense of pride in the community. Houses were painted and lined inside, plumbing was installed, and some attempt made to land-scape the front yard. As more of the houses improved in appearance those occupied by the unenterprising became more conspicuous. Clear social lines formed between the more and the less respectable. Persons active in local community affairs, and possessed of a sense of social responsibility, came increasingly to determine the character of the area.

Riverdrive Park remained, however, almost wholly cut off from the world outside. Status could be secured by a late model car sitting in the driveway, a new coat of paint on the house, or a well landscaped front yard, but it was a status almost wholly lacking support from outside the local community. For the most part, these people were nobody in the world beyond Riverdrive Park. They had no important jobs, and they had no affiliation with important organizations. Few could even boast an attachment to a church. There was an intense isolationism which the passing of time did little to lessen.

In a very real sense, in settling in Riverdrive Park these people had escaped from the whole secondary structure of urban society. Here sewer lines could never reach, nor streets and sidewalks, running water, and such. This population could be made no part of an urban tax-paying world. But neither could it be made a part of an urban world of work. Opportunities for employment remained as far off as ever; nor did there develop any means of strengthening the position of people within the labour market. The economic marginality of the population maintained its state of social marginality. Ten years after Riverdrive Park was occupied the only social resource was still the primary group association imbedded within the structure of the local community.

Even less did the society of a residential area like Wilcox Lake become with the passing of time a part of the urban social complex.

Here the movement out and in of population brought practically no settling down whatsoever. People moving out were social misfits but so as well were the people moving in. The failure to establish the associations of the family and neighbourhood on a secure basis led to a failure to establish any meaningful identification of the population with the local community. Isolationism extended down almost to the level of the individual. No real part of the local social world, the population of Wilcox Lake could become no part of the social world outside. There was an almost complete escape from the whole complex of urban social institutions and forms of social organization.

It was not only in residential areas like Riverdrive Park and Wilcox Lake that there was something of this failure of the suburban community to develop beyond a certain point. Charges of high-minded civic leaders that certain suburban areas would in time develop into slums certainly were exaggerated, but they had nevertheless some basis in fact. The truth was that the Toronto urban community by the end of the nineteen-fifties had not yet extended far enough out to justify semi-detached residential developments twenty-five or more miles from the city. The low price of the land and the crowding together of semi-detached houses on very narrow lots made possible down-payments so low that there was attracted a population which could not really afford home-ownership under middle-class urban conditions. Residential areas of this character tended in time to become poorer rather than better off. Few urban services were offered to begin with and not many could later become established in face of the urgent necessity to keep down the tax rate. In such areas there could be very little settling down of the population. They had been easy places to move into but they became exceedingly hard places to move out of. Many of the original purchasers, not really able to afford the houses they had bought, defaulted on their payments and homes coming on the market in this way were usually in a poor state of repair and could only be re-sold by making the conditions of their sale even more attractive than had been the case in the first instance. By the intrusion of second and third mortgage vendors, down-payments in such areas were reduced often to as low as $300. The result was that they continued to attract people buying houses for the first time and people whose position in the housing market was even more marginal than that of the original purchasers. What persisted was a housing market with still very much of a mass character. There could thus be no development of a socially homogeneous population. The very people who had the largest equities in their houses, and thus the greatest stake in the community, were the people who socially least belonged. The new people moving in widened rather than narrowed the differences between groups of residents. Under circumstances such as these, the sense of attachment of the population to the local community did not strengthen. It was as socially undifferentiated a population which occupied such areas three or four years after they were settled as in the first year.

To some extent, such forces of residential mobility acted throughout the suburban community to arrest the development of stable forms of social organization. So long as the suburban residential area remained a considerable distance from the built-up areas of the urban community it faced the threat of declining property values and intrusion into the area of people less well off financially than the original home-owners. Indeed, after 1958, with the declining demand for housing, new residential construction could have no other effect than to depress property values in older-developed suburban areas that were still far distant from the urban community. Throughout the suburban community there were to be found social misfits, people who did not feel they socially belonged in the areas where they lived but had no easy means of escape. By the end of the decade of the nineteen-fifties almost all suburban residential areas, except those that by now were an integrated part of the urban community, had become places easier to move into than out of.

But to say this is only to give emphasis to the fact that wherever there is a movement of population into new areas of development considerable social risks are involved. Not all the people who settled in the Western Prairies in the years 1880–1910 found themselves prospering in the first decade or two of their settlement. Some, guessing wrong on the route to be followed by the railway, were left with no access to markets of the outside world. Others, caught at the beginning of a prolonged period of drought and depression, were left at the end considerably poorer than when they had started. Where the direction of development takes a sharp turn, whether for geographical, economic, or other reasons, whole communities of people can be left for a long time isolated from the world outside and made as a consequence socially poor. Dogpatch had an existence outside the Li'l Abner comic strip. It would have been remarkable, indeed, had the North American Continent become occupied without considerable numbers of people being stranded in out-of-the-way places, and it would have been little less remarkable had suburban development occurred without the establishment of some residential areas that only very slowly and haltingly were made a part of the larger urban social complex.

Yet this very character of the suburban community, where parts of it remained for an indefinite time only slightly integrated into the urban society, was a character of the urban community itself. There was no great difference between a residential area like Riverdrive Park or even Wilcox Lake and certain downtown areas of the urban community. Large segments of the urban population lived almost completely divorced from the whole secondary structure of the urban society. It is questionable, indeed, whether any example could be found in the suburbs where a body of residents lived in greater social isolation than some bodies of residents in the urban community. Active participation in the larger world about them was an attribute of only the more favoured social classes of the urban society; and so it was of the suburban society.

In truth, what suburban development meant was the reproduction of the city in the country. The reproduction came about fitfully. Some parts of the urban complex were more easily transferred than others. Indeed, some parts got transferred in such a way (as in the case of the packaged suburb or what became known as suburbia) that they failed to be recognized as urban at all. In the end, however, there was not much of the urban society that was not reproduced in the suburban. The balance for long may have favoured the middle classes—it was people of the middle classes who could most easily afford the kind of houses being built—but the suburbs were not without their poor (and as well, of course, their rich), and, as the type of development shifted from the building of single-family dwellings to the building of apartment houses, row houses, duplexes, and the like, a point was eventually reached where few elements of the urban population could not be accommodated in the suburbs.

At this point, of course, the suburbs had clearly ceased to be suburbs. Only from the political scientist could they longer claim the title, and then only if the municipal boundaries of the city had not been extended to include them. But if this was so, it would seem apparent that before this point was reached the only usefulness of the title suburban was to give emphasis to the character of the society as an urban society coming into being. The suburban could be nothing more than a new urban society. It was in its character as a new urban society that as a social phenomenon it gained significance.

8 | The New Society

THIS STUDY has been concerned with how the suburbs developed. Its main thesis has been a simple one. People moved out to the suburbs in search of space. They wanted a house, and the only place they could find a house was in the suburbs. What views people had about suburban living had little to do with their becoming suburbanites. If there was a selection, it was one largely of a negative character. There were far from enough houses in the city to go around. People determined to remain in the city were able to find residential accommodation there, but only because people who did not care too much where they lived got out. It was in the city rather than in the suburbs that was most likely to be found people with a strong commitment to a way of life.

This is not to say that the suburbs had to develop in the way that they did. Nor is it to say that such a development was a "good thing." The spread of urban population out into the country could have been prevented; or it could have been controlled in such a way that there would have been far less dispersal of suburban residents. Governments are not helpless in dealing with a problem like urban growth. Indeed, it was government policy to some extent which determined the pattern of growth that did take place. Mortgage money was made readily available for the building of houses in the suburbs. A different policy might have discouraged such building and led to a greater effort to provide residential accommodation within urban boundaries. Suburban development came in the years after the war without much thought having been given to where such development might lead. Had governments been more ready to plan and direct, the kind of suburbs we know today might not have come into being.

What could have happened might have been a "better" kind of development. Certainly, it would be difficult to argue that the development which did take place produced the best of all possible worlds. There was much about this development that was appallingly wasteful. It is not difficult to estimate some of the economic wastes involved: the provision of transportation, sewerage, water, fire protection, education, shopping, police, and other such services in areas far removed from the main concentrations of population; the using up of people's time and energy in getting to and from work, in shopping and in performing household tasks that might better have been done by persons professionally qualified; the exclusion from the labour market of women unable to accept employment, particularly of a part-time character, because of distances involved or the difficulty of providing for the care of their children. The social wastes, though less easy to measure, were probably no less great. Society was the poorer as a result of the deprivations suffered by the suburban population. The isolation of suburban people, the weakening of kinship ties, the absence among the population of persons older and wiser in years, the constant struggle to finance, the lack of means of intellectual or cultural expression exacted their toll. Indeed, it is scarcely possible to escape the feeling that there was something almost fraudulent about the whole vast enterprise directed to the object of persuading people to move to the suburbs. Many of the costs of such a movement were hidden: by municipal councils, in passing on to future tax-paying publics a part of the burden of providing services for the suburban population; by the new residents themselves in postponing, through first and, even more, second mortgages, the charge upon their earnings of the house purchase; by the federal government in using financial aid to housing as a fiscal device; and by society at large, in applauding the accomplishment of providing housing for the population, without reckoning the price paid. Suburban development may not have produced a society as disagreeable as the one pictured by David Riesman. But there was much certainly that could be deplored about this society, by persons concerned about aesthetic values or about simply the economies to be obtained from a rational plan of residential dispersement.

Yet suburban development cannot be judged a mistake because it damaged certain aesthetic values or even because it resulted in certain economic and social wastes. There is much that people do that is aesthetically damaging, or wasteful, but they do it nevertheless because they want to. They would consider the alternative unacceptable. A good deal of the discussion about suburban development has been carried on by persons who have not liked the suburbs. Their use of such terms as "suburbia," "urban sprawl," and even "middle class" when applied to suburban people has revealed a biased view of the character of suburban development. Such persons have been against the kind of unplanned growth which created the suburbs, or they have been against the manner of life of suburban people. As a consequence, they have found no good in suburban development.

What has to be demonstrated, in passing judgment upon suburban development, is whether under different conditions of development people would have got the kind of residential accommodation they wanted. It might certainly have been less wasteful to have housed the new post-war urban population in high-rise apartment buildings and it would certainly have been more aesthetically pleasing had it been housed in residential areas of the Thorncrest Village type. But this population was one possessed of certain very definite social preferences in terms of the way it wanted to live. That is not to say that it had any precise ideas about housing designs or qualities of construction. Nor is it to say that it got precisely what it wanted in the housing market that developed. But it would seem clear that the vast majority of people who moved into the suburbs wanted to live much, in fact, as they found themselves living. People who moved to the suburbs wanted a house of their own and they wanted the sense of freedom and anonymity that a home in the suburbs afforded. Though they may not have fully counted the costs—the fatiguing and expensive daily trip to work, the onerous and mounting burden of mortgage payments and property taxes, the loneliness of subdivision life, the trials and tribulations of keeping a house in repair, particularly if it was improperly built, the lack of recreational facilities for children who had passed beyond school age, and the like—there was a readiness to accept the disadvantages of suburban living for the sake of the advantages. In another society people may want to live differently, and what thus was conceived by the suburban dweller as the good life could there be considered intolerable. We can learn much from the experience of city building of peoples in other lands but only if we recognize the differences as well as the similarities of the materials out of which the building is done. It was people with North American, middle-class, values of home-ownership who had to be provided with housing in the Toronto area after the war.

Critics of suburban development could not be expected, perhaps, to ask the question whether people in the suburbs were living as they wanted to live. But such critics could be expected to ask the question whether the lives of people in the suburbs were really as they were made out to be. The stereotype of suburbia has done more than simply amuse the reader of the popular magazine or paperback book. It has entered into a good deal of the thinking about how our cities should be planned and what measures should be taken to assure a more satisfying urban way of life. We have in the last few years gone almost full circle in our conception of what is good and worthwhile in urban society. The time was when we deplored the congestion, disorganization, and impersonal character of big city life. Then the railway and the horse-drawn street-car forced population, and industry, near the urban centre. From such a development emerged the downtown slum, presenting to the outside observer a picture of squalor and dirt, disease, broken homes, juvenile delinquency, and crime. The city was condemned because it crowded people together, compelled them to accept inadequate residential accommodation, and made its streets and back alleys the only playground for children. The major concern of urban reformers, not more than thirty-five years ago, was the devising of means by which urban people could be given more living space.

The automobile and super-highway have brought into being today a new kind of urban complex, far-flung in its dimensions, and scarcely any longer having a centre. People now can live and work many miles from what was once the city, and if they want to play or shop, dine, or attend musical concerts they need not even then go near the city centre. We have been fast making the whole North American Continent into one great urban community where we no longer know who is city man and who is rural. The city man commutes to work but so does the rural man, and, if the farm is still linked to a farm home, it is a farm home that is becoming equipped with all the household conveniences once associated with the city home. In large parts of the North American Continent rural society has disappeared, and with it has disappeared what long was known as urban society.

The reaction to such changes has often been one of dismay and disapproval. Developments that have sharply reduced the size of the farm population and turned what farmers are left into people living like city persons have been viewed almost as a national disaster. Speeches about the passing of rural society can always be counted upon to arouse deep emotional feelings associated with a romantic view of what rural society is supposed to be like.

Similarly, developments which have threatened to destroy the slums of the downtown urban community have been deplored by those very people who a generation ago would have welcomed their passing. The slum has been discovered to have a "society." It is not a disorganized area as sociologists had once mistakenly supposed. We talk now of urban "villagers," not slum-dwellers, and concern is expressed about disturbing the way of life of these people, their norms and values, forms of social control, their culture.

I am not suggesting that the society of the slum, or rural society, has no real existence. Nor is there any suggestion that forces of change should be permitted to ruthlessly destroy these societies. But the sociologist can easily get himself into the same position as the anthropologist, where sentiment dressed up in a functional theory of society is permitted to rule over good sense. The anthropologist has had good reason to deplore the way in which outsiders have interfered with, and tried to make over, the societies of primitive peoples. But too often the concern with what more advanced civilizations were doing to primitive societies has led him to view any attack upon the way of life of primitive peoples as something to be deplored. Similarly, in the case of the sociologist, so great has been the fascination with a functional theory of society that almost any functioning society has come to be viewed as a society which should be preserved. The world would not be poorer if there were no slum societies—or primitive or rural societies—and, though certain people might be hurt with their passing, probably no change has taken place in human history that has not brought hurt to some people.

The simple truth is that as a consequence of the making over of urban society in the past quarter-century urban people—and rural people now become urban in their way of life—are living better. They are enjoying a standard of housing—and a general standard of living—far in advance of urban or rural people a generation ago. And nowhere is this general well-being of people more in evidence than in the suburbs. The Toronto suburban population today is larger than was the total population of the Toronto urban community before the Second World War and almost the whole of this population is provided with very substantial and modern dwellings, spacious lots, and all the conveniences of modern living. It is a population that must be judged well off.

Yet nothing that has happened to the city in the past quarter-century has aroused more lament than the spreading of its population out into the surrounding countryside. It would almost seem that the better off people are the more cause there is for concern. People who are prospering, it appears, no longer permit their lives to be ruled by the Protestant ethic, or they become "other directed" rather than "inner directed" in the governing of their conduct. To the person intellectually or culturally sensitive the suburbs might appear a dull place to live. Most people who took up residence in the suburbs were not strongly interested in intellectual and cultural pursuits. But neither were the people who made up the great part of the population of the city. The only difference between the city and the suburbs in this respect was that the population of the city was a mixture of middle class and working class, rich and poor, while the population of the suburbs was predominantly middle class. The poor of the city had the virtue of being sociologically interesting. The middle class of the suburbs could only appear stuffy in their enjoyment of a state of material and social well-being.

It would, of course, be unfair to the critics of present-day urban society to suggest that everything they have said about suburban development grows out of an unfounded and biased view of the character of suburban living. Life in the suburbs could have been made richer and more meaningful, as, indeed, could have life almost anywhere man has been found. What should be insisted upon, however, is that the measure by which a society is judged be understood and fully made known. Too often hidden biases and false conceptions of what is have been built into the measure used. Canadians are fond of comparing themselves to Americans, and few Canadians are not convinced that because Americans possess more bathtubs, refrigerators, cars, and super-highways they are somehow culturally inferior. Yet if history teaches anything, it is that material well-being is a necessary condition of intellectual and cultural advancement. In terms of the very measure used to judge them, suburban people were almost certainly better off as a consequence of their move to the suburbs. After a period of adjustment and settling in, the move brought an advance in their material well-being. There could not help but result an advance in their intellectual and cultural well-being as well.

Index